OLD SOUTH BATON ROUGE

The Roots of Hope

"A View of Old South Baton Rouge" by local artist, Wayne Jones, 2006.

Old South Baton Rouge

The Roots of Hope

Petra Munro Hendry
and Jay D. Edwards

with Carolyn Ware, Pat Smith, Gwen Hamilton,
Elecia Lathon, Dorian McCoy, Guiyuan Wang

Foreword by former LSU President, William Jenkins

Featuring photography by James W. Terry, III

University of Louisiana at Lafayette Press
2009

University of Louisiana at Lafayette Press

P.O. Box 40831
Lafayette, LA 70504-0831

ISBN: 1-887366-86-5

Library of Congress Cataloging-in-Publication Data

Hendry, Petra Munro, 1958-
Old South Baton Rouge : the roots of hope /
Petra Munro Hendry and Jay D. Edwards ; with Carolyn Ware ... [et al.].
p. cm.

Includes bibliographical references and index.

ISBN 1-887366-86-5 (pbk. : alk. paper)

1. Old South Baton Rouge (Baton Rouge, La.)--History. 2. Baton Rouge (La.)--History. 3. Old South Baton Rouge (Baton Rouge, La.)--Social life and customs. 4. Baton Rouge (La.)--Social life and customs. 5. Community life--Louisiana--Baton Rouge--History. 6. Social change--Louisiana--Baton Rouge--History. 7. Community development--Louisiana--Baton Rouge--History. 8. Housing--Louisiana--Baton Rouge--History. 9. Old South Baton Rouge (Baton Rouge, La.)--Social conditions. 10. Baton Rouge (La.)--Social conditions. I. Edwards, Jay Dearborn. II. Ware, Carolyn. III. Title.

F379.B33H46 2008

976.3'18--dc22

2008038060

This book was printed in Canada on acid-free paper.

Made Possible Through a Grant from
LOUISIANA ENDOWMENT FOR THE HUMANITIES
State Affiliate of the National Endowment for the Humanities

Table of Contents

Foreword

Just outside the north gates of the Louisiana State University main campus is a two-and-one-quarter square-mile area between LSU and downtown known as Old South Baton Rouge. Once a vibrant neighborhood of successful and flourishing African-American restaurants, stores, and theaters where music greats such as B.B. King, James Brown, and Sam Cooke performed, today, every one out of two residents of Old South Baton Rouge lives in poverty. It is home to McKinley High School, which in 1927 became the first public high school for African Americans in Louisiana. Some of the earliest stirrings of America's Civil Rights Movement, such as the 1953 Baton Rouge Bus Boycott, sprang from residents of homes along its tree-lined streets.

Much of the history of Old South Baton Rouge has been obscured by time and distorted by the prism of defacto racism. In 1994, however, LSU, working alongside community activists, launched an effort to revitalize the area by forming the Community University Partnership. Over the years LSU architecture students and faculty took part in collaborative urban renewal research and construction projects. The Baton Rouge Area Foundation initiated additional re-development endeavors as part of a master plan to revitalize this important part of Baton Rouge, now poised to reclaim its rich heritage.

This book chronicles not only the proud history and hard times but also the rise of hope for Old South Baton Rouge. More importantly, it is an uplifting narrative about fulfilling the American Dream and the promise of future prosperity born from a partnership between Louisiana's flagship university and the long-neglected community at its doorstep, a community in transition and being transformed into a better place to live.

Dr. William L. Jenkins, Past President
Louisiana State University System

Photo courtesy of Jim Zietz, LSU.

Chapter One

Community, Culture and Social Change

I suppose people were poor, but you never knew anybody that was poor because on Sundays people would dress up and on weekends they would go out and [enjoy] a real great social life.

~ Joe Delpit

Community studies are as old as sociology and anthropology. Their professional beginnings are to be found in the last quarter of the nineteenth century. Literally thousands have been written. Each community study is an examination of the people of a place unlike any other. Some have contributed theoretical insights and others have penetrated deeply into the human condition. In Louisiana, however, detailed community studies are relatively scarce. Those that exist have mostly focused on Louisiana's first city—New Orleans.[1] With the exception of the historically-oriented *The Forgotten People* about the Cane River Creoles of Natchitoches Parish, few broad scholarly studies of predominantly African American communities outside of New Orleans have been undertaken (Mills 1977). No legacy of scholarship stands for what in the post-Katrina era has become the largest city in the state—Baton Rouge.

In contrast to New Orleans, the popular image of Baton Rouge has been that of a utilitarian and rather pedestrian working capital city, a university town, a petrochemical center, a place which lacks the rich culture and history of its downstream cousin. Indeed, the Capital City has often been characterized as no city at all, but rather a conurbation of specialized urban places scattered along the banks of the Mississippi River with more sprawl than center. It is a place which has borrowed its culture from Europe, Africa, Native America, the Caribbean, and even from China. Most people are familiar with European contributions to the culture of Baton Rouge. Yet its creolized multi-ethnic African American culture lies sequestered—accomplishments largely unrecognized, a narrative untold.

We are going to recount for you the story of one of the most complex and resilient parts of the Capital City—the neighborhood called Old South Baton Rouge (OSBR). It is a predominantly African American community that lies between the southern edge of the central business district (CBD) and the northern edge of the Louisiana State University (LSU) campus, about one and a half miles to the south (**Map 1.1**). Today, OSBR is considered by many to be a blighted neighborhood suffering from poverty, crime, the ills of public housing, and urban decline. Few in Baton Rouge remember that this was once a thriving multi-ethnic community boasting its own central business district, fine homes, excellent educational and medical institutions, many active churches and civic clubs, and a site which drew the best in live entertainment from around the entire country. It was a place which thrived and developed into a strong and vibrant community on its own terms in the face of economic deprivation and the restrictions of racial segregation.

Old South Baton Rouge emerged after the Civil War, flourished during the "Jim Crow" era, and reached the pinnacle of its development during the 1940s and 1950s. It experienced economic decline thereafter. OSBR's evolution is an integral part of the greater history of the Capital City, but seen from a special perspective. Because it is viewed through the lens of minority ethnic group history, our story places emphasis on events and cultural processes essential to the African American perspective. The story of OSBR is more turbulent, more stained with the burden of disadvantage, neglect and struggle than would be the story of, say, Beauregard Town, the original center of the

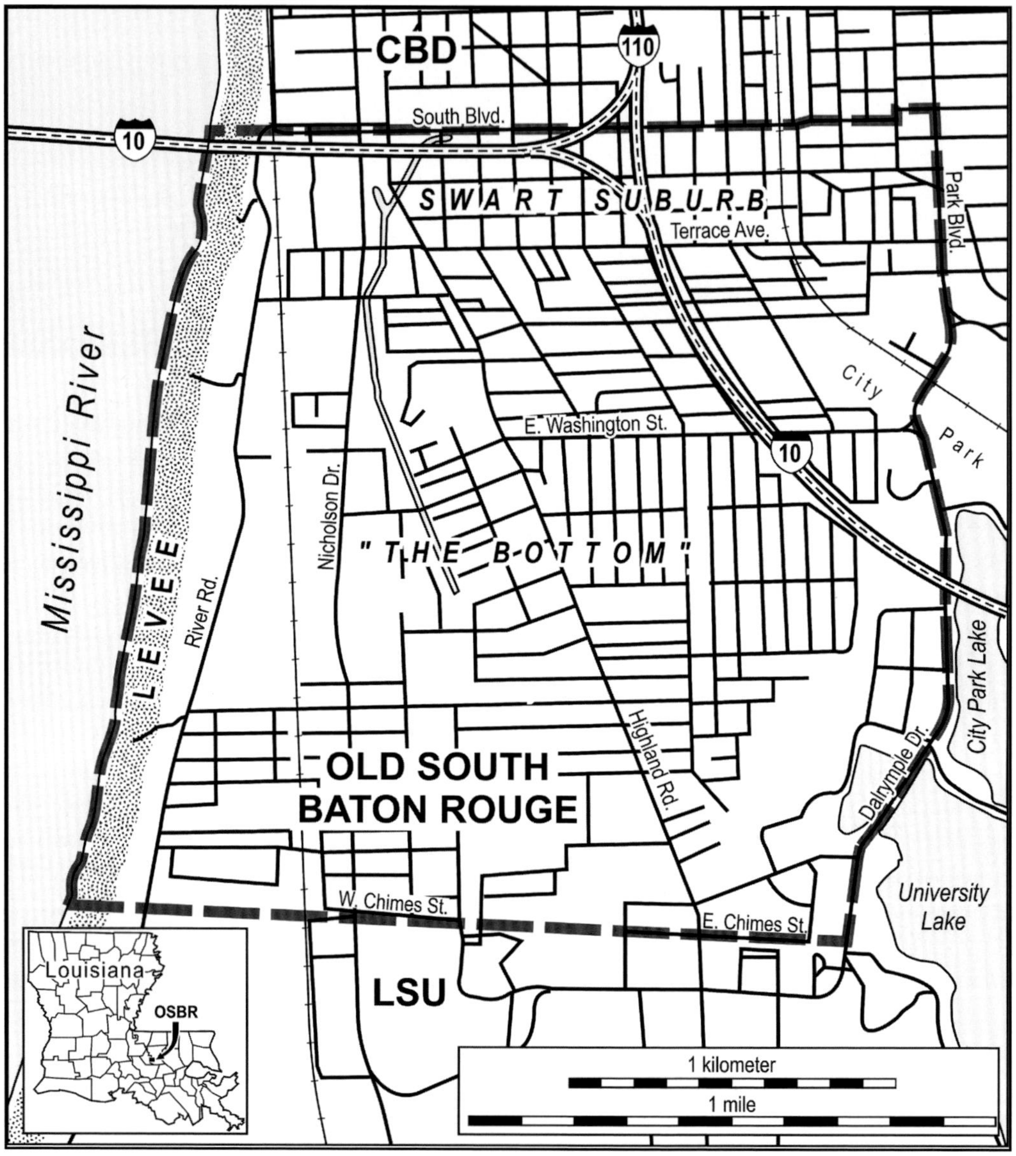

Map 1.1. A general location map of OSBR.

Capital City. But this is not an overwhelmingly negative story. True, it is the story of the evolution of a community under stress, but it is also a story of surprising and largely unheralded successes and of unique strengths and accomplishments. Herein we glimpse universally valid truths about human resilience and the will to succeed in the face of dominating and sometimes impossible circumstances.

The story we tell arises largely out of the voices of members of this community. In the early 1990s a grassroots initiative to revitalize the neighborhood began with several projects, including an oral history project. One aim was to encourage youth to invest in rebuilding the community by making them aware of its largely unappreciated cultural, political, and social history. Memory was seen as essential in the process of community revitalization. Between 1995 and 2005, a collaborative team from LSU, McKinley High School, and the OSBR community, began to record and transcribe oral histories. No one had ever collected the stories of those persons central to the successes which the community had once enjoyed. Hundreds of hours of tape recorded interviews were obtained from families and friends by diligent high school students. Like archaeologists, these interviews began to uncover another South Baton Rouge—one not in the memory of the young people conducting the interviews or of their generation. Tape by tape, stratum by stratum, they pulled the curtain back on a way of life now forgotten by all but a few living in Baton Rouge: stories of the struggle for the first public high school for African Americans in Louisiana; stories of the Baton Rouge Bus Boycott in 1953—the first mass public civil rights protest in U.S. history; stories of how politicians and community leaders had worked together to build strong public institutions, businesses, clubs, churches, and civic organizations within a segregated community; and stories of how people of many different ethnic groups lived together and cooperated as neighbors and friends under the restrictions of institutionalized racial segregation.[2] In addition to the oral histories, community residents also shared numerous historic photographs from their private family collections. Many of these photographs are published here for the first time. They provide an intimate visual portrayal of community life and an otherwise unavailable window into the past.

So dramatic have been the changes in social life and in the built environment that few remember, and many remain skeptical of, accounts of life in this community prior to 1960. What was life under segregation really like for black people living in the urban South? What kinds of successes and failures did they experience, and how did they adapt to the cruel rigidities of a segregated social system? It is a story which may well surprise you and force you to reassess your preconceptions about the lives of people of your parents' and grandparents' generations. Let's begin with a few sample accounts typical of this now lost and under-appreciated world. They are tiny vignettes drawn from the larger story of Old South Baton Rouge.

Voices of Old South Baton Rouge

J.W. Vaughn:

When I was thirteen in Baton Rouge, we organized a club to help young boys in this area like ourselves to have self-esteem and to be something, go to school everyday, because we knew then that times were very difficult for us people of color.

We had to excel in order to be accepted in the job market. We called our club the Golden Gophers Social Club. I was the president, and we were right here in Baton Rouge. We played basketball on the [Masonic] Temple roof garden—that's on North Blvd. That was the only place we had to play, it was the fourth floor. [It] was windows all around this big place and during the basketball games we had people stand around the windows to make sure the players wouldn't fall out—[we'd] push 'em back.

We brought bands to town to make money for our club and for projects. Of course during that time when you brought a band to town, the club would make about fifty dollars. The band itself cost about $350.00 to come from New York. We started all of that [when we were only] thirteen; I knew then that the Lord had put me on this earth for more than just walking around and doing nothing. So, when I left McKinley High School and went into the service and stayed two years and six months, came out and finished my work, and then went to work for thirty-five years. I only missed fifteen days from work in that thirty-five years (Vaughn 2003).

Joe Delpit:

I suppose people was poor, but you never knew nobody that was poor because on Sundays people would dress up and on weekends they would go out, you know, and [enjoyed] a real great social life.

And at that time you know things were segregated. You had white and black restaurants. Three restaurants were owned by blacks and primarily served blacks: the [Delpit] Chicken Shack, Bernard's Chicken Loaf House, and Percy's Bar-B-Que. But even though segregation was in place, a large number of whites would be coming to those restaurants to want to eat and sit down, because the food was just that good.

Everybody loved my man Joe Cascio [an Italian]. He was a plumber and he had a hardware store there [on East Blvd.] and people would go to his hardware store. . . . It was there for years, and he would always give people credit and let them get their plumbing and stuff done and he was the kind of people that I would say wouldn't rip people off. I mean he was of honest people, and he helped a lot of black men learn how to be plumbers in working with them. And when blacks couldn't [legally] get their licenses to be plumbers [due to racial discrimination], he would get the permit and let the black do the work, and everybody start from him, I guess. That's how some blacks got to be plumbers.

Later during the years, McKinley Theater [on East Blvd.] was changed to what was called the Rhythm Club. The Rhythm Club was the largest club probably at that time in Baton Rouge, and possibly in the state, that black people went to. They had all sorts of nationally known artists—Sam Cooke, James Brown, B.B. King—I mean any and everybody who was on the charts or who was hot performed at the Rhythm Club.

I remember when Sam Cooke had come in the [Chicken Shack] business, and I got his autograph, along with James Brown and Ike and Tina Turner. Mr. Alvin Guidry and all of the stars would usually stay either at the International Hotel or the Boulevard Motel. The Staple Singers, I remember when they came to town they stayed over at the Boulevard Motel—Bobby Glen, and all the big groups. . . . You know it was segregated, and you couldn't stay in any other hotels. Mr. Fred Williams was the one who really made something great. He had movie actresses and actors come to Baton Rouge, and they would promote those movies and they were primarily black movies. Mr. Williams was really responsible for all of that, Fred Williams (Delpit 1996).

Fred C. Matthews, Jr.:

For public transportation the city operated trolley cars, similar to the ones used in New Orleans and San Francisco. The two main routes, Third Street, out North Boulevard to East Boulevard, down East Boulevard to Howard Street, serving the South Baton Rouge section. I believe the fare was five cents. There was practically no taxi service. The streets were mainly gravel in South Baton Rouge. In the early years the streets were just plain dirt. Some people owned a horse and buggy. Walking to town was a common practice—few people complained. Candles, kerosene lamps and lanterns were popular. For heat in the winter we used fireplace wood for fuel; potbelly stoves also used wood for fuel. Some years ago South Baton Rouge had a flooding problem. On many occasions McKinley High School had to close because of high water. Mr. Joseph Delpit, first black city councilman, spearheaded a program to correct the drainage. (Matthews, 1996).

What Is Unique About This Community Study?

How does one write the history of a community which for all practical purposes has been invisible to outsiders and even to its own younger generations? There aren't any standards for writing community studies. Every author selects his or her favorite subjects and these are informed by the kinds of information which are available. It is appropriate then, right at the outset, that we set out those organizing principles which we feel to be the most important to the development of a well-grounded understanding of Old South Baton Rouge history. Gradually, out of years of research, a number of perspectives and themes began to stand out. We believe that each is useful and important in appreciating the formation and resulting character of the community. Some developed out of archival investigations in libraries and private records, others from the oral histories and remembrances of the people of the community. We group these perspectives under four general themes: Geography; Place; Culture and Creolization; and Change and Revitalization.

Geography

This study is unlike almost any other in certain respects. In Chapter II we begin with a more detailed exploration of the geographical setting than you might find in other community studies. Our rational for what at first glance might be considered an excursion, rests on the supposition that people's lives are importantly and profoundly shaped by where they live. Even rather subtle changes in the land often result in large-scale changes in the life-ways of those who settle upon it. Regions and their specializations are defined by the nature of the landscapes they contain. Significant topographical features such as the Mississippi River may produce both enormous opportunities for success, and potential liabilities which may ruin the lives of the unlucky or unwary. Topography also provides place names and even personal identities for those who reside in distinctive geographical locals. Environmental racism refers to politically and socially motivated attempts to systematically disadvantage those who reside within certain places and to benefit those who reside in others. Social segregation may be based on geographically determined differences in land values. Complex

Fig. 1.1. The levee looms above the houses of OSBR.

patterns of settlement may evolve directly out of nearly invisible or innocuous geographical factors such as differential access to highly valued places. We will find that all of these and others have shaped the community of Old South Baton Rouge. It is our hope that exploring them may cause us to reassess and to broaden our conceptualizations of how communities develop.

Place

For the purposes of this study we define OSBR geographically rather than applying other criteria such as ethnicity or census tract boundaries. Old South Baton Rouge is bounded by South Boulevard on the north, Park Boulevard and the LSU University Lakes on the east, Chimes Street and the LSU campus on the south, and the Mississippi River on the west. The levee—an enormous barrier of earth over twenty-five feet tall—separates the entire community from the Mississippi and

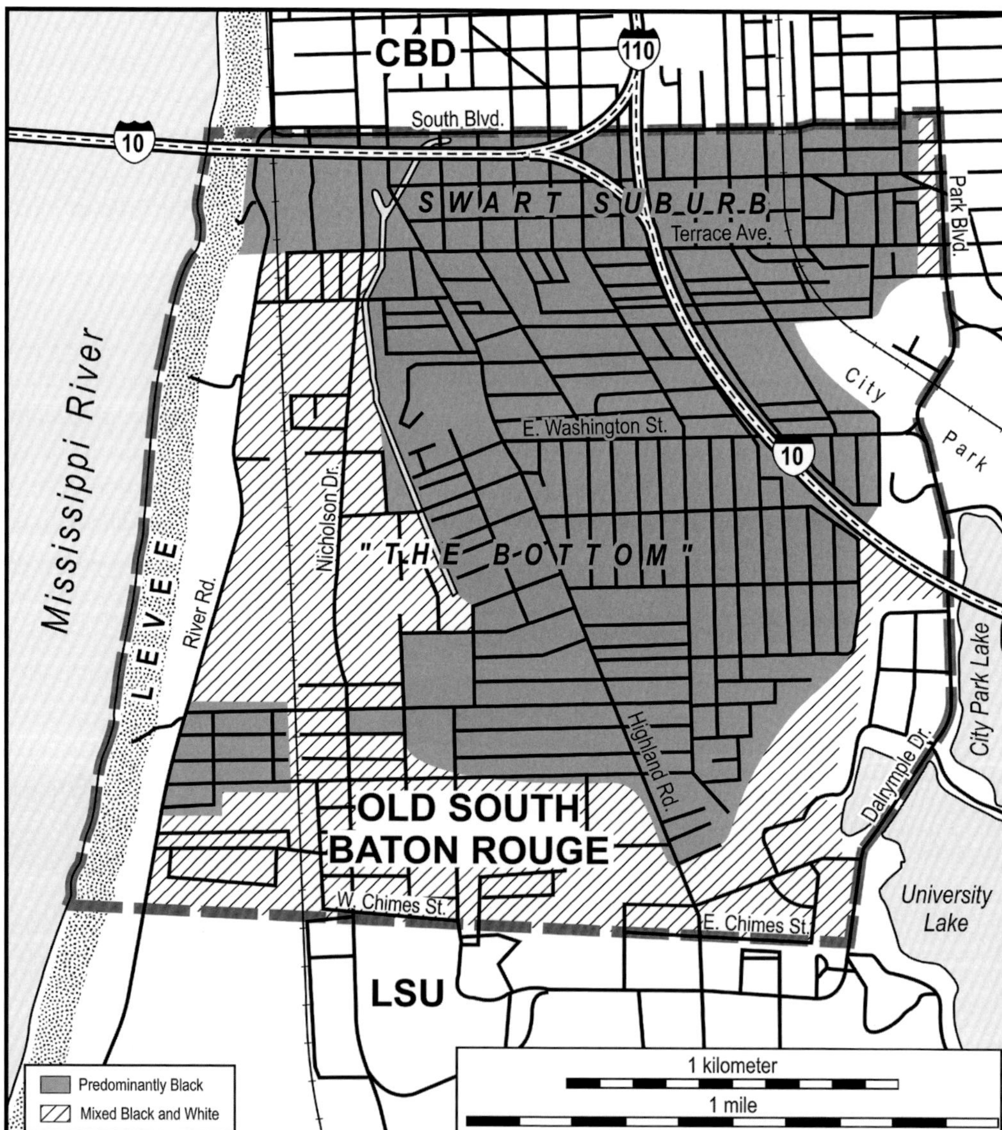

Map. 1.2. Ethnic settlement in OSBR, 2007.

Fig. 1.2. Lois Payne, Knight of Peter Claver.

Fig. 1.3. Evelyn Baranco, Teacher at McKinley High School.

dominates the low-lying houses of OSBR (**Fig. 1.1**). The total area of OSBR amounts to about 2.25 sq. mi. This geographical zone is divided into a central core of African American settlement, and a periphery of mixed ethnic settlement on the west near the river (Nicholson corridor), the south close to the LSU campus area, and the east along Park Boulevard-Dalrymple Drive and University Lakes suburban settlement (**Map 1.2**).

We believe that it is not unreasonable to argue that African Americans in the South have a special kind of relationships with their places of residence that other ethnic groups do not share, at least not in the same way. Centuries of discrimination and separation meant that African American

Fig. 1.4. King and Queen, Purple Circle Social Club, 1940s.

Fig. 1.5. Lutheran cemetery, OSBR.

Fig. 1.6. Rural cemetery near St. Mark, Haiti.

institutions were largely self-constructed in place. The social and educational institutions of each locale were more personally and intimately theirs (**Figs. 1.2-1.4**). They were often shaped by the often more visually expressive culture patterns of their forebears, including generalized traditions arising out of Africa and the Caribbean (**Figs. 1.5-1.6**). OSBR illustrates this relationship perhaps better than almost any other place we have studied.

Historically, places in the South have been defined by race. Between the beginning of the eighteenth century and the end of the twentieth, race was the single most important determinant of identity. Race shaped and enforced where one lived, what jobs one took, and the nature of one's relationships with those in the society at large. Race was a Durkheimian "social fact"—something external to and coercive upon the individual (Falk 2004:17).[3]

> In the South, as nowhere else for blacks in the United States, blacks were not a novelty but rather were, in some ways, the very definition of the place. That is, one could only understand the place in light of their presence. No blacks, no slavery. No blacks, no cotton [or sugar] industry. No blacks, no Civil War. No blacks, no Reconstruction. No blacks, no *Plessy v. Ferguson*. No blacks, no "race as the most vexing question in the twentieth century." No blacks, no civil rights revolution, no school desegregation, no integration of all public facilities, no affirmative action. In short, no blacks, no continual reminder to *all of America* about how far is the reach to "e pluribus unum." (Falk 2004:119).

Fig. 1.7. McKinley Alumni Center.

Fig. 1.8. Chicken Shack Workers, 1937, corner of East and Lettsworth.

For African Americans, life in a particular place was more than simply a convenience. Settlement was often characterized by violence and the struggle for control of land resources. Economic disadvantage meant that it was difficult to hold onto places which were desirable. Zoning and tax laws could be manipulated to exert the power of the dominant class against the subjugated. And then, even if a place was assigned or otherwise agreed upon by the existing power structure of the community, the development of that place into a fortress of protection and self support, to say nothing of pride, required the efforts and skills of all members of the community working together over decades. In a climate of relative powerlessness and discrimination, the effort invested in a place of one's own was greater, but so was the corresponding pride of success. Even if a community appeared to be flawed or blighted to outsiders, from the perspective of the insider it was *their own*, warts and all. First class institutions such as McKinley High School (**Fig 1.7**) or thriving businesses (**Fig 1.8**) were experienced in a different light because they had been created against the odds by the people of *this* community. They were shaped by and invested with the personalities of community members. These were highly visible people whom everyone knew. Even the anti-establishment activists—the H. Rap Browns of the community—had placed their distinctive stamps on the larger American consciousness (Brown 1969; **Fig. 1.9**). Their voices were significant.

Each community is a social construction established and maintained by a history of innumerable relationships given meaning by its residents. One's place within a web of relationships becomes the all-defining forge of one's being. It is there that one was raised with friends and kin; there that all of the life experiences of growing up and becoming adult were stored as memory and as nostalgia. The institutions which shaped and strengthened one's life experiences were rooted there, in the homes, the churches, the schools, the clubs, the sports leagues and the work places. Even if every experience was not a good one, they were unique and personal, and they could never be taken away. They shaped identity. Each individual personality was rooted in thousands of such place-defining experiences, many of them shared due to the character of the place.

Fig. 1.9. H. Rap Brown, 1967.

Architecture and landscape become powerful aspects of this rootedness in place. In interviews with residents raised in OSBR, what was often fondly remembered was the front porch of the house. There, many good, relaxing and pleasurable hours were spent working, socializing, courting, and just greeting neighbors who were passing by. Until the 1950s, OSBR was very much a pedestrian community. Front porches, found on almost every house—even the smallest shotguns—abut directly on the sidewalk or the street (**Fig. 1.10**). News traveled up and down those sidewalks, and the porch sitter was privy to every bit of it—who was ill, who got a new job, who recently died, what news was electrifying the community at the moment. More than any other place, during the week it was the porch which became the locus of interaction and conviviality. Even the tiny shotgun

Fig. 1.10. Shotgun Row, Julia Street.

Fig. 1.11. Painted shotguns, 17th Street.

house, seen as a disadvantaged lodging by those from the outside, was experienced very differently and with considerable pleasure by its residents (**Fig. 1.11**). Owning a piece of property and a house became a powerful symbol of self-validation, pride, and earned participation in the community. OSBR boasted a high level of home ownership. And we must remember that disadvantage itself provided a certain sense of camaraderie, *communitas* and a shared moral perspective on the wider world. In all of this, place played a central role in helping people define who they were and how they related to others of their community.

Culture and Creolization

Another organizing principle central to this study is the concept of creolization. Most pictures drawn of the South before integration emphasize the stark contrast between the black and white cultures of the two major populations. Anthropologists and historians have gone to great pains to point out the ironic and often tragic inequalities in life-ways and life-chances of residents of segregated communities. While remaining mindful that systematic differences existed, in this study we emphasize a somewhat different perspective. We prefer to focus more specifically on the dynamic interrelationships which enriched each of the multiple ethnic communities of South Baton Rouge. It is a portrait not drawn simply in black and white, but rather in many colors of cooperation and conflict between members of several ethnic groups.

Fig. 1.12. Descendants of enslaved Africans on the Beaubeneau Plantation, Louisiana. Marion P. Walcott photo, 1930s, courtesy of the Library of Congress, Prints and Photographs Division.

Creolization refers to a special form of culture blending which destabilizes the traditional binary (black and white) view of race (Palmié 2006). It is a form of cultural change which takes place under special historical circumstances such as colonialism, segregation, and institutionalized racism. In these circumstances where one group is subjugated by another, culture forms and grows in complex ways. Some people adopt the dominant culture and copy it with enthusiasm, some accommodate it without much enthusiasm, some reject most of its values, but remain passively without inspiration or goals, and some actively struggle against the values of the dominant culture by searching for outside cultural sources and alternate inspirations. In anthropological theory, creolization refers to those aspects of culture change which circumvent or subvert the binary model of power and cultural relations, striving instead for the construction of unique and independent ways of life.

Under conditions of cultural domination, the best path to success is often unclear. Culture growth may be fluid and beset with advances, innovations, rejections, and detours. Identity politics becomes complex. Local society may become plagued with opposing agendas and segmented by factionalism. Cultural creolization may produce a kaleidoscope of institutions and sub-cultures, one filled with unresolved dualisms and contradictions. Old culture traditions are knotted together in new ways, only to be cut apart and rearranged once again. Because the forms and values of the dominating culture become tainted with mistrust and despair, use is made of the traditions of many alternate sources. Patterns of culture change become multi-cultural and multi-ethnic. Rather than accommodating to a bipolar or linear view of the world, influences and models for success may diffuse into what Edouard Glissant refers to as "cultural diffraction . . . a never-ending *métissage* (cross-breeding) without limits . . . bearing unpredictable consequences." Creolization "suggests a comprehensive and dynamic phenomenon of cultural give and take, of invention and reinvention, of dialogue and disagreement" (Glissant 1989:28). This dynamic—the creation of entirely new layers of technical and symbolic adaptations out of the fabric of once disparate cultures—is what we will focus upon under the label of cultural creolization. Together with the more common process of adopting and perhaps reshaping the values and models of the dominant culture, creolization characterized significant periods in both the growth and the unraveling of OSBR between 1900 and 1965.

Fig. 1.13. Italian American residents, Servio Cascio and bride.

In our historical sketch of the development of OSBR we focus upon the two interrelated concepts of culture and community. Culture provides the conceptual tools which humans use to overcome their obstacles and disadvantages. Out of the struggles of the past, OSBR has forged its own unique variety of a larger minority culture, and of a larger Baton Rouge culture. As late as the late eighteenth century no vestiges of native culture survived in OSBR. Rather, elements of nineteenth century rural African American plantation culture were brought together and mixed with the cultures of European Creoles, French speaking Afro-Creoles, Sicilian Italian immigrants, Anglo-Americans, Scotch-Irish, Canary Islanders, German Dutch highlanders, Cajuns, and American Indians (**Figs. 1.12-1.14**). These eventually blended into a local repertoire of practices which served the growing

Fig. 1.14. Barn dance at the Temple Theatre, 1940s.

population of the area. In the African American community the merged patterns resulted in a unique ethnicity which would distinguish itself in the cultural character of OSBR.

The importance of African American culture in the South, and in Louisiana specifically, has been largely ignored by historians and educators. The contributions of African Americans are those of the African diaspora and those of subsequent generations of creative inventions and reinventions. At the level of vernacular and folk culture, diaspora-derived patterns were to be found everywhere in the Caribbean and in Louisiana in the nineteenth century. Creolized African American cultures consisted of a core of knowledge carried from Africa, overlain with European technologies and practices which had been acquired on the plantations of the New World. The legacies of these cultural blendings are expressed, even today, in the landscapes of OSBR.

Anthropologists have described how Africans contributed substantially and obviously to the creolized architectures of Louisiana (Vlach 1975; Edwards 2001; 2002). The idea of open-air living through the placing of a broad living gallery on the front of a common person's house is a widespread and essential part of coastal West African indigenous architecture, but it was essentially unknown by Europeans before they began visiting and building trading posts along the Guinea Coast (**Fig. 1.15**). The shotgun house, so popular in Louisiana, has been traced by Vlach to a syncretism of indigenous African spatial and dimensional traditions and Caribbean Indian forms (Vlach 1975). The result was the "*ti kay*," or small (shotgun-like) house, so popular in both colonial and modern Haiti (**Fig. 1.16**). Construction techniques such as the use of mud in the walls of Creole houses (called *bousillage*) were selected in Louisiana from a repertoire of French construction methods largely because of the prior experience of West Africans with similar technologies. Of course, it was largely African Americans who constructed most of the buildings in the Louisiana colony and thereafter. Evidence of the legacy of African Creole architectural traditions is still recognizable in the dominance of shotgun style houses in many parts of OSBR (**Fig. 1.17**).

Fig. 1.15. Indigeneous West African homestead, Liberia, circa 1724.

Fig. 1.16. Decorated *ti kay* house, Haiti.

Fig. 1.17. Shotgun house, Terrace Street, OSBR.

Another form of creolization occurred in religion. Plantation folk religion had contained a highly variable amalgamation of magical beliefs and medicinal practices, Louisiana Catholic religious culture, Afro-Caribbean religious traditions and increasingly, Protestant folk religion. All of this was carried into Baton Rouge in the second half of the nineteenth century. Enslaved Africans were commonly used as medical doctors and surgeons in Louisiana due to their skills in herbal medicine (Hall, 1992). According to Hall, "they [whites] participated in an acculturation process that was a mutual exchange of knowledge, perceptions, and techniques—an exchange in which Africans, as well as Indians, were often more influential than whites."[4]

Yet another example of creolization becomes apparent as we trace the linguistic contributions of the rural African Americans into Southern Black English and eventually, American dialect English. Enslaved Africans arrived in the South speaking a variety of languages from the coasts of West and Central Africa. While the majority of this vast lexicon was lost, some was retained, providing Southern and eventually American English with a special flavor it would not otherwise have. Much of what survived did so because it filled gaps and social needs not covered by standard American English. Beyond language forms, African American culture provided an abundance of verbal riches. Special naming practices are still common to the community.

Proverbs, folktales such as Brer Rabbit, Anansi, and Bouqui and Lapin tales, legends (High John the Conqueror) and entire styles of speaking such as fancy oration and stylized verbal dueling provided a special flavor to street corner verbal encounters or informal evening gatherings.

Fig. 1.18. Large kitchen garden, Royal Street.

But how did these Creole cultural traditions and technologies survive into the nineteenth and twentieth centuries? While many African American traditions prevailed on the plantations of Louisiana, large numbers of freedmen moved into the cities of the South, including Baton Rouge, following the Civil War. They carried their traditions with them. Not surprisingly, much of this culture was retained at first in the urban environment. For example, a culture of provision gardening shared along the quarters lanes of the plantations persisted in the widespread use of urban gardens in OSBR. In 1940, about 63 percent of African Americans in Baton Rouge relied on a kitchen garden for nourishment (Louisiana State University 1940:56-75). Private and neighborhood gardens were common throughout the community, and ritual practices such as planting by the moon continued unabated (**Fig. 1.18**).

At the same time, entirely new institutions were emerging in the urban environments. The culture of the OSBR community (and, indeed, of all of Baton Rouge), owed its existence to waves of earlier cultural amalgamations from the plantations, augmented by new layers of traditions acquired from neighbors and co-workers in multi-ethnic urban settlements. New institutions and new adaptive responses had to be forged in this very un-plantation-like environment. The resulting transformed institutions and the adaptive responses of the new urbanites contributed substantially to the building of Baton Rouge.

Change and Revitalization

In many important ways the lifestyle of the majority of the people of Old South Baton Rouge in 2006 bears little resemblance to that of their forebears. Today, one is hard-pressed to find vegetable gardens, for example. In 1940, almost half the families raised chickens and many kept other kinds of small livestock as well. People walked everywhere. Only one in ten families had a bicycle, and only the elite had an automobile.

To begin the story of the transformational changes which were to impact OSBR, it is worth briefly revisiting the community at the peak of its early twentieth century development:

> By 1940, it was a flourishing minority and immigrant neighborhood, a jambalaya of culture like so much of Louisiana. At its peak, Old South Baton Rouge had thirty-two churches, twelve grocery stores, eight restaurants, and forty-one specialty shops. According to parish records, home-ownership was at eighty-three percent, with many of the resident families also running local businesses, including names that are still found on buildings and streets in the neighborhood: Delpit, Mellini, Divicenti, Butler, and Vicaro (Housing Authority of East Baton Rouge Parish 2002:7).

The success of this economic activity was in part due to Jim Crow. The irony of segregation was that it forced blacks to create their own institutions. Within the boundaries of this neighborhood

Fig. 1.19. Shiloh Baptist Church, 14th Street.

Fig. 1.20. Masons Parade on East Boulevard, 1950.

Fig. 1.21. A Night in June, Purple Circle Club, 1950s.

the black community shaped its own world. For example, black churches were to be found on almost every street corner (**Figs. 1.19, 5.1-5.2**). They still are. Over the previous generations Hoodoo beliefs had gradually been replaced with the practices of established religions and medical professions. A belief in the power of the spirits of the dead, or signs of disaster such as the hooting of an owl, were increasingly set aside in favor of the power of prayer and Christian charity.

Fig. 1.22. Bars in OSBR, *Sepia Socialite*, 1942.

Outside of the churches, civic associations flourished. The Masons, the Odd Fellows, the Daughters of Ruth, and the Elks had black lodges in or around OSBR (**Fig. 1.20**). The single most active civic association was the National Association for the Advancement of Colored People, which had thousands of members (Louisiana State University 1940:115). The Colored Civic Association of Baton Rouge, Inc. was the principal business organization. Other beneficial and service societies, such as the Purple Circle Social Club, and sororities, such as the Deltas, also played increasingly larger roles in the cultural life of the community. Typical events included "a Night in June" and the annual presentation of the king and queen (**Fig. 1.21**).

In OSBR, as the segregated community expanded in the 1930s and '40s, a larger clientele became available to African American businessmen. Black restaurants and night clubs sprang up in and just beyond the boundaries of OSBR. Numerous bars, pool halls and dance halls were available for those who enjoyed nightlife, and increasingly after World War II, nightlife boomed at the Blue Room, the Brown Derby, the Green Parrott, Two Gat's Jazz Room, and the Apex Cocktail Lounge (**Fig. 1.22**). The excitement of this period has been captured by one of Louisiana's most famous authors:

> Phillip could remember when Chippo and he used to come here to gamble and dance. Everything they had wanted from a woman to a good barroom fight could be found on East Boulevard or nearby. It was a dangerous place, you could easily get yourself killed there . . . (Gaines 1992:140).

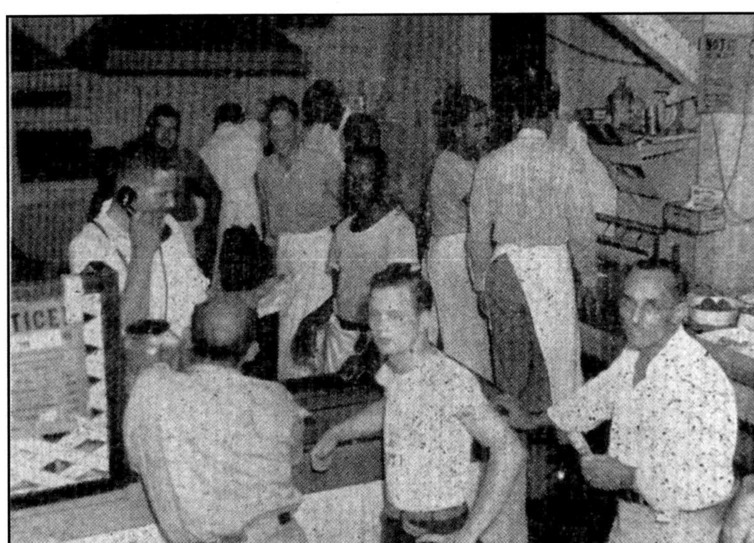

Fig. 1.23. A multiethnic clientele inside the Bernard Chicken Loaf restaurant, *Sepia Socialite*, 1942.

Dydees's Duck, Delpit's Chicken Shack and the Bernard Chicken Loaf restaurants carried on their culinary magic (**Fig. 1.23**). All were popular with both black and white clientele throughout Baton Rouge and far beyond.

If popular culture was your thing, movies could be seen at local theaters. Perhaps the earliest motion picture theater available to black Baton Rouge residents was the McKinley Theater on East Boulevard (now Thomas Delpit). It opened in 1939 and finally closed around 1960. By 1945, two additional "colored" theaters were available: East End Theater on N. 33rd, and the Temple Theater on

Fig. 1.24. The Lincoln Theatre, 2005.

Fig. 1.25. The original sign of the Lincoln Theatre.

North Boulevard. In 1951, Dr. A.L. Chapman's Lincoln Theatre opened on Myrtle Street with 600 seats, a single screen, and a stage for live concerts. It also housed a barber shop which still operates (Hendry and Edwards, et. al. 2005: Appendix 3, No. 6). The two previously mentioned theaters were owned by a Nashville, Tennessee firm, but they hired local managers. The favorite films were musicals, westerns, and gangster movies (Louisiana State University 1940:117). Colored theaters could not get a first run movie until sixty to ninety days after the film had been shown at the white Paramount Theater. The price of admission was ten to fifteen cents. Movies were, perhaps, the single favorite recreation for blacks in Baton Rouge in 1940. Sundays were the most popular day for going to the theater. From the 1950s on, the Lincoln Theatre was the most prominent venue (**Figs. 1.24-1.25**). It played host to many of the great musical names, including Otis Redding, the Four Tops, Hank Crawford, and Louis Armstrong. Besides movies, there was a black-oriented radio station, WXOK (white owned), and an all black newspaper, the *Weekly Press*. But, unfortunately, all of this was about to change.

New Challenges and Difficulties

The rather miraculous cultural and economic success of OSBR was not to last. Like many other inner city neighborhoods across the United States, this community underwent economic decline in the 1960s and '70s, as a result of suburbanization and other social factors.

> Twenty years ago it was lively, now it was dead. Many of the bars, cafés and other businesses had shut down. The remaining buildings looked old and dilapidated. The street [East Blvd.] had never been lighted well, but it looked even darker now. The sidewalks were paved in some places, dirt and gravel in others (Gaines 1992:140).

Three factors contributed to the economic decline of OSBR beginning in the 1960s. First, the construction of the I-10 corridor through the middle of the neighborhood in 1963 resulted in the dislocation of many business and private properties including the all black and very modern St. Francis Xavier Catholic High School, only four years old at the time. The erection of an elevated highway, an interstate interchange, and the approach to the high Mississippi River Bridge, resulted in a blighted zone that extended through what had originally been some of the most affluent parts of the African American community (compare **Maps 1.3 -1.4.**). The result was that many of the older educated and professional families simply left the community, relocating to the new suburbs then opening up in Baton Rouge and other Southern cities. OSBR lost many of its leaders and activists.

Second, the building of the I-10 Interstate had ramifications far beyond the specific roadway corridor. The elevated throughway sliced the eastern part of the neighborhood off from its larger

Map 1.3. An aerial photograph of OSBR from 1932.

portion to the west (**Figs. 1.26-1.27**). This type of environmental racism was prevalent in the 1960s and '70s throughout America. Suburban growth at any cost was seen as the price of economic development and advancement, and it was often minority communities which were most severely impacted by the urban planners. The partition of OSBR resulted in two local segments, neither of which was self-sustaining and neither of which could support the other. Minority school children could no longer walk to their local schools. Local businesses, already operating on very narrow margins, had depended heavily on pedestrian traffic from all parts of the community.

Third, and ironically, desegregation, which followed quickly after the construction of the interstate, had the also unintended effect of further destroying the locally-owned businesses and institutions. Small, local black-owned businesses could no longer compete in the larger urban market as residents now had more access to more modern and better financed white-owned commercial outlets, chain stores, and new shopping malls. Much of that clientele was lost.

Map 1.4. An infrared aerial photograph of OSBR from 1990s.

For generations, African American children from OSBR had attended neighborhood schools. The large-scale social changes which accompanied desegregation meant that many black children would no longer attend "their" schools. Instead, they were bussed, sometimes for hours, to remote locations across town. Teachers, as well, were forced to cross-over. Many of the highest ranking and most experienced black teachers were plucked from the OSBR neighborhood schools to teach in predominately white schools across town (Davis 1999). Schools which had once functioned as a

Fig. 1.26. Heavy traffic over OSBR.

Fig. 1.27. Wide interstate corridor divides OSBR.

cohesive social force in the community were dismantled. A spirit of community was lost. Pride of place turned into frustration and disappointment.

These factors combined to undermine the economic self-sufficiency and social independence of the OSBR community. As opportunities for jobs and careers opened up for young African Americans in other cities of the South, many of the better trained youth left Baton Rouge. What had once been a resilient and self-supporting community began to decline economically (**Figs. 1.28-1.29**). OSBR transformed into an urban zone of impoverished young families, too poor to relocate, and of elderly people who no longer had the will or resources to move to other neighborhoods. The strength of the extended black family, once a foundational institution of the community, now waned with dislocation of its young people and the increasing residential separation of the generations.

Fig. 1.28. Blight: abandoned house on Myrtle Street.

Fig. 1.29. Blight: abandoned automobiles and overgrown yards.

That segment of the younger generation which remained in place found few opportunities for local employment. They turned their attention to other available ways of making money or just surviving. Unemployment soared. By the 1990s, most residents of Baton Rouge thought of OSBR as a drug-infested, run-down neighborhood. With little knowledge of its better days and the vital role that OSBR had played in the development of the greater Baton Rouge community, this area was increasingly viewed as expendable by outsiders.

While only a shell remains of this once lively and successful place, its geographical position has remained central to the larger Baton Rouge community. City planners increasingly came to realize that the presence of a large blighted community standing directly between the economically expanding CBD and the state's growing flagship university could no longer be ignored. In 2005, OSBR was in the midst of a major urban revitalization effort launched by Plan Baton Rouge, an initiative of the non-profit Baton Rouge Area Foundation (BRAF). The BRAF has partnered with community residents, the city, LSU, and the Community University Partnership, to develop a master plan for revitalization.

Community Revitalization

> At certain times during our gatherings, there was an exchange of ideas, somewhat of a dialogue, that I believe will serve to overcome some of the inequities yet untouched by the powers that be. Yes, this was a new and beautiful experience. For me the diversity of this project gave a flavor to my life. These relationships without a doubt will linger in our lives forever (Fred C. Matthews, Jr., 1998 Community Liaison for CUPs McKinley High School Oral Project).

A final purpose of this book is to recount attempts by various organizations to address some of major pressing inequities "untouched by the powers that be." In chapter VI we chronicle the fifteen-year collaborative effort between local community activists in Old South Baton Rouge (OSBR), its state university neighbor, and, eventually, the city of Baton Rouge. The principal aim of this cooperative endeavor has been to stimulate revitalization of the community. It is the belief of these cooperating entities that aspects of the vitality of the historic community can be recaptured, resulting in a newly energized community.

Why revitalization? Although this community shaped the history and the culture of the state through its unique African American and multiethnic heritage, many who drive through the streets of Old South Baton Rouge today see only dilapidated houses, boarded up businesses, vacant lots, and drug dealers on street corners. Commuters who drive between downtown and LSU on Highland Road, the main artery connecting these two sections of town, glimpse only tantalizing vestiges of what once was an important part of their city. The common perception is that this neighborhood has no value and should be torn down to make room for upscale condominiums, fast-food restaurants, and strip malls that will service LSU and the expanding downtown area. Indeed, at the south end of Highland road, this is taking place (**Fig. 1.30**). Like many other cities across the country, a central issue in revitalization is determining the value of these historic neighborhoods.

What role does maintaining historic homes, buildings, and sites play in economic revitalization? In the larger senses of history and place, what role does preservation play? What happens when

Fig. 1.30. Highland corridor looking north from near Roosevelt intersection, 2007.

the history of an entire community is erased? Unlike post-Katrina New Orleans where whole neighborhoods have been devastated, OSBR still maintains much of its earlier integrity.

As the greater Baton Rouge community undertakes its revitalization project a pressing issue is the determination of what will remain and what will be bulldozed. Who will decide what survives, outside specialists or community leaders? How will decisions be made? This book recounts the story of a community's attempt at renewal, but also of the political and intellectual struggles involved in the making of large-scale decisions which will continue to affect the lives of many throughout the entire greater Baton Rouge community far into the future.

The authors believe that the preservation of a revitalized OSBR provides us all with a vital link to our common history. Our purposes here are two-fold: recounting the history of collaborative efforts by community stakeholders in an urban revitalization project, and documenting the historical, geographical, architectural, and cultural significance of this under-appreciated community. These two goals are naturally intertwined and interconnected. Stimulated by the threat of total urban renewal, the citizens of the OSBR neighborhood are acquiring a more in-depth understanding of their own history. Through many public meetings and articles in local newspapers and magazines, there has begun a virtual voyage of rediscovery into the history of the life of their community, the stories of its people, the patterns of its growth and development, and the role of its central institutions—the churches, businesses, and schools. Hopefully, this book will contribute to this awakening. Our hope is that the portrait we paint of this important community will convey something of its significance in the larger cultural history of Baton Rouge and the state of Louisiana.

Notes

[1] Classic studies of African American communities within New Orleans include: *Children of Bondage* (Davis and Dollard 1940), *The Eighth Generation* (Rohrer and Edmonson 1960), and *Black New Orleans 1860-1880* (Blassingame 1973). Four excellent books of readings on African Americans and Creoles of color in New Orleans have expanded our understandings: *Louisiana's Black Heritage* (MacDonald, et al., eds. 1979), *Creole New Orleans* (Hirsch and Logsdon, eds. 1992), *Creoles of Color of the Gulf South* (Dorman, ed. 1996), and *Creole: The History and Legacy of Louisiana's Free People of Color* (Kein, ed. 2000).

[2] The name "Jim Crow" is believed to derive from a routine in a minstrel show which toured the South in the antebellum period. In the skit Thomas "Daddy" Rice danced an awkward jig in blackface while singing lyrics which included "Weel about and turn about an do jus' so, Ebery time I weel about I jump Jim Crow." The term became a popular pejorative in reference to African Americans. In the 1850s it was generalized to refer to segregated railroad cars. Following the Civil War and Reconstruction periods, rights of legislation were returned to the Southern states. Almost immediately they began passing laws requiring the separation of the races. These restrictive regulations became popularly known as Jim Crow laws in the South. They specified penalties for racial mixing in private housing and in public accommodations. They created poll taxes to prevent poor blacks from voting, and they outlawed miscegenation. Many of these laws continued to be enforced until the Civil Rights Act of 1965.

[3] Emile Durkheim defined social facts as "ways of acting or thinking with the peculiar characteristics of exercising a coercive influence on individual consciousness." Social facts are constraints that are enforced by collective social sanctions and social will (Layton 1977:19-20; Durkheim 1938:liii).

[4] The role of the descendants of enslaved Africans as co-constructors of the culture, landscape, and history of Baton Rouge is detailed below in Chapters II through V.

The People
of Old South Baton Rouge

PHOTOS BY JAMES W. TERRY, III

ST. FRANCIS XAVI
THOLIC CHURC

SOUTH
ALL-STARS
POLE

Chapter Two

Shaping the Cultural Landscape

In 1920 when my family moved to Baton Rouge, the city limits extended to Terrace Street (then Reddy Street). South Baton Rouge, as we all know, has many rolling hills. Much of the land in South Baton Rouge was used for cultivating small farms and gardens. A few houses were scattered here and there.

~ Fred Matthews

As with many places, geography is the key to understanding the development of the Old South Baton Rouge community. Historical geography answers questions such as: "Why do people live where they do?" and "How was the history of a community shaped by its physical environment?" Even today much of OSBR is still popularly known as "the Bottom," but a thoroughfare called "Highland Road" transects the entire community—a seeming contradiction in terms. Within the community, residents distinguish between those who reside in the Swart community, closest to downtown Baton Rouge, and those who reside in the Bottom, closer to the campus of the Louisiana State University in the south (**Map 1.1**). In this chapter we chart the settlement of Old South Baton Rouge from its earliest beginnings through the mid-1960s. In order to place OSBR in the larger historical setting of East Baton Rouge Parish and, indeed, in Louisiana, we begin our story with a brief look at the cultural geography of Baton Rouge and OSBR.

Geographical Setting

Baton Rouge would not exist without the Mississippi River, but it is not just any river city. Its specific location is determined by the relationship between the water body and the surrounding topography—an interconnection with the "Father of Waters" which is complex and worth recounting. Today, most people who live in Baton Rouge turn their backs on the great river. It lies hidden behind levees which rise about twenty-five feet in height along the western edge of Baton Rouge (**Fig. 1.1**). Even to see the river, one must climb the levees or into the upper floors of a multi-story building. So we often forget what an amazing phenomenon this mile-wide juggernaut is as it relentlessly twists and turns its way southward. After engorging itself on the Missouri, the Ohio, the Tennessee, and the Red, it has become fat and lazy, but not torpid. South of Natchez it winds like a running snake, with a floodplain as much as fifty miles wide, but always constrained by the high lands along its eastern flank. These are the terraces and taller loess soil blufflands, laid down from billions of tons of wind-blown and water-borne glacial dust, ground from the igneous rock of Wisconsin and Illinois some 20,000 years ago. They represent pulverized trash caste off by the great glaciers. In southern Mississippi, the Pleistocene (glacial age) tablelands rise hundreds of feet directly out of the river bank flats. They form a continuous south-running wall which gradually diminishes in elevation the further one continues towards the south.

Each time the mighty river turns to run east, it smashes into this rampart of earth and is rejected, turning back to the west once again. At the loess hills of Fort Adams, just north of the Tunica Hills in southern Mississippi, the river is turned back, and again at Tunica, just south of

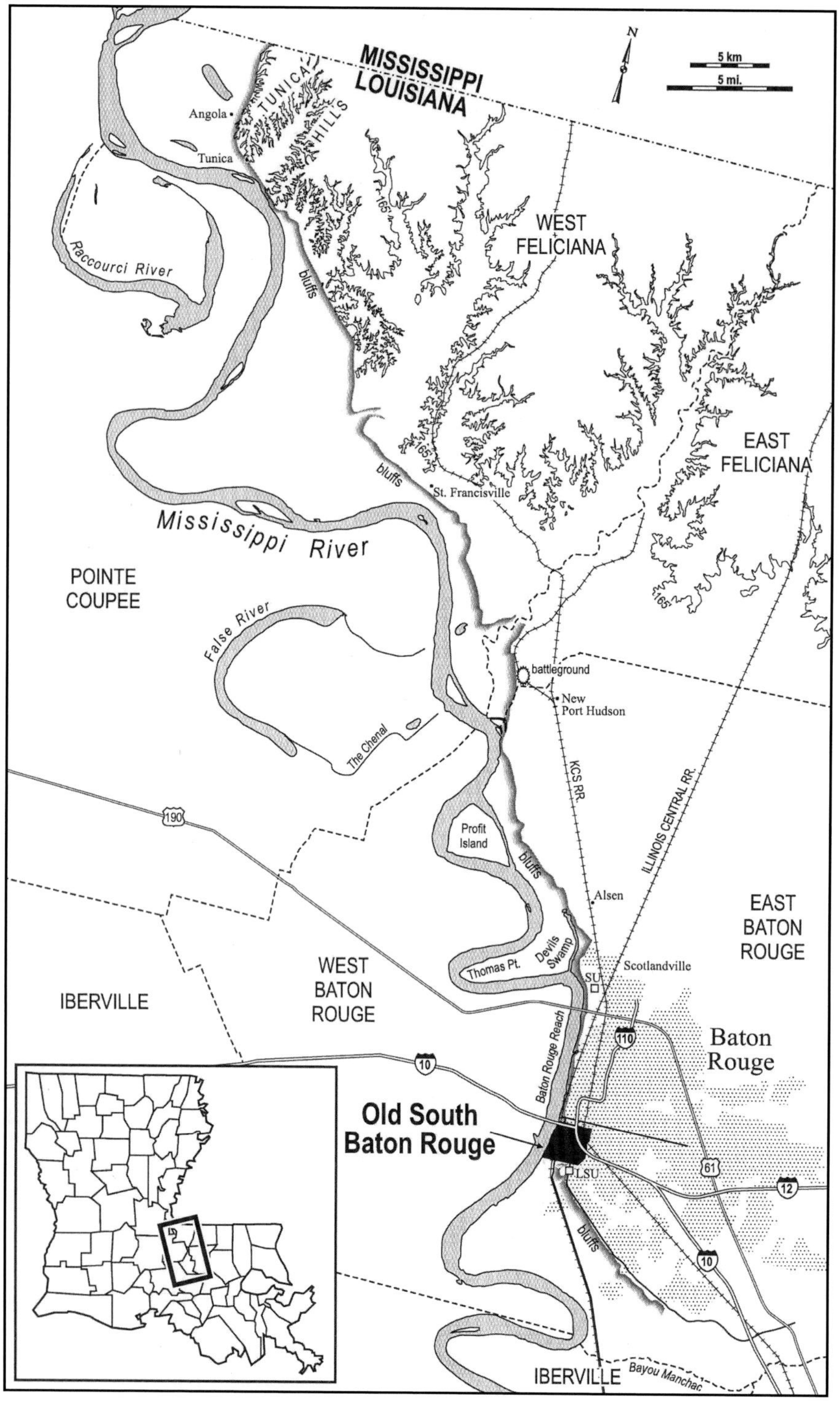

Map 2.1. Baton Rouge and the River.

the Mississippi-Louisiana state line (**Map 2.1**). It tries to ram its way east again at St. Francisville, and again at the highlands of Port Hudson, where so many Americans, including African Americans, fought and died in 1862. There it once made a mighty circle to the west, turning back upon itself to attack the highlands head-on from the southwest. It was here that the river was cut off forming the great ox-bow lake named False River but, though turned away again, the river has not yet given up. As its separates and rejoins around Profit Island, it sideswipes the eastern blufflands at the tiny town of Alsen. Here, it gathers its strength for one final assault on its seven hundred mile long foe. Running three and one-half miles to the southwest, it twists sharply around Thomas Point and Devil's Swamp and charges northeast again, directly at the blufflands at Southern University on the northern edge of Baton Rouge. But, once again the ramparts hold. Rejected one final time and out of will, the Father of Waters appears to give up, turning uncharacteristically south for eight miles almost straight as an arrow through the Baton Rouge Reach. About three miles along it rolls past the old historic center of Baton Rouge and immediately passes under the I-10 bridge. Here it begins to curve ever so slightly towards the west, rolling past Old South Baton Rouge along its eastern flank (**Map 2.2**).

Ironically, it is at this very point, at just the place where the river seems at last to have lost its will to attack its eastern highlands that the eastern bluffs die out in Old South Baton Rouge. One flank of the diminished highlands turns inland towards the southeast and continues running further on for several miles down to Bayou Manchac, where it finally disappears into alluvial bottomlands at the southern end of East Baton Rouge Parish. The old eighteenth century "High Lands" wagon road took advantage of this elevated topography, running from Baton Rouge southeast along the crest of the gradually diminishing terrace in order to connect the farms and plantations of the German-and-Anglo settled area south of Baton Rouge.

Closer to the river, the terraces extend only about a mile to the south of the I-10 bridge before breaking up in an irregular complex of gullies and steep-sided salients. This forms a series of small hills and valleys at the center of OSBR. While the relatively rugged terrain was unsuitable for farming, many people today consider this area to be one of the most picturesque in the city.

Complicating this picture is another geological feature—the Baton Rouge fault (**Map 2.2**). This east-west running fault marks the place where a geologically less stable delta is sliding slowly downslope into the Gulf of Mexico. North of the fault, the Pleistocene terrace is stable. What geologists refer to as the up-thrown block of the Baton Rouge fault stands at about fifty-five feet of elevation. It had not been subjected to flooding for perhaps as long as 20,000 years (Haag 1975:1). Though much

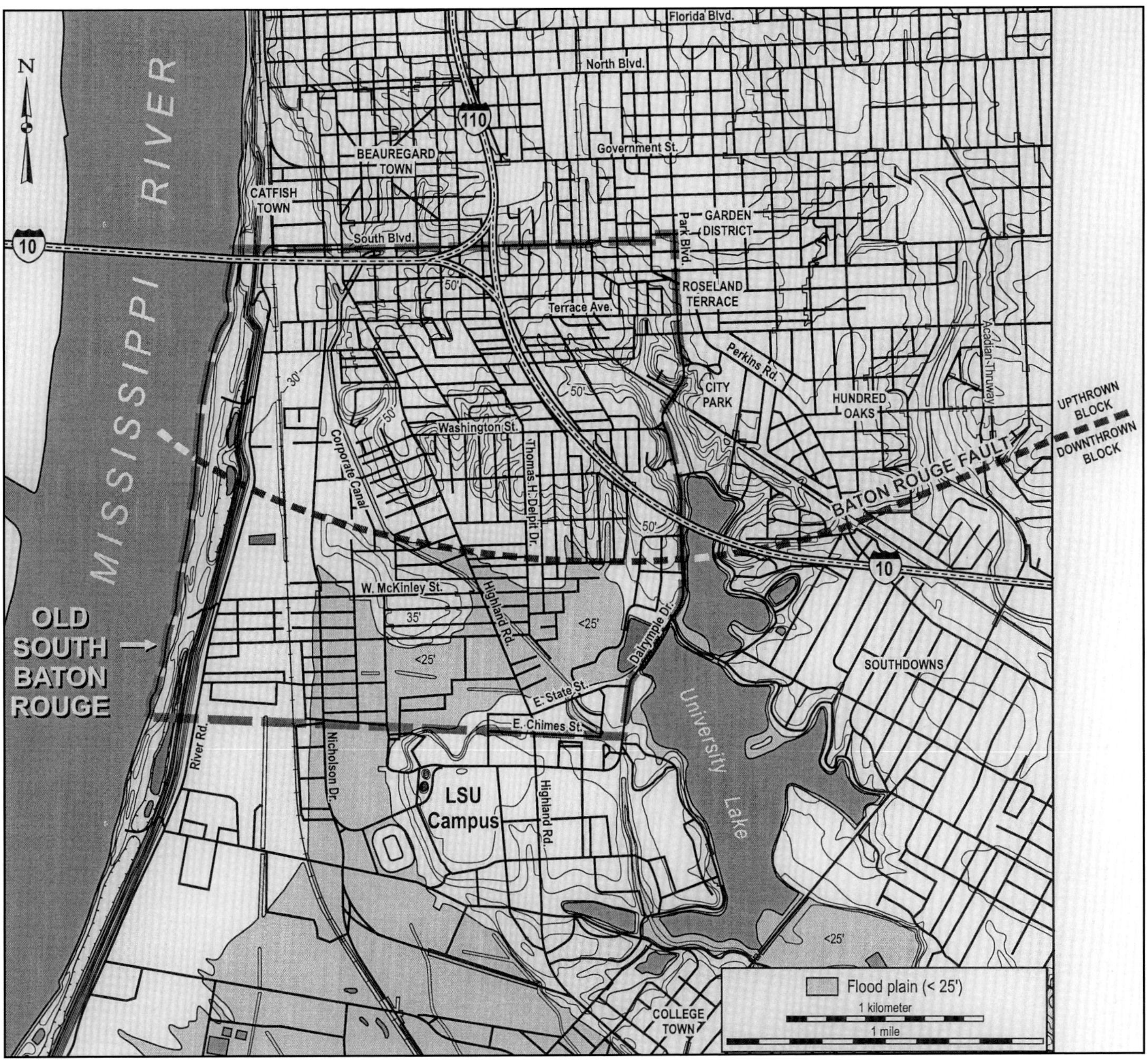

Map 2.2. The geomorphology of OSBR.

diminished from their northern neighbors, the terraces of Baton Rouge have been of considerable significance for its settlement. The city was founded here precisely because it was the southernmost place along the river where the terraces could be utilized. They represented a natural defense against the annual spring inundations so, since aboriginal times, they were populated first.

South of the fault, the downthrown block rests only as high as about thirty-five feet above sea level (Shuman 1993:12). To the north, the higher land supports the stable Pleistocene terraces. The alluvial bottom lands are another story. The fault causes a topographic anomaly beginning in OSBR just to the south of Washington Street. Behind the natural levee of the Mississippi this land was originally swampy and covered by cypress forests. This is the easily flooded zone which become known as "the Bottom" to the residents of OSBR (shaded area on **Map 2.2**).[1] Here, the narrow eastern floodplain of the Mississippi River blends with the drainage basins of the tributaries of the Amite River (Dawson Creek and Bayous Duplantier and Fountain), draining most of the runoff water away from the eastern bank of the Mississippi towards Lakes Maurepas and Pontchartrain. Lying as low as twenty-five feet, the floodplains which flank the Mississippi are prone to almost annual flooding, so its settlement came much later.

The Geopolitics of European Settlement

While the terraces in the Baton Rouge area had been thinly settled for thousands of years by Native Americans, the first great international struggle which would determine control of the Baton Rouge era came during the Spanish colonial administration. To make sense of the multi-ethnic nature of this portion of Louisiana, we briefly review the geopolitics of eighteenth century Louisiana. Geopolitics is that branch of history (combining geography and political science) which charts struggles between different nations over the control of vast stretches of land. In Louisiana, it explains how particular pieces of territory became so important along the colonial frontiers, and how landforms helped or hindered control and settlement by different groups and nations.

The French exploration party into the trans-Mississippi region by La Salle and Tonti in 1682; and the lower Mississippi explorations of 1699, by Iberville and Sauvolle—both sailed past the future site of Baton Rouge on the Mississippi River without noting anything particular about it. Rather, it was several miles above downtown Baton Rouge, where the great river flows straight eastward towards the bluffs at Southern University that the second party of French explorers found a group of thatched Indian huts and a tall red pole.

> From there we went five leagues higher and found very high banks called *écores* in that region, and in savage [Indian language] called Istrouma, which means red stick, as at this place there is a post painted red that the savages have sunk there to mark the land line between the two nations, namely: land of the Bayagoulas which they were leaving and the land of another nation-thirty leagues upstream from the baton rouge—named the Oumas . . . Along the shore, there were several huts covered with palmetto fronds, and a branchless maypole, which is reddened by the attached sacrificial offerings of fish and bear heads. The countryside is absolutely beautiful (Rodrigue and Phillips 2006:6).[2]

This pole was situated at the mouth of Bayou Baton Rouge, about one mile straight west of the bluffs at Southern University (near river mile 236). It marked the division between the hunting lands of the Houmas (crawfish red people) to the north, and the Bayou Goulas (bayou people) to the south (Edwards and Kariouk 2004:24). It would not be until 1718 that a small settlement on the French concession to Bernard Diron Dartaguette was established on the site of the present capital city. However, that venture failed by 1727 and no further settlement occurred under the French administration.

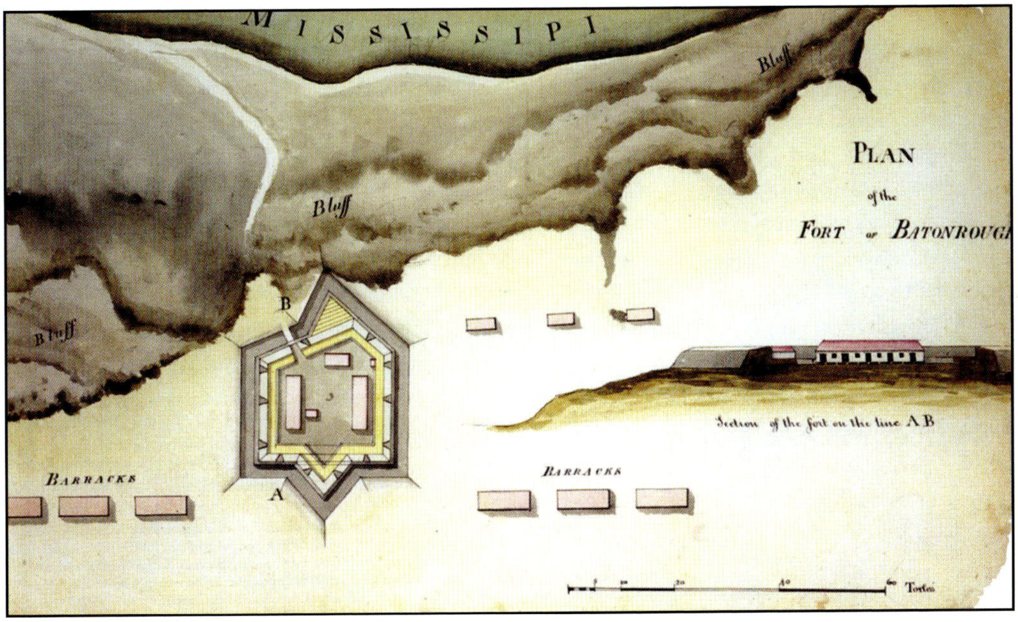

Map 2.3. 1806 Barthélemy Lafon plan of the British Fort at Baton Rouge. Courtesy of LSU Special Collections.

In 1763, following the British triumph in the Seven Years' War, France initiated the process of conceding parts of greater trans-Appalachian Louisiana to the British while transferring the remainder west of the Mississippi and the Isle of Orleans to the Spanish. The Treaty of Paris, ratified February 10, 1763, granted Great Britain the lands east of the Mississippi River down to the Iberville River, now called Bayou Manchac—the southern border of East Baton Rouge Parish. Because it now stood at the southwestern corner of British holdings in North America, the strategic importance of Baton Rouge was suddenly magnified. Under their military commander Capt. George Johnstone, New Richmond, a star-shaped fort with six points, and a trading post, were constructed near the site of the Pentagon Barracks (Lemmon et al., eds. 2003:101; Draughon 1998:4; **Map. 2.3**).

The new village of Baton Rouge contained an uneasy mixture of Americans, English, Scots, Irish, Germans, Spanish, French, Acadians, Native Americans, and both free and enslaved African Americans (Draughon 1998:5). Many of the European whites of East Baton Rouge were small farm owners holding a few slaves in the surrounding countryside. The village was equally dependent for its survival on the agricultural labor provided by these enslaved Africans as well as on their technological knowledge in cultivating rice and indigo. Baton Rouge was a perfect location for promotion of the new contraband trade which sprung up between the newly arrived Acadians living in Spanish territory below Bayou Manchac and the new English settlements to the north of the Iberville River.

Between 1779 and 1783, the Spanish successfully attacked the British. They acquired West Florida, including the present Florida Parishes and Baton Rouge. When Baton Rouge fell to the Spanish forces from New Orleans in 1779, new governor Bernardo de Gálvez repaired the fort and renamed it Fort San Carlos for Don Carlos de Grand Pré, the new district commander. Gálvez, himself, is said to have retained the galleried British commandant's house for his personal residence (Edwards & Kariouk 2004:47). Under Spanish rule, the Baton Rouge settlement began to grow, albeit slowly. Five years after the end of the American Revolution, in 1788, the population still only stood at 682—not even a good-sized village (Carleton 1981). Residents congregated primarily in what is today called "Spanish Town."

If Spanish Town was the foundational neighborhood of Baton Rouge, Beauregard Town was its second, and eventually, most central and important neighborhood. In the later years of the eighteenth century, Capt. Elias Beauregard had purchased two plantations for his proposed Beauregard Town. He envisioned an entirely planned and self-sufficient community complete with plazas, parks, and a formal system of interconnecting streets, not unlike the l'Enfant plan for Washington, D.C. in miniature. It was to be surrounded by broad boulevards: North, East, and South, with the river on the west (Franz 1993). His town was established atop of the bluffs south of the fort. By 1805 the streets of Beauregard Town had been laid out, but Beauregard had failed to sell many lots.[3]

The Florida Parishes continued to be held by Spain following the Louisiana Purchase in 1803. After the West Florida rebellion by Anglo-Americans against Spanish dominion in 1810, Baton Rouge became the capitol of the new West Florida Republic interregnum for several months. Soon it was incorporated into the American Territory of Orleans, and then, eventually into the new state of Louisiana in 1812. Still a small but strategically important village on the bluffs, as a new American city, Baton Rouge was on the cusp of momentous changes.

Baton Rouge and Its Plantations

The first steamboat to stop in Baton Rouge, the *Orleans*, chugged into port in 1812. Ten years later, in 1822, eighty-three steamboats, plus 174 barges and 441 flatboats docked at local wharves (Draughton 1998:8). The steamboat revolutionized the Baton Rouge economy, eventually transforming the riverfront from a landing area into an industrial zone.

The riverfront battures and their adjacent terraces and blufflands were just two of the triad of topographic landforms appropriated by settlers and essential to the economic and social development of the Baton Rouge area (**Fig. 2.1**). The third was the natural levees of the Mississippi. Annual inundations and springtime riverbank overflow resulted in the deposition of alluvium

Fig. 2.1. The Old State Capitol building, atop the Prairie Terrace in Beauregard Town.

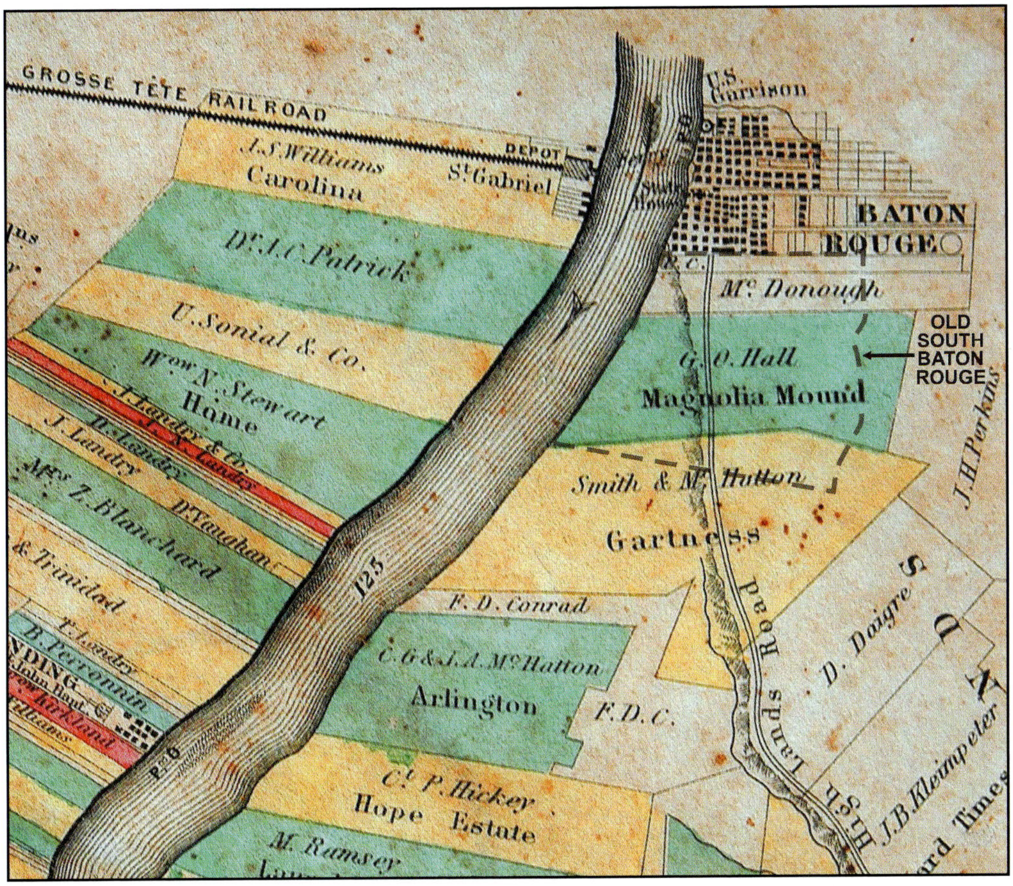

Map 2.4. 1868 Norman's Chart, Baton Rouge. Courtesy of LSU Special Collections.

from the muddy river waters as they flooded over the river banks. Eventually this produced natural levees parallelling the banks of the rivers and bayous. On large rivers like the Mississippi, the elevated lands might rise as much as fifteen feet above the mean water level. They were often a mile or more wide, providing an excellent location for large-scale agriculture. Plantations soon spanned the natural levees and adjacent low-lying flatlands along every major water course in southern Louisiana—particularly along the Mississippi. Beginning in the late eighteenth century, plantation agriculture grew into a nearly continuous settlement form paralleling both sides of the river from above Baton Rouge to well below the city of New Orleans (**Map 2.4**).

A map of land claims for the federal government, probably drawn ca. 1830 shows claims around Baton Rouge dating back to 1805. The purpose of the map is to document colonial holdings, including a number of sections claimed by the heirs of Armand Duplantier, previous owner of Magnolia Mound Plantation. These holdings include various sections located in Township 7 South, Range 1 West, Sections 53, 54, and 75 (1,125.62 acres; Edwards & Kariouk 2004:198). Magnolia Mound Plantation would eventually become the major part of Old South Baton Rouge. The Magnolia Mound Plantation house, a raised Creole-style home, remains on its original Spanish land grant in Section 75 (Sternberg 1996; **Map 2.5**; **Fig 4.37**). The property was first recorded in 1786 as belonging to James Hillin. With six enslaved Africans, he cleared 1,054 superficial arpents, equal to 948.6 acres. A small house (no longer standing) and several outbuildings were constructed, and land was prepared for the planting of indigo (Perkins 2004; Rodrigue and Phillips, 2006:10). Tobacco and corn were also planted, later cotton, and eventually sugarcane (Rose 2006). In this area, plantations were dependent for survival on the agricultural skills provided by enslaved Africans as well as

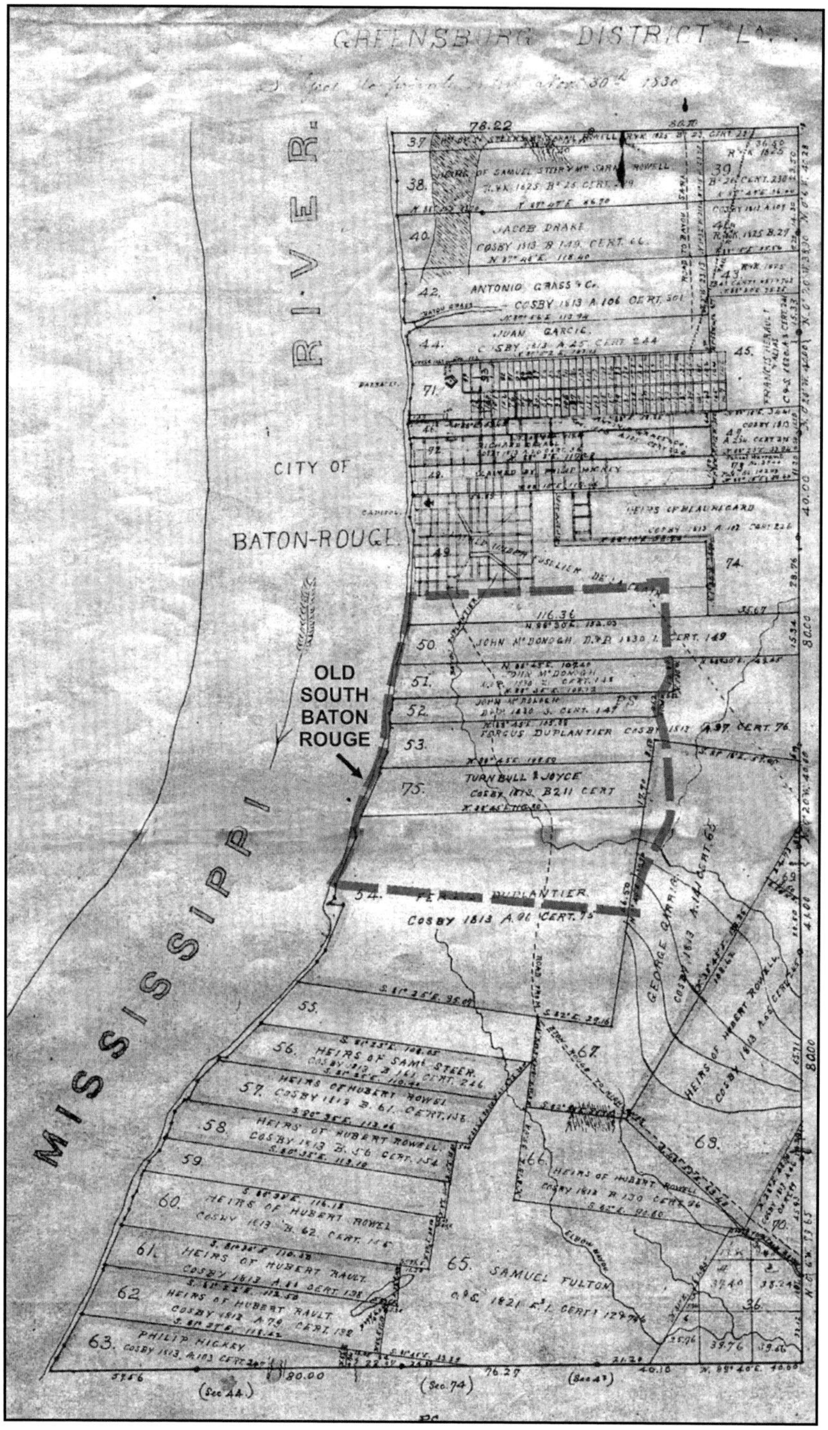

Map 2.5. 1830 Baton Rouge Land Districts.
Courtesy of LSU Special Collections.

their technological knowledge in cultivating rice and indigo.

Names of some of the first African residents of Old South Baton Rouge have survived in the archival record. In 1789, the succession of Constance (Hillin's wife) listed the names of the six enslaved Africans: Thomas, age forty, of the "Caramanty" (Caramantin) nation; twenty-eight-year-old Lucia and her two-month-old daughter of the Arfanti (Fanti) nation; Chiny, age twenty of the Chamba (Champa) nation; Caterina, age eighteen, of the Samba nation; and twenty-year-old Ana of the Mandinda (Mandingo) nation. In addition, there is evidence of at least three ex-slaves of Magnolia Mound Plantation, Charlotte Duplantier, Catchie, and Narcisse Duplantier, settling in OSBR in 1870 (Rose 2006). What has remained obscured in historical accounts is the interdependence between the races and cultures that was necessary in rural Louisiana during this plantation period, and, specifically, the role that enslaved Africans played in shaping Louisiana culture. The resulting Creole traditions in housing, gardening, religion, music, and the arts would be passed on generation-to-generation to shape the African American community that emerged as OSBR.

The development of OSBR may be followed through a sequence of maps made in the nineteenth and twentieth centuries. In 1880, Charles Greene surveyed Magnolia Mound Plantation lying just to the south of the urban zone of Baton Rouge. This rather accurate topographical map, now set against a modern map dating from about 1960, shows the principal buildings of the plantation situated atop an isolated remnant of the Pleistocene terrace—its top elevated at above thirty-five feet (sections colored green, **Map 2.6**). This piece of a terrace is the very southernmost expression of that system of Pleistocene bluffs which run northward along the eastern flank of the river. This map shows with considerable accuracy the location of the Magnolia Mound big house (labeled A), the sugar house (E), the slave quarters (G) and other structures, and a slave cemetery located on the slopes of the easternmost point of the terrace remnant (H). Vegetation is not depicted, so the alley of Live Oak trees which borders the lane leading straight from the

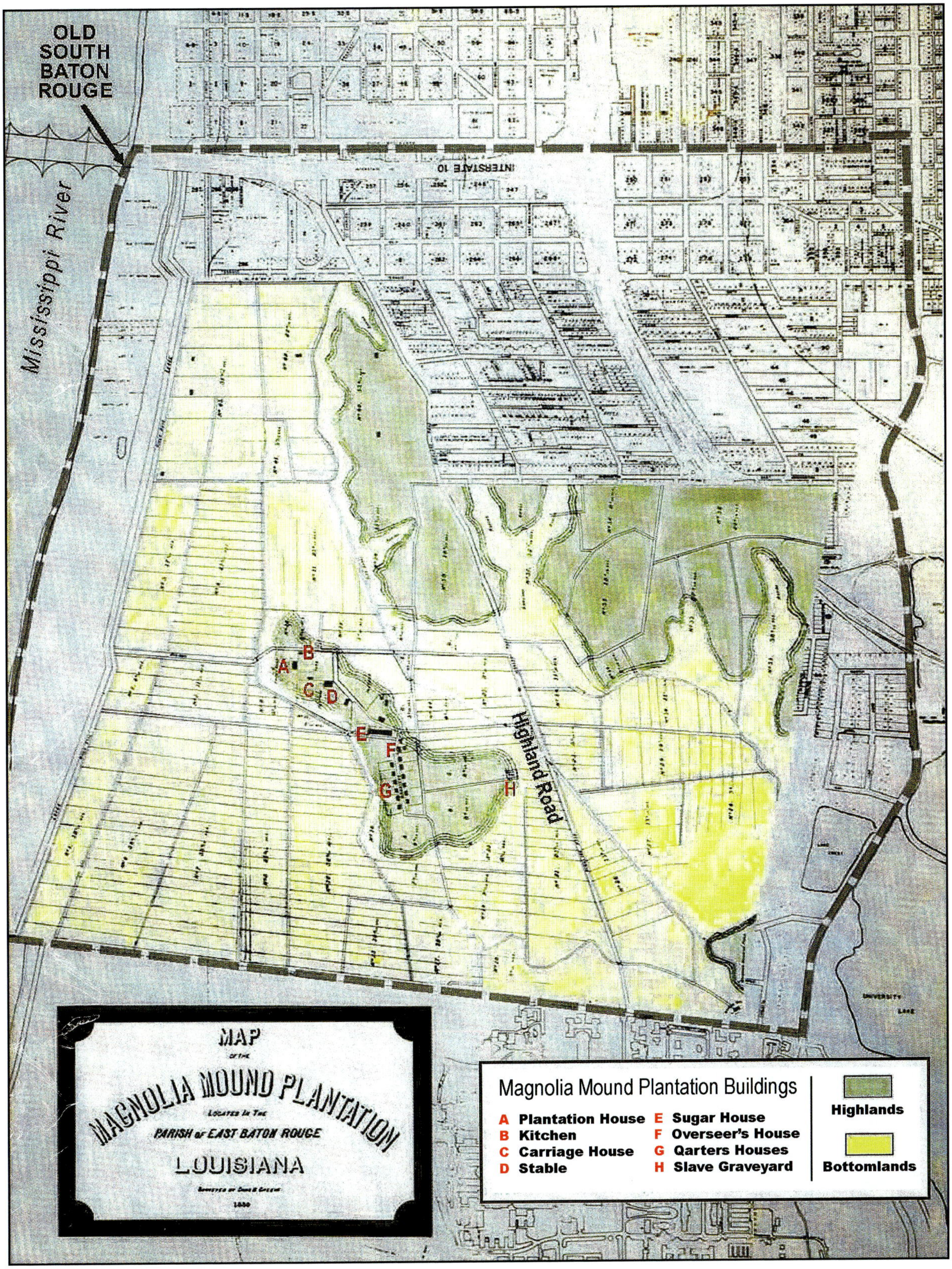

Map 2.6. Charles Greene map of the area around Magnolia Mound, ca. 1880.

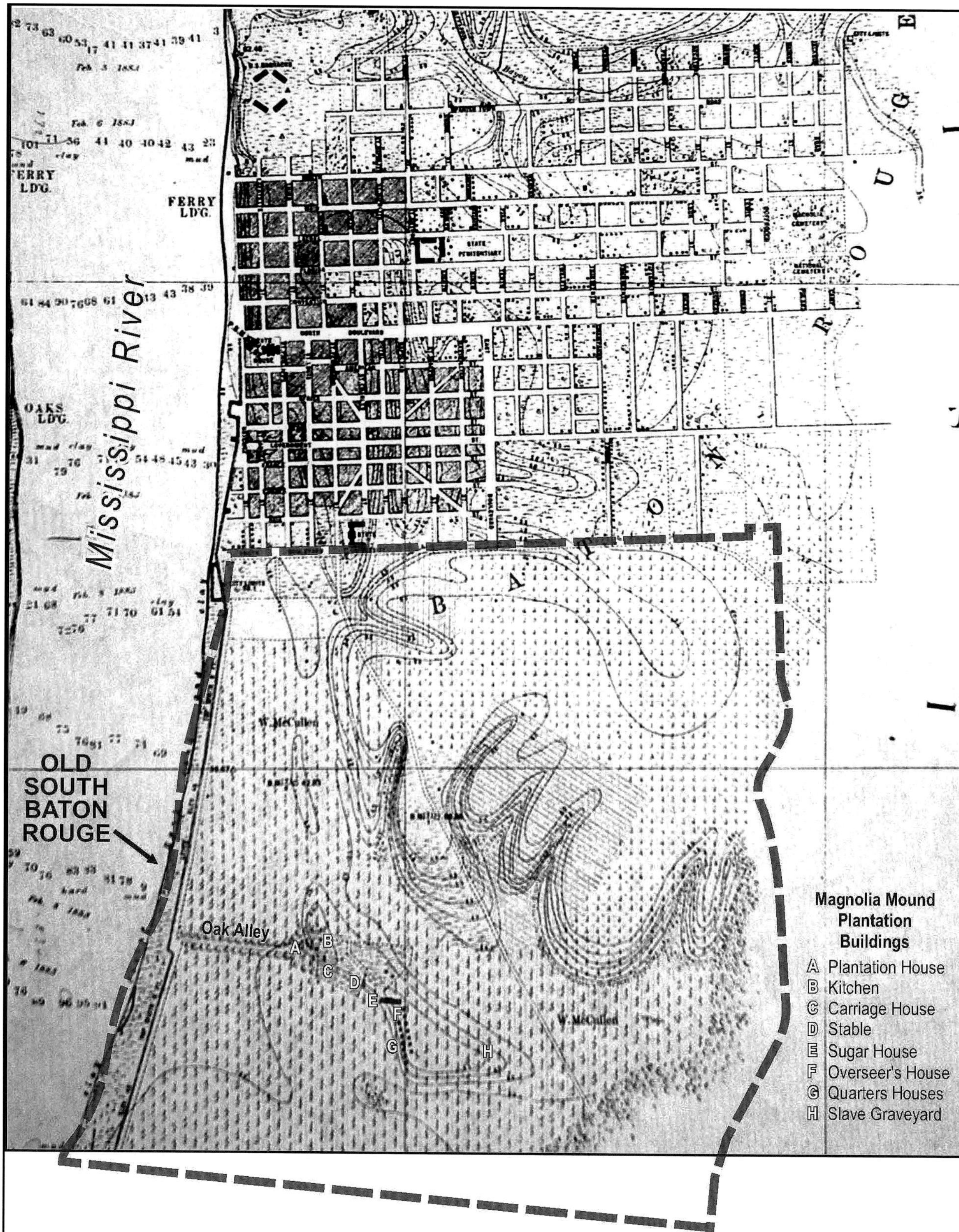

Map 2.7. 1881 Mississippi River Commission, Baton Rouge Area.
Courtesy of LSU Special Collections.

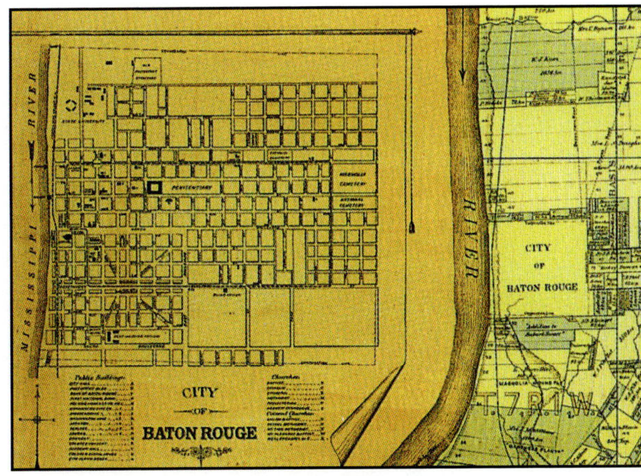

Map 2.8. 1895 map, EBR Parish, Baton Rouge Insert. Courtesy of LSU Special Collections.

big house to the river is not represented. We know it existed from an earlier map. "High Lands Road" extends across the plantation from north to south, and the alluvial lowlands which will in future years be referred to as "the Bottom" are clearly delineated (in yellow). They are elevated at between twenty and thirty feet.

Beginning in 1879, the United States Mississippi River Commission made a series of accurate survey maps of the river between St. Louis and its mouth. These included culture features on both sides of the river, running back from the batture for a mile or so. Topographical features are also shown. The 1881 map of Baton Rouge clearly shows the W. McCullen (Magnolia Mound) property with its alley of oak trees running to the river, and with the big house complex, sugar house, and slave quarters exactly as shown in the Charles Greene map of the previous year (**Map 2.7**). The extent of Spanish Town and Beauregard Towns are depicted with settlement areas shadowed. Note that Old South Baton Rouge will eventually expand to more than three times the area of the two original neighborhoods, combined.

Between 1876 (Mrs. Helen Walworth McCullen, owner) and 1889 (L. Barillier, owner), property lines of Magnolia Mound Plantation changed several times. In 1899 it was acquired by Baton Rouge Mayor Robert A. Hart. The Hart family would retain possession until 1965, when the plantation would be acquired by wealthy Texas developer Al German and then by the City of Baton Rouge. However, by that time the old plantation was a much-diminished version of its former self. Robert Hart had begun selling large sections of the northern part of the plantation to developers soon after he acquired it. The developers subdivided the sections in anticipation of selling many small lots to newly arriving African Americans.

The first indication of the expansion of urbanization into the sugar cane fields south of Baton Rouge is to be found on the 1895 property holdings map of East Baton Rouge Parish. Sandwiched between the southern limit of the city and the northern edge of Magnolia Mound Plantation are two lots marked "Addition to Suburb Swart" (right side of map below "City of Baton Rouge;" **Map 2.8**). The blocks between South Boulevard and Myrtle are just being laid out (left side inset plan in orange). This marks the beginnings of surburbanization of the city of Baton Rouge.

Swart Suburb, The Beginnings of Old South Baton Rouge: Black Migration in the Early Twentieth Century

In 1860, Baton Rouge was considered a typical medium-sized town in the South. Its 5,428 people, black and white, were eager to advance themselves and their town (**Fig. 2.2**). In 1862 Baton Rouge fell to federal forces. They held it during the duration of the Civil War. The accurate street map produced to record the Battle of Baton Rouge (August 5, 1862) provides an excellent view of the city in that period (**Map. 2.9**). The city extends south only to South Boulevard, and east to East Boulevard; Main Street and Florida Boulevard extend eastward to about 22nd Street. Highland Road runs south from Ferdinand Street into open lands beyond the "Deaf, Dumb & Blind Asylum" property. To the east, Perkins Road curves from Government Street to the southeast. Plantations with open sugar cane fields stretch south of the city. The majority of Magnolia Mound land holding remained intact until after the Civil War.

At the beginning of the war, 23 percent of the total population was enslaved (1,247) and about 10 percent (532) were free persons of color (FPC). After the Civil War and during Reconstruction, blacks migrated from plantations into Baton Rouge, establishing a sizable community along the

Fig. 2.2. 1858 Norman's Map—cartouche of Baton Rouge.

Map 2.9. 1862 Battlefield Map, Baton Rouge. Courtesy of LSU Special Collections.

Mississippi River at the foot of what is today Government Street. Here the flood plain is about 400 yards wide between the edge of the water and the bluffs. When it flooded, people found fish in the drainage ditches next to their homes, and occasionally even inside their flooded houses. Soon, the low-lying community was being called "Catfish Town" (Haag 1975; Rodrigue & Phillips 2006:34).

Fig. 2.3. Catfish Town as viewed from the Old State Capitol looking south, ca. 1920. Courtesy of LSU Special Collections.

Governmental and residential growth continued atop the adjacent bluffs. This dual-elevation settlement pattern was not unique to Baton Rouge. All along the river the well-established European settlers took the upper crest of the bluffs as the favored zone for their communities. People working at the river, on the river, and because of the river, took the lowlands—the "batture" area as it is called in Louisiana—and the floodplain. We see the same pattern in St. Francisville, where the Bayou Sara community, infamous for its sporting houses, sat at the riverbank, with the adjacent commercial capital of West Feliciana Parish residing atop precipitous bluffs. As steamboat travel stimulated increased commerce with the plantations and farms of the interior and industrial growth along the riverbanks, taverns and houses of prostitution sprang up on the battures to "service" the stevedores, laborers, and the weary travelers. The most famous of these was, perhaps, Natchez under the Bluff.

In Baton Rouge, following the Civil War, the flood plain between Government Street and South Boulevard became the settlement site for ex-slaves. This was part of what Suzanne Turner refers to as the "first great internal migration" of African Americans within the United States—"a migration that, played out in the local context, resulted in the creation of the South Baton Rouge Community" (2000:1). According to historian Mark Carleton, in 1865, "The whole flat down in Catfish [South Baton Rouge along the River] is covered with little Negro Shantyes and the [public] Schools are very full of Negroes" (1981:111). By 1870, Baton Rouge was more than half black.[4]

In 1883, the New Orleans & Mississippi Valley Railroad was constructed along the riverbank and across the western side of Magnolia Mound Plantation. It became the Yazoo and Mississippi Valley Railroad by 1898. In the city it ran along Natchez Street and through the developing river front industrial zone. The area south of Catfish Town (south of South Boulevard between Natchez—now River Road—and Nicholson) was the site of several new industries including the Burton Lumber Company & Saw Mill (313 Natchez), the Capital City Oil Mill, and the Baton Rouge Brickyard (913 Natchez, owned by Garig, Reddy & Co., Proprietors; **Fig. 2.3**).[5] This location was ideal for these businesses because it offered easy river access and was in close proximity to the railroad whose depot was located just to the north. Lumber could now be shipped out of the Burton Lumber Company mill by rail, and new industries sprang up along the tracks (on the site of the present day Illinois Central Gulf; ICG). One of these was the Baton Rouge Standard Sugar Refinery, built in 1885 south of South Boulevard near the levee.

This industrial zone was among the first areas in Old South Baton Rouge to be developed. Throughout the 1890s the land that constitutes OSBR remained for the most part undeveloped and rural, except for this south of Catfish Town area. Established industries began constructing company towns in miniature for their workers. By 1898, Sanborn maps indicate numerous shotgun-style houses in the alleys by the Brickyard and the Capital City Oil Co. (**Map. 2.10; Fig. 2.4**). Tiny properties on St. James Alley, Brickyard Alley, St. Louis streets, along the railroad line on Natchez Street, and along the River Road, all housed local African American workers.[6]

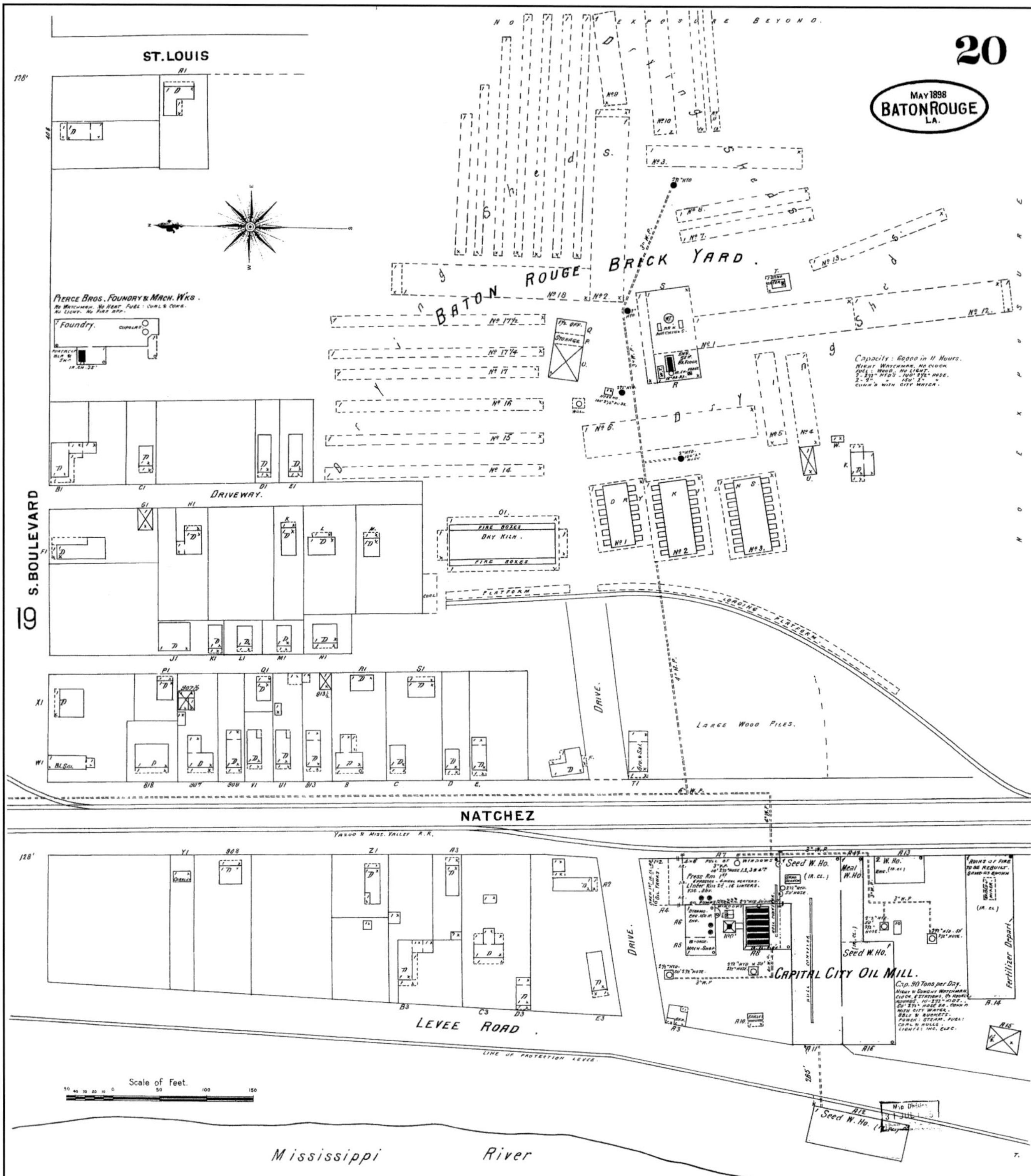

Map 2.10. 1898 Sanborn Map of Brick Yard and Houses, OSBR.

Fig. 2.4. The Baton Rouge Brick Yard.

The African American population had risen dramatically in the 1880s and the early 1890s. The city had become almost 60 percent black in the 1880s. While free people of color and town slaves had lived in pockets in Spanish Town and Beauregard Town, the black population now spread southward, below South Boulevard, into new areas contiguous with the industrial properties. These fringe settlements conflicted with the growing industrial zones along the railroads and the battures below the central city. Historian Mark Carleton described a "reign of terror" in the 1890s designed to force African American residents to sell their properties to the industrialists and land developers. Obviously, many remained there as late as 1910. Baton Rouge would not become a majority white city again before about 1920.[7]

Sometime before 1910, Renier Swart, a Dutch engineer, laid out the first suburb in what is now South Baton Rouge. A 1908 Sanborn map shows the beginnings of streets being extended

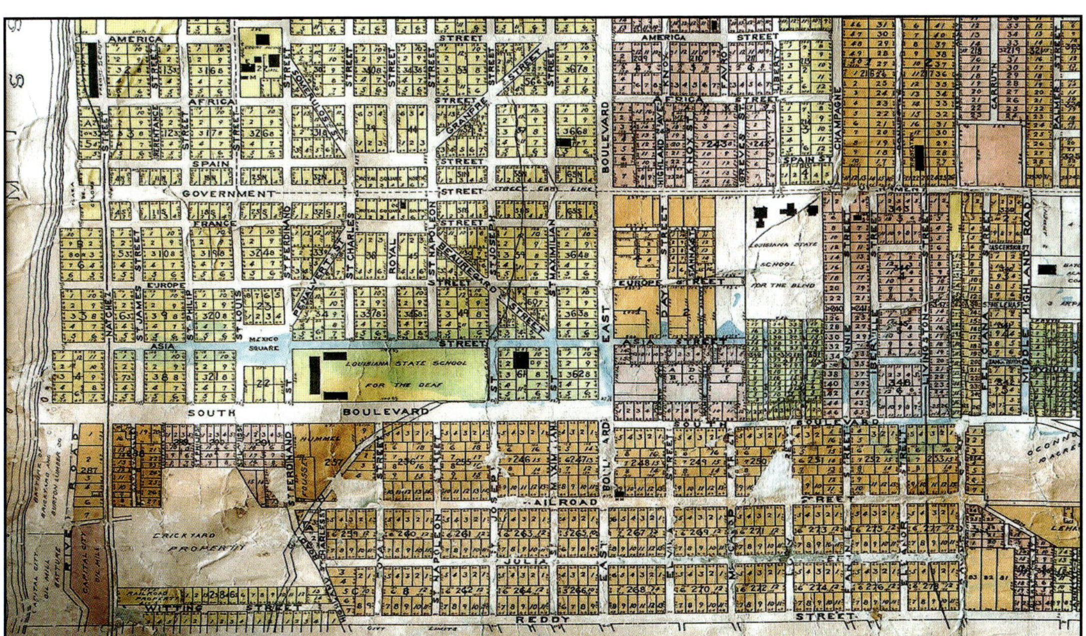

Map 2.11. 1910 Swart Map of Baton Rouge. Courtesy of LSU Special Collections.

southward from South Boulevard. Swart was apparently inspired by the way in which the French Quarter had been laid out by the French engineer Adrien de Pauger in 1722. Swart's basic blocks are almost the same size as those of the French Quarter—300 feet on each side (though he is using the slightly smaller English foot). And like the French Quarter, they are arranged with five standard lots in each block facing north and five facing south, and two (or more) "key" lots in the middle running east and west (**Map 2.11**). Key lots are longer than the standard lots by about thirty feet each. Between South Boulevard and Myrtle (called Railroad then), engineer Swart inserted three sets of key lots instead of only one. The industrial character of the riverbank area west of Highland Road/St. Ferdinand Street, described above, is obvious from the 1910 Swart map. Properties are labeled "Brickyard Property," "Capital City Oil Mill," "Burton Lumber," and "Railroad Property."

The new Swart subdivision contained over 427 suburban lots, each sixty feet wide. The subdivision was clearly planned as an extension of the older urban neighborhoods in Beauregard Town and that section of the city which was spreading east of it. The southern boundary of Baton Rouge had now moved to Reddy (Terrace) Street, three blocks south of South Boulevard. Already in 1910, new subdivisions were being planned for African American families, as evidenced by the indications of streets running southeastward below Reddy. In 1916, most of the lots in the area between South Boulevard and Julia Street do not yet have houses on them.

The dramatic expansion of Old South Baton Rouge into the former Magnolia Mound Plantation is documented in the 1916 and 1923 Sanborn maps. By 1916, a series of large parallelograms have been laid out, mostly to the east of East Boulevard (Thomas Delpit). Major streets running southeast have been extended to about the location of today's Washington Street. Smaller streets running east-west connect the thoroughfares. Very narrow lots, mostly running northwest-southeast are beginning to fill between the connecting streets (**Map 2.12**).

Map 2.12. 1916 Sanborn Map of Baton Rouge.

Map 2.13a. 1923 Sanborn Map of Baton Rouge.

These properties are, for the most part, still on the terraces. West of East Boulevard, the subdivisions are only beginning to be laid out. There is reason to believe that the large subdivisions to the south of Washington Street have already been planned and located, though they do not appear on the 1916 Sanborn map. However, they do show up, fully planned, on the 1923 Sanborn.

The central theme of the decades between the two world wars is rapid urbanization. By 1923, dramatic changes are seen (**Map 2.13a**). All of the parallelogram area between Reddy (Terrace) and Washington Boulevard had been subdivided east of Highland Road. About 580 residences were already in place, particularly in the northern sections adjacent to Swart (north of Reddy). Assuming one house per lot, the subdivided area within the parallelograms was 93 percent settled (**Map 2.13b**).

Urbanization had spilled over the southern end of the terraces south of Washington. A grid pattern had been laid out upon the landscape without regard to elevation. In a sense, Baton Rouge had expanded beyond the boundaries of its original *raison d'être*. New settlement expanded out across the flood plain so carefully avoided by previous generations of settlers (**Figs. 2.5-2.6**). Suburban development had now invaded the Bottom, with most of the new tracts lying on low and easily flooded alluvial lands below the Pleistocene terraces.

The area between Washington and Monroe had been completely laid out with north-south running streets named for states and the blocks subdivided into narrow east-west running lots, mostly thirty-five feet wide by ninety-five feet deep (**Fig. 2.7**; **Map 2.13c**). These are clearly intended for low-income laboring-class residents. Subdivisions also extended south of Jefferson (now Polk) to about Buchanan. A subdivision just east of Highland Road had somewhat larger lots, and a rectangle east of East Boulevard (called Texas south of Washington at that time) had been laid out with small lots equal to those in the subdivisions just to the north. The streets running west

Map 2.13b. 1923 Sanborn Map, between Reddy and Washington showing parallelograms.

Fig. 2.5. Intersection of the terraces and the bottom on Washington Boulevard.

Fig. 2.6. A shotgun house set on edge of terrace in the bottom.

Fig. 2.7. A shotgun house fitted to a narrow lot.

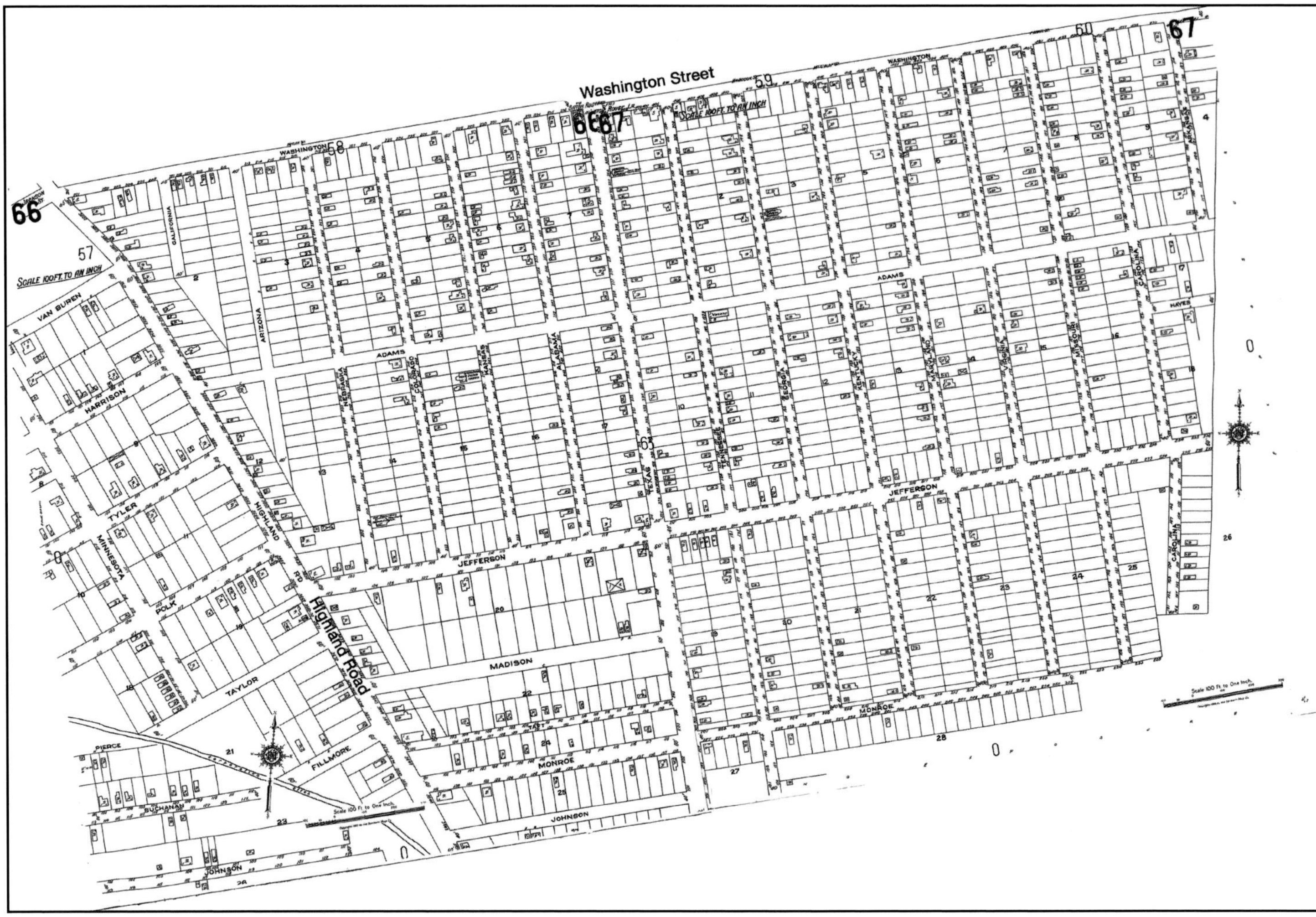

Map 2.13c. 1923 Sanborn Map: area south of Washington Street showing extent of development at the time.

connected with Highland Road down to about McKinley Street and were being extended west of Highland Road. This pattern ran south on Highland Road to about where the corporation canal (old Bayou Duplantier) crossed under it. There were about 350 houses established by this year, and the area was about 30 percent settled.

Settlement expanded westward of Highland Road up the steep eastern flank of the Magnolia Mound terrace remnant where the old Magnolia Mound slave cemetery once lay. Somewhat less than half of the lots in this western zone have houses on them, and the lots are slightly larger, with sixty-foot by 150-foot footprints, mixed with lots forty feet wide by the same depth. The densest and most successful newly settled zone in 1923 was the area immediately south of Reddy (Terrace) between East Boulevard (Thomas Delpit) and the L&N Railroad line (now the ICG). Most of the area west of Highland Road and South of McKinley Street remained to be settled at this point. A number of the streets in OSBR have experienced name changes since 1923. For example, Buchanan was called Monroe, Harding Street was called Madison, and East Polk Street was called Jefferson. Thomas Delpit south of Washington was originally called Texas.

Between 1925 and 1932, LSU made its move from its second Baton Rouge campus at the Pentagon Barracks, near the State Capitol, to the present site south of Chimes Street.[8] The southern limit of expansion of OSBR had now been established. The entire southern half of the community rested largely in a bowl between the highlands of the central LSU campus and the highlands north of Washington Boulevard. An examination of the excellent 1932 aerial photograph of OSBR reveals that, with the exception of the lowest-lying ground, most of the lots in the area south of Washington Street had now been filled in with houses (**Fig. 2.8**). The cane fields of Magnolia Mound still extended along Nicholson Drive and north and west of the LSU campus.

Fig. 2.8. A 1932 aerial photograph of OSBR.

Jim Crow and the Checkerboard Pattern of Settlement

Economy and race both played important parts in the establishment of the positioning of the new suburbs which were expanding to the east and south of the central city in the 1910s and '20s. Patterns of settlement were strongly shaped by the increasingly restrictive rules and norms of racial segregation. Since before the beginning of the twentieth century, African American men and particularly women had worked as laborers and domestics in the houses of affluent whites in Louisiana cities. Lacking much formal education, they worked as cooks, nannies, maids, personal servants, and as gardeners, chauffeurs, carpenters, stable hands, and handymen. Before the rise of the single-family automobile in the 1940s and '50s, most domestics walked to work, meaning that they could not live too far from their places of employment. A distinctive pattern of racially dominant neighborhoods grew up in many Southern cities as a result of residential segregation. In his geographical study of New Orleans, Peirce Lewis refers to the resulting pattern of segregated housing as "superblocks" (1976:46-47). In Baton Rouge, we refer to it as a "checkerboard block pattern," with white- and black-settled zones interspersed and interconnected. More affluent white families established their residences along the major boulevards. African American neighborhoods stood conveniently close behind these white residential strips because opportunities for permanent employment were locally available. A 1940 map of housing by race in Baton Rouge (discussed below), illustrates the nature of the racial settlement in that year (**Map 2.14**).

Although the Swart neighborhood was originally intended as a middle-class expansion of Beauregard Town, it quickly began to function as a service neighborhood for this northern neighbor and for the riverside industrial complex. By the early 1920s, African American families were moving into all sections of Swart. The eastern end of Swart now functioned in a similar way for the growing Garden District and Kleinert Terrace neighborhoods. Those Swart blocks between 15th and 18th streets, east of the ICG Railroad, were convenient to the comfortable middle-class professional, business, and university-oriented families which were moving in along Park Boulevard—the eastern border of OSBR, and the western edge of the Garden District and Kleinert Terrace. Park Boulevard, a divided street with a "neutral ground," was laid out in about 1925. It was connected southward with Dalrymple, the University lakes, and the LSU campus before the end of that decade. A similar part of the checkerboard-like pattern is to be seen in the southern part of OSBR, where employment connected with the construction of the LSU campus brought many African American workers to the area. In the early 1920s they settled in suburbs close to LSU in the area of the presidents' streets (McKinley, Grant, Garfield, Jefferson, Madison, Monroe, etc.).[9]

In 1927, Baton Rouge commissioned a map of the sanitary sewers of the city (**Map 2.15**). Sewage lines extended only as far south as the Swart subdivision, although subdivision settlement had been extended over a mile south as far as Roosevelt Street. South of the relatively middle-class Swart neighborhoods north of Terrace, almost no sewage service was available to OSBR residents. Presumably out-houses and septic tanks were the rule. McKinley High School was constructed in this year, and East Boulevard was becoming a successful commercial strip with Italian and African American owned stores and businesses lining the street between Terrace and Washington. Highland Road also supported a number of businesses. Nicholson Drive was being laid out, extending about halfway down to the LSU campus area. A railroad spur now ran the length of Railroad (Myrtle) Street, connecting the L&N (later ICG) railroad with the Yazoo and Mississippi Valley line which ran along the river. A trolley line used this spur to bring commuters into downtown Baton Rouge.

In 1929 the Higginbottom Street Map of Baton Rouge shows how settlement finally extended to the bottom of OSBR (**Map 2.16**). Park Boulevard/Dalrymple Street had been extended past the University Lakes to State and Chimes streets. Alaska Street had been connected to the LSU campus,

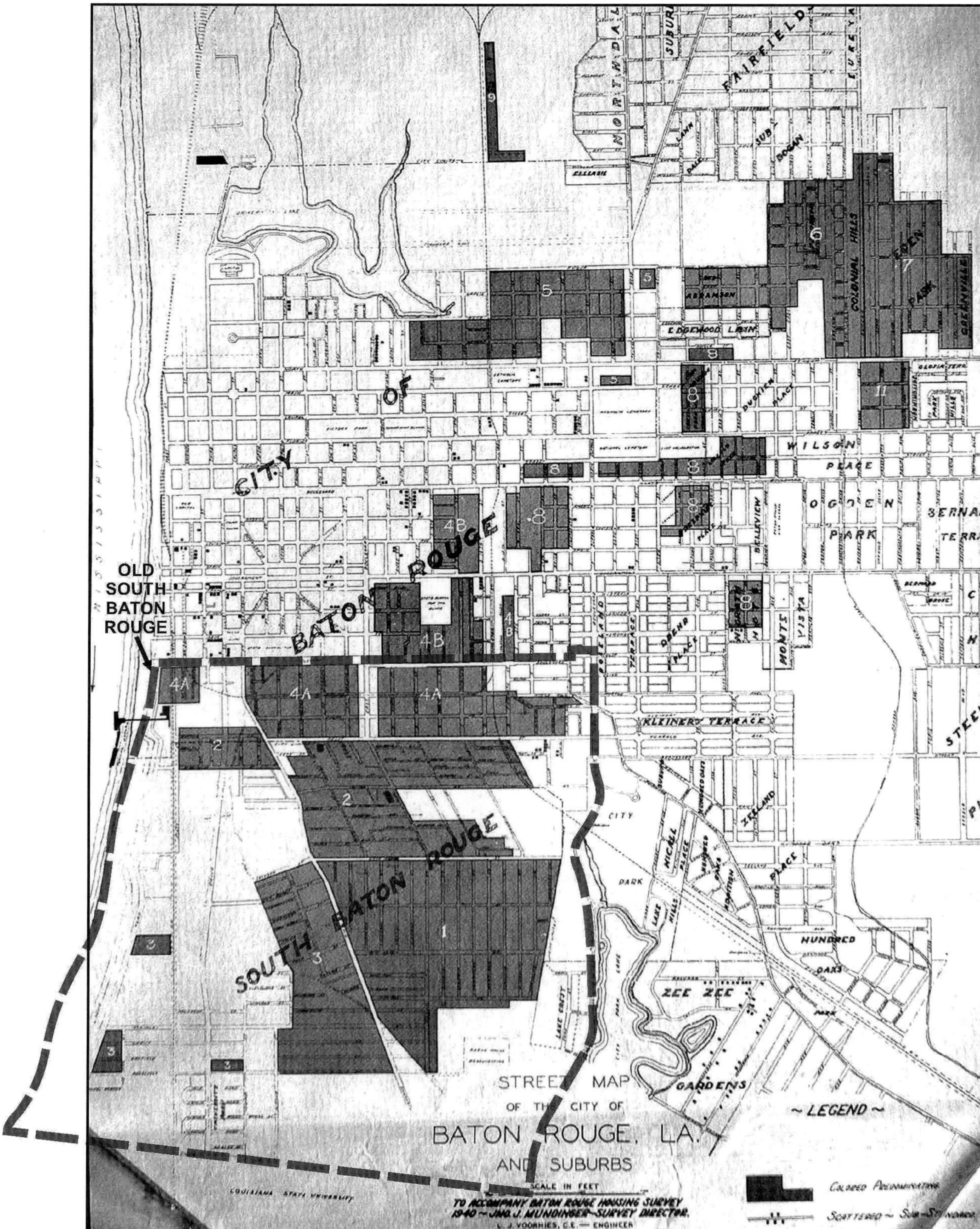

Map 2.14. 1940 Voorhies Housing Survey map of Baton Rouge, showing checkerboard pattern of racial settlement. Courtesy of LSU Special Collections.

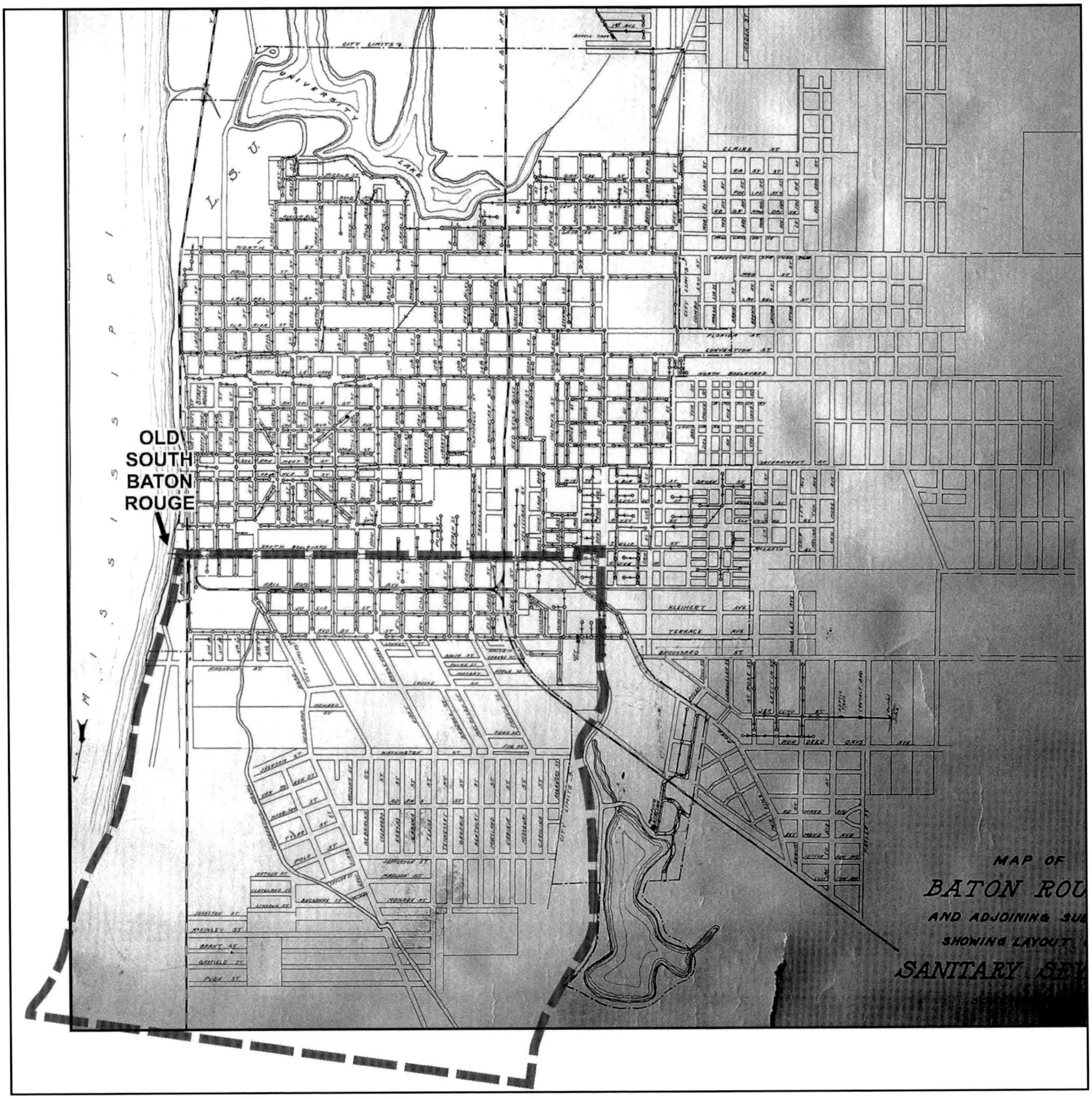

Map 2.15. Voorhies 1927 Sanitary Sewer map of Baton Rouge, detail.

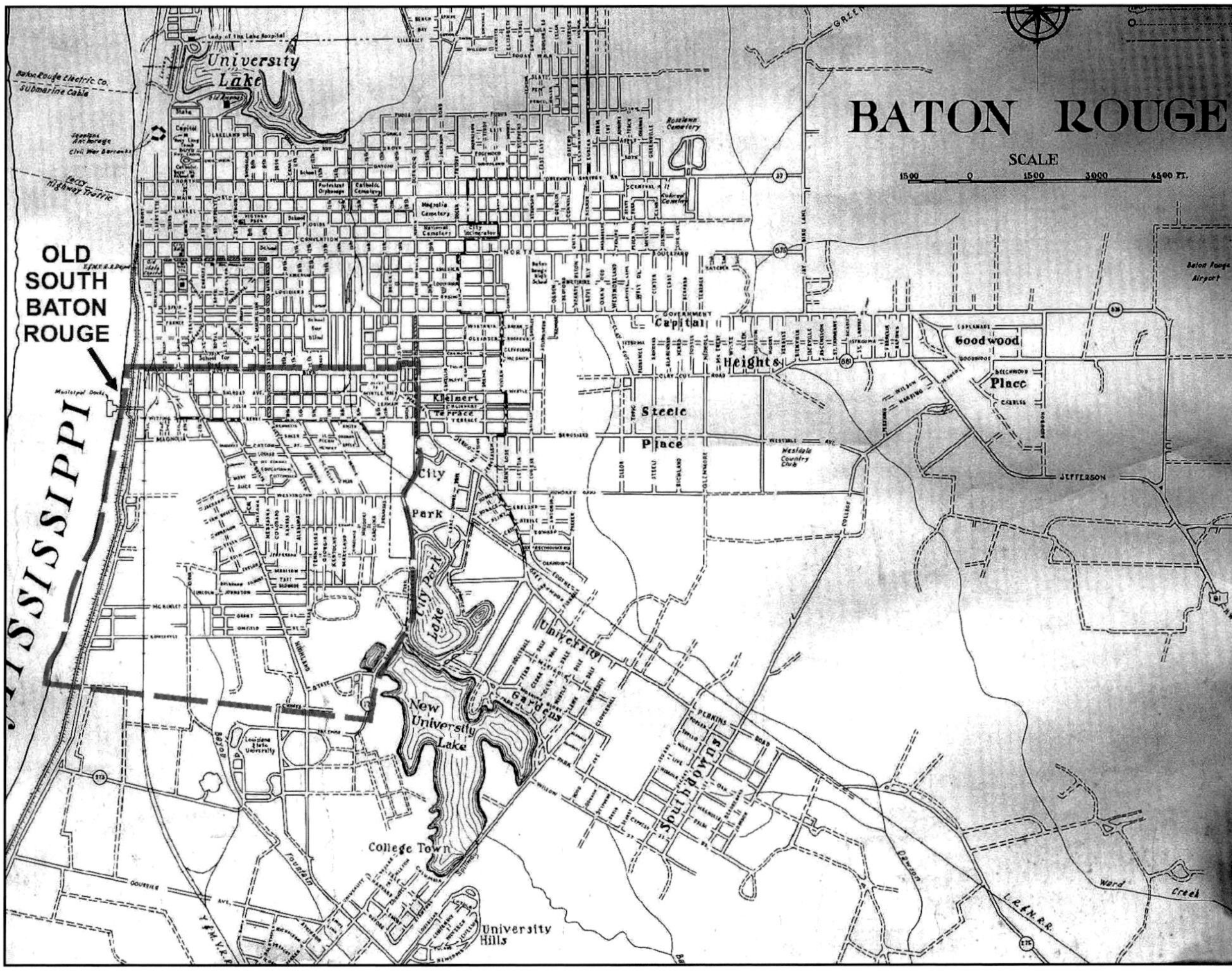

Map 2.16. 1929 Higginbottom street map of Baton Rouge.

as had Nicholson Drive. The connecting thoroughfares between the CBD of Baton Rouge and the LSU campus were now complete.

A highly detailed subdivision map of OSBR was completed in 1930. The Pillet map shows the blocks of almost continuous settlement from Reddy (Terrace) all the way to Roosevelt Street, near the southern end of OSBR (**Map 2.17**). Areas not completely laid out include those north of Washington Street (the eastern parallelograms), the southeastern corner near the lakes, and much of the area between Highland Road and Nicholson Drive. Development west of Nicholson Drive was minimal, though Grant, Garfield, and Roosevelt had been extended over to the River Road. The small Magnolia subdivision where the WJBO radio station is located is in place.

A housing survey of all of Baton Rouge was undertaken in 1940. This fascinating map clearly shows the patterns of ethnic population density in Baton Rouge (**Map 2.14**). By this time, housing had become much more segregated, and neighborhoods could be designated as either "white predominating" or "colored predominating." OSBR was divided into a number of zones of black settlement. The new subdivisions at the southern end of OSBR on either side of Nicholson Drive remained white, for the most part. Interestingly, the mixed, residential/commercial area on East Boulevard (Thomas Delpit) between South and Reddy (Terrace) was also a narrow island of white settlement, almost certainly in reference to the Italian community in that area. This was the

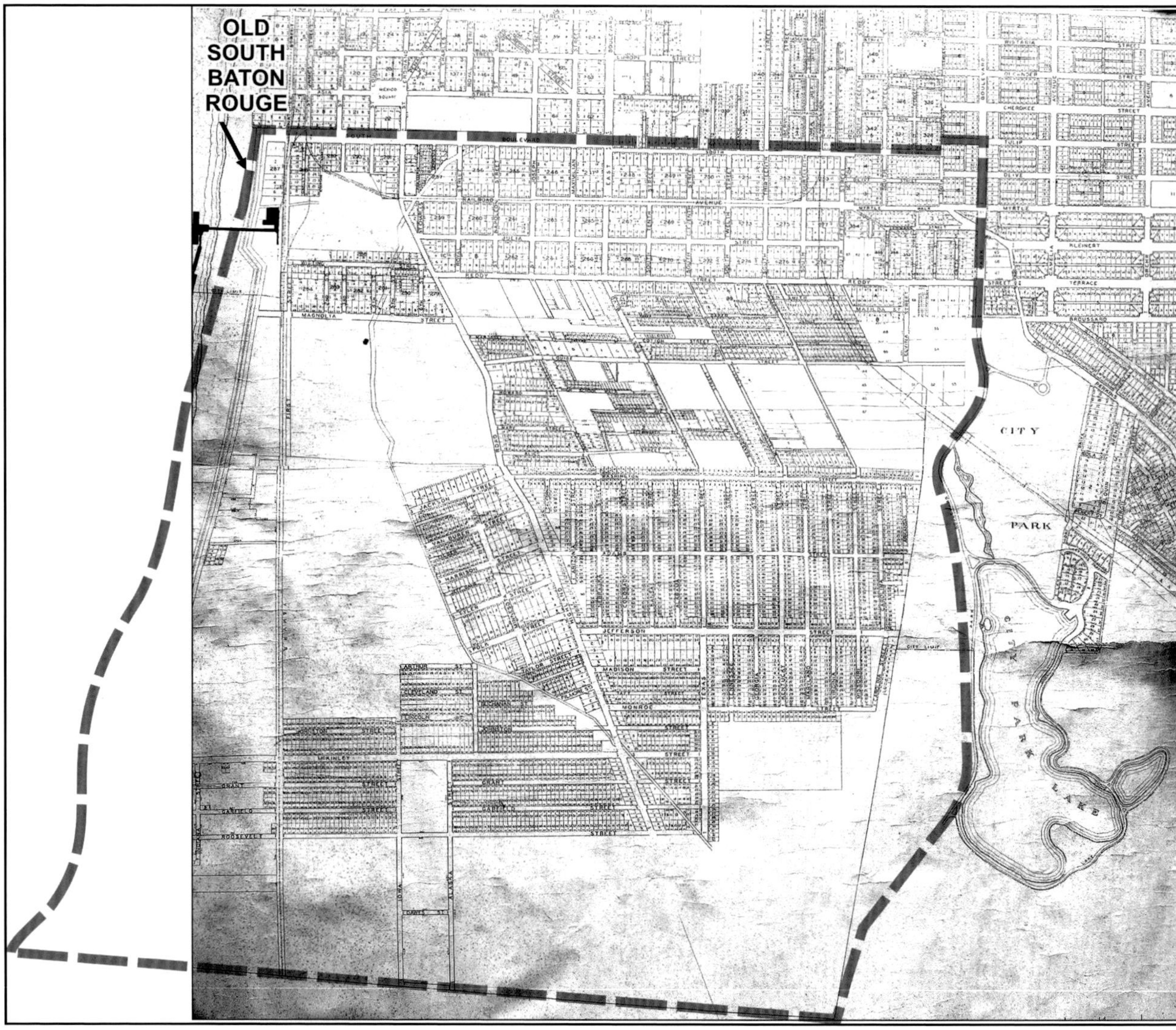

Map 2.17. Pillet Street Map of OSBR in 1930 showing development of the subdivisions in OSBR.

developing commercial area at the heart of OSBR. Most of the rest of the Swart neighborhood was designated "colored predominating." Highland Road had become mostly black, except for a small area at the intersection of Terrace and Highland.

The last Sanborn Insurance Company map to be published was a composite of maps made between 1923 and 1951 (**Map 2.18**). Like the previous Sanborns, it is incomplete in that it leaves out certain areas where settlement was not yet dense. Settlement was still not continuous across OSBR, though it had increased and expanded into formerly vacant areas. Hundreds of wooden shotgun houses and bungalows now filled the central bowl of the community between Washington and Roosevelt streets. Most of the lots in the Swart neighborhood were filled, and about half of the area between Terrace and Washington had been settled. New white residential neighborhoods have been laid out along Dalrymple Drive near the University Lakes, and along State and Chimes streets, to the east of Highland Road, near the University. This was OSBR at the height of its growth, before the triple impact of desegregation, interstate highway construction, and the flight of jobs to other areas of the city had been felt.

Map 2.18. The last Sanborn map of Baton Rouge, a composite of the 1923 through 1951 surveys.

The Geographical Impact of Nationwide Changes in the 1960s

By the early 1960s the automobile had become king in the U.S. The interstate highway system was being laid out across the country. Baton Rouge was no exception. A major bridge was planned across the Mississippi River near the center of the city, but the problem of how to connect that structure to the highways running east towards Hammond, and southeast towards New Orleans had to be solved. At the time, New Orleans was in the midst of a titanic preservation struggle called "the Second Battle of New Orleans" (Baumbach 1981). A large-scale effort was under way to prevent the construction of a riverfront expressway which would have cut the French Quarter off from its access to the river. This was a battle which the preservationists eventually won, due to a fortuitous combination of political might excerised by residents of the French Quarter, the preservationist community, and commercial and tourist-oriented interests. No such confederation of constituencies stood to protect African American communities of OSBR and Valley Park (between Acadian and College, a mile to the east). Dr. Baranco and other prominent OSBR citizens complained that the northwest running section of the expressway should be placed above the existing railroad line to minimize the impact on the community (Turner et. al. 2000:9).

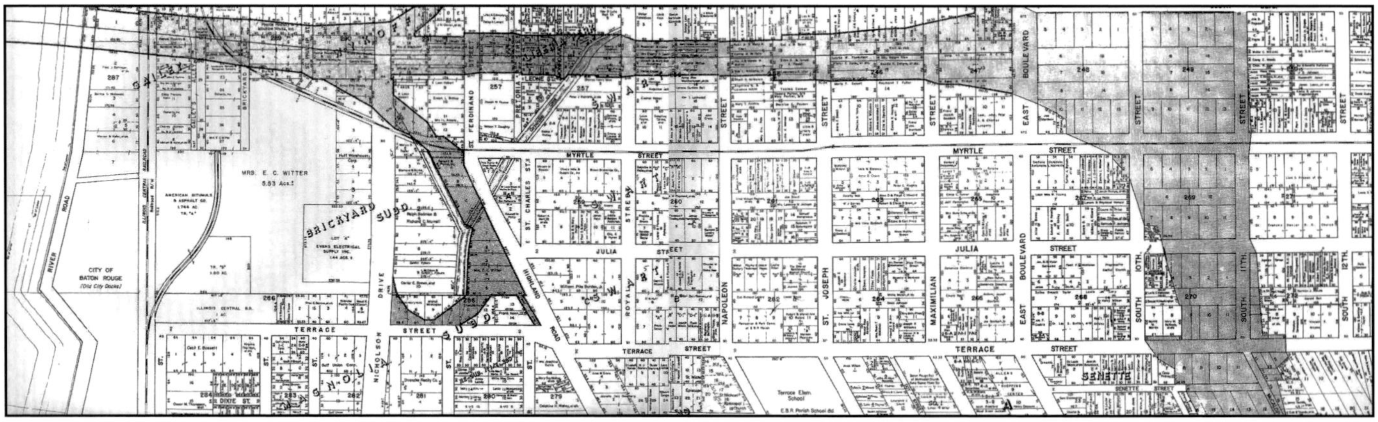

Map 2.19. 1960 map showing the planned route of the I-10 expressway through OSBR.

Inexplicably, some of the densest settled residential land was selected for the thoroughfare by the Louisiana Department of Transportation and Development. It was land owned preponderantly by African American residents. This was in spite of the fact that there was a shortage of housing available for blacks in the segregated city of the time. About 400 dwelling units and the brand new colored St. Francis Xavier High School were destroyed to make room for the six-lane elevated highway and the massive I-10-I-110 interchange (**Map 2.19**).

Bridget Jackson Brister, a member of St. Francis Xavier who had grown up in OSBR, was displaced with the building of the interstate. She recalled:

> It wasn't until they built the interstate and split the community in two that people actually left what had been their home-base since, I guess, their families first came to this area. That had a very devastating effect on our parish. When that interstate came through it really changed my life. Our house was taken when the interstate came. A lot of families experienced that. Some continued to reside in the South Baton Rouge Area. Most people though ended up moving. And to leave everything that you're familiar with and kids that you've grown up with, a neighborhood where you felt comfortable walking out your door and around the corner or down the street or a group would get together and you would walk over to the YMCA or to the Lincoln Theatre. It had a devastating effect on all of us.

Members of St. Francis Xavier Church were particularly affected. In 1956, the new St. Francis Xavier High School the parish's only all black Catholic high school had been dedicated. More than 3,000 African Americans were on the church rolls, and the classrooms were filled to capacity. Only six classes graduated from St. Francis Xavier High School. Interstate 10 carved a path straight through the building. Parishioners Percy Franklin and Johnny Little went to Washington, D.C. to discuss the situation with federal highway officials, but plans remained unchanged. St. Agnes and First Methodist were saved, but St. Francis Xavier experienced a tragic loss.

Others in the community organized to stop the interstate going through the heart of the community. Dr. Beverly V. Baranco maintained that "what we really would prefer would be for the interstate to follow the KCS L&A tracks and not displace us. Most of us would like to stay in this area. We own our homes." Despite the protests the interstate was completed in 1964. Rosella Williams recalled "I remember we were the last people on the block to leave. People would come during the night to take the pipes to sell for the copper. We would hear the rattling on the pipes and we'd say 'we haven't gone yet.' This would let them know they couldn't destroy our house yet."

The effect of ramming the highway through the community delivered a blow from which it has never recovered. Construction for the highway and bridge approaches destroyed most of the northernmost tier of squares in the original Swart neighborhood, one of the most economically successful zones of the community. Not only did the construction slice off the northeastern corner of OSBR from the rest of the community, it created a continuous blighted zone which suffers from the pounding noises of heavy traffic without cessation twenty-four hours a day. School children were separated from their segregated neighborhood schools, or forced to run dangerous gauntlets across lower portions of the new interstate. In response, the interstate was fenced. A bridge was constructed across the highway one mile to the southeast to connect two halves of Valley Park, which had also been bifurcated by the I-10 construction. But in OSBR the interstate zone became a place to avoid—a powerful impetus for many of the more successful and affluent families to desert the community for new suburbs in the southern and western portions of Baton Rouge. It was the beginning of a loss of leadership and a slow decline in the political effectiveness of the community. The final legacy of the interstate consists of abandoned businesses and deserted homes and schools.

In retrospect, we now see how geographical realities such as landform elevations and access to America's major river, regional trends such as the movement of large populations from plantation to city, Jim Crow segregation, and industrial and economic opportunities, all combined to shape the development of OSBR. In Baton Rouge, geography was destiny. The complex interrelations between the several geographic landforms of East Baton Rouge Parish profoundly shaped the kinds of human settlement which was to be laid out upon them.

Notes

[1] From the river, the fault progresses eastward across the northern edge of the University Lakes (a former cypress swamp). It crosses Acadian Throughway at the Catholic Life Center (below Hundred Oaks Avenue) and at Corporate Boulevard just north of the Wards Creek bridge. Its topographic signature extends eastward as far as Livingston Parish.

[2] The Parisian linear league (*grande lieue ordiniare*) referred to was equal to 3.0277 English miles or 15,986.26 English feet (Edwards and Kariouk 2004:126).

3 One of the forty plots laid out in Spanish Town, was listed as being owned by a "Mobile negro *libre*," a free person of color.

[4] The initial increase in the black population was due to the mass migration of blacks into the cities in search of work when slavery came to an end. The drop in the black population is due to the resettlement of African Americans to other communities, often times they moved back to the plantations from whence they came to become tenants or sharecroppers.

[5] The Baton Rouge Lumber Company employed large numbers of African Americans. Formed in 1885 and eventually owned solely by William Garig, a prominent Baton Rouge businessman, the Baton Rouge Lumber Company was located on the bank of the river at 602 1st Street in Catfish Town. Great stacks of lumber may be seen on its property in a photo taken from the top of the Old State Capitol (Fig. 2.3).

[6] These houses were built as company houses for African American laborers (Haag, 1975). The 1899 Baton Rouge city directory lists in the "colored" section Joseph Gedry, William Scott and Samuel Williams, among others, as laborers who lived on Brick Yard Alley. Several African Americans, including Samuel Carter, residing at 604 Europe, were listed as employees of Burton Lumber. Stephen Collins, who lived at 205 Penalvert, lists his place of employment as the Capital City Oil Mill.

[7] In 1920, 61 percent of the population was white and 39 percent was black.

[8] The first LSU campus was in Pineville, Louisiana.

[9] Later, in the 1950s, Valley Park developed as another nearby south Baton Rouge community, located so it might conveniently be of domestic service to the affluent neighborhoods situated on the up-thrown block of the Baton Rouge fault, between College Drive and Acadian and south of the old Baton Rouge Country Club (now Webb Park Golf Course).

Chapter Three

Remembering the History of Place: 1885-1965

The one whose shoulders we stood on are dead and no one knows about them.

~ David Whitten

Throughout the early part of the nineteenth century, Baton Rouge remained a small and rather insignificant town perched along the banks of the Mississippi River. The city was officially incorporated in 1817, with its eastern boundary at 22nd Street, though actual settlement only extended to 5th Street. Within a few years a new military post, centered on the Pentagon Barracks, was built on the north side of the city. Spanish Town and Beauregard Town continued to grow slowly as did the population of Baton Rouge. Although the population was only 1,463, a town had emerged alongside the many plantations that lined the Mississippi riverbanks north and south of Baton Rouge.

Baton Rouge entered a new phase of growth shaped by the exchanges between town and country plantations. Although slave life on the plantations changed little, the growth of the town provided space for an emerging class of free persons of color, many of whom resided in Beauregard Town. Under France and Spain, the Louisiana colony had a larger black population than the British colonies to the north and east, and it also had a higher level of racial mixing, referred to as *métissage* in French Louisiana. The Baton Rouge area was no exception to this generalization. Almost from the beginning, Baton Rouge was a multi-ethnic society. A smaller Afro-Creole class descended largely from the mixed parentage of eighteenth century Africans, Franco and Hispanic whites, and American Indians. In the plantation system of the time, the descendants of this group of largely domestic slaves received certain legal and economic privileges and inheritances not available to other enslaved African Americans. It gradually came to consider itself racially and ethnically distinct from both whites and blacks—a kind of middle class in the overall social structure of the colony. Because of the liberal manumission policies of the Spanish administrations, a considerable number of mulattos were able to purchase their freedom. They became free people of color, or *gens de couleur libres*, as they were still called in the nineteenth century. Their children often received the benefits of formal education and professional standing. In 1805, of the forty plots laid out in Spanish Town, the original Baton Rouge, one was listed as being owned by a "Mobile negro *libre*," a free person of color. Creoles of color specialized in crafts, trades and professions such as carpentry, house building, blacksmithing, plastering, wagon and buggy making, coopering, cabinet making and barbering (**Fig. 3.1**). Their children were educated in the Catholic schools of New Orleans, or even in France. Some became lawyers and doctors.

Fig. 3.1. Blacksmith at work. Courtesy of the Leo S. Butler Center, OSBR.

By 1850, 10 percent of Baton Rouge's population was comprised of free people of color and 25 percent were enslaved Africans. Some male slaves in Baton Rouge were foundry and sawmill workers. Many were apprenticed or hired out by their plantation owners to carpenters, bricklayers, and other craftsmen. They worked as painters, wagon makers, shoemakers, bakers and butchers. Female slaves labored primarily as cooks, maids, laundresses and nurses. Free people of color in Baton Rouge worked in various occupations including: barber, blacksmith, brick mason, butcher, carpenter, cooper, cigar maker, mechanic, engineer, grocer and shoemaker. In 1850, there were seventeen free black carpenters. Especially prosperous was carpenter Willis Carney, well known for his skill in building sugar refining houses (Sykes). In 1851, Carney purchased a 120-acre farm just north of town. A white planter, John B. Kleinpeter, co-signed the loan of $1,000. In 1850, Theopile Bertrand opened a mercantile house on Church (now Main) Street, just north of Harney House, Baton Rouge's premier hotel, and owned property totaling $14,500. Working out of rented property on Lafayette Street (still standing), Victor Vincent was one of Baton Rouge's two free black "master barbers." Free persons of color also ran black boarding houses.

Slaves from neighboring plantations like Magnolia Mound were often "hired out" to Baton Rouge businesses. Thus, enslaved Africans experienced life off the plantation and engaged in the social life of the town which included dances, Sunday afternoon horse racing, and a variety of other social and religious activities. Although the lives of African Americans were regulated and clearly defined within racial boundaries, residential areas within Baton Rouge were racially mixed and blacks participated in all spheres of life. This co-existence would be radically altered with the Civil War and Reconstruction.

A brief period of political and social equality was ushered in during Reconstruction. The years after emancipation were hopeful ones as former slaves who came to Baton Rouge went about establishing churches, schools, clubs and various societies. The 1895 *Baton Rouge City Directory* lists the following colored organizations in downtown Baton Rouge: seven churches (two Methodist and five Baptist); six Masonic lodges, including the Mispah Lodge No. 2045, Stone Square Lodge No. 8, Ajax No. 45, Third Mount Pilgrim, Star of Bethlehem, and Gethsemane Commandary No 4; and one club, the Capital City Literary and Social Club located at 212 St. Louis Street.

The hopes of emancipation were gradually dispelled by white efforts to impose racial supremacy. The new Louisiana legislature in 1865 quickly adopted a resolution "that this is a Government of white people, made and to be perpetuated for the exclusive benefit of the white race" (Gill 1997: 76). Despite white efforts to reinforce a racial hierarchy, by 1867 black voters outnumbered white voters in Baton Rouge. They preceded to elect two Republican African Americans, Louis François, and Victor M. Lange—a free man of color from Baton Rouge—to the state's constitutional convention (Rodrigue and Phillips 2006: 21). In 1868, Lange went on to serve a term in the House of Representatives. White Democrats, with the help of the White League and paramilitary groups like the KKK, quickly organized to reinstitute white control of the city. By 1876, with the withdrawal of the federal government and end of Radical Reconstruction, participation in the political system by blacks was ended for all practical purposes. The counterrevolution against racial equality, and the imposition of white supremacy, extended beyond political rights to encompass every aspect of daily life. By the 1890s measures to ensure the segregation of the races by law and stringently enforced custom regulated almost every conceivable situation in which whites and blacks might come into social contact: "from public transportation to public parks, from the workplace to hospitals, asylums and orphanages, from the homes for the aged, the blind, deaf, and dumb, to the prisons, from saloons to churches" (Litwack 1998: 233). Signs denoting "white only" and "colored" appeared over the entrances to parks, theaters, boardinghouses, waiting rooms, toilets, and water fountains. In white stores, black women were forbidden from trying on dresses, hats and shoes. Even the use of sidewalks was regulated by custom: blacks were expected to step aside when white adults approached. Segregated residential patterns also emerged resulting in the emergence of Old South Baton Rouge. Within the confines of segregation, blacks persisted in finding ways to assert their humanity and dignity through the creation of their own institutions: schools, churches, businesses, social and civic clubs. These institutions pursued the ideals of equality and the promises of emancipation. This community, while marked by segregation, was not defined by it.

Progressivism: Progress for Some

> The paradoxical combination of white supremacy and progressivism was not new to the region, but it never ceased to be a cause of puzzlement and confusion . . .
>
> C. Vann Woodward, 1951: 373

By 1900, Baton Rouge began to make the transition from "country" town to "corporate" town. According to Carleton, Baton Rouge's values were "those of the emerging urban-industrial middle-class: taxation wisely spent and honestly accounted for, responsible and scientific management of government, observance of proper governmental forms and procedures, and above all, decorous behavior on the part of public officials" (1981:126). Baton Rouge now saw itself as a modern and forward-looking community. The 1898 election of Robert A. Hart as mayor of Baton Rouge exemplified this shift (**Fig. 3.2**). Hart, a wealthy property owner and real-estate developer, encouraged positive growth and civic improvements. He was vice-president of The First National Bank of Baton Rouge; president of Fuqua Hardware Company, Limited, a hardware wholesaler; and the owner of S.M. Hart and Son, a general insurance and real estate business. According to the 1898 city directory, he was "one of the most progressive Mayors that Baton Rouge has ever been blessed with" (Baton Rouge 1899: 25).

Hart was representative of Southern progressivism, which according to C. Vann Woodward was "essentially urban and middle class in nature and the typical leader was a city professional man or businessman" (1951: 371). He persuaded local property owners to approve bond issues for a new city hall, a school, and the paving of Third and Main Street. Bond issues in 1905, 1912, and 1914 paid for more paving, and the construction of a white high school and a black public school (Perkins Road School, eventually named Baton Rouge Colored High). Bonds also permitted the purchase of the old state penitentiary buildings, plus sewage and drainage works. In 1898, it was Mayor Hart who bought the entire remaining property of Magnolia Mound Plantation. He started selling off pieces of the property to developers, who in turn subdivided them and sold them to individual families. By 1929, Hart had sold all but seventy-five of the original 800-plus acres.[1]

The opening up of lands south of downtown Baton Rouge resulted in rapid residential development south of South Boulevard between 1891-1911. Three residential developments: Suburb Swart (1889) in the north, and Magnolia Suburb (1891) and Wykoff Suburb (1891) bordering Highland Road, appeared in the northwest portion of OSBR. The urban landscape of Baton Rouge was shifting significantly. Before and immediately following the Civil War, African Americans were scattered throughout the city. The first step in the establishment of the large contemporary black community was the creation of urban clusters at the outskirts of the city. According to John Kellogg (1977), landowners who held land near the edge of town quickly seized the opportunity for profit by dividing up their fields into small lots and selling them to poor black migrants. By far, the most common sites for these new settlements were the bottomlands, the damp, poorly drained lowlands that were of considerably lower value. This describes well the area, formerly part of Magnolia Mound Plantation, that would become "Old" South Baton Rouge or the "Bottom." Increasingly blacks settled in the area south of downtown Baton Rouge including Swart suburb and the industrial section of town south of Catfish Town.

Fig. 3.2. Mayor of Baton Rouge, R.A. Hart. Courtesy of LSU Special Collections.

The Death of W. Leroy Stewart on August 5 took off the Refinery rolls the name of one of its most popular colored men. Stewart, a brickmason ever since he joined the Refinery organization the first time on March 29, 1911, had almost 30 years of accumulated service with the Company. He was born September 3, 1887, in Baton Rouge and was to have retired on August 19 had he lived until then. He was married to the former Elizabeth Tyler and the father of four children. His residence was at 1081 South Boulevard.

Fig. 3.3. Article on W. Leroy Stewart, the *Standard Oil Stanicolan*, Aug., 1947. Courtesy of Exxon, Baton Rouge.

One purpose of expansion south of South Boulevard was to accommodate the increasing influx of black migrants to the city. New businesses emerged that relied heavily on black labor. By the early twentieth century, Louisiana led the nation in Spanish moss production. Sidney B. Webb's moss factory, located in a black residential section in the southern part of the city near the railroad, employed many African Americans. The industries located in the western section of Swart Suburb, Capital City Oil Mill, Burton Lumber Company and the Baton Rouge Brickyard, employed many of the new African American "immigrants" to the city. In 1903, Standard Oil opened a refinery in Baton Rouge and employed more than 700 people, many of them black.[2] Blacks were employed as brick masons, concrete workers, coke handlers, still cleaners, tube cleaners, in the loading rack and barrel rack as well as in the lubricating and paraffin departments. Many of the workers like Louise Payne, Leroy Stewart, Philip Griffin, Fred Mathews, and Adolph Wiggins, among others, resided in Old South Baton Rouge and worked for the company their whole lives. Some, like Adolph Wiggins and Leroy Stewart were active as elected representatives of the colored divisions in the company governance (**Fig. 3.3**). At the time, all aspects of the company were segregated. While the company was forging a "company life" by creating sports teams (baseball), a band, a choir (known as the minstrels), mutual benefit societies, and company holiday celebrations, all of these activities and events were segregated. The company newspaper the *Stanocolan* reported in a separate section for "colored" all news regarding company election results and conferences. Also under "colored" news were the results of the Socola baseball team which played games with teams as far away as Beaumont, Texas, Bogalusa, New Orleans as well as Scotlandville, Port Allen and Baton Rouge. Many of these games were played in the heart of Old South Baton Rouge at Ethiopian Park across East Boulevard from McKinley High School (**Fig. 2.8**). Even training for workers in first aid and the safety association were segregated. The Labor Day Picnic described in the July 31, 1924 *Stanocolan* (Vol. 1, No. 6, p. 4) was held (annually) at Maryland Farm, with dancing, music provided that year by Toots Johnson, sports, (including baseball, boxing, foot races, pole vault, greasy pole and greasy pig), and food. The picnic was segregated. The company arranged for a special train to take employees and their families from Baton Rouge to the picnic grounds. In all parts of the plant black workers worked as skilled labor and participated in the corporate life of Standard Oil, but did so under strict segregation. The company provided steady employment, benefits such as investments in the Stock Acquisition Plan, and continuing education. These opportunities, according to Fred Matthews, a thirty-year employee with Standard, were pivotal to the growth of OSBR. He recalled in 1996:

> My family moved to Baton Rouge in October 1920, at which time the Baton Rouge City limits extended to Terrace Street [then named Reddy]. The Standard Oil Company had recently been located in the parish and was in need of men with various skills. Having worked at the refinery for several years the majority of the employees began to buy homes. Few remained on rent. The population increased by leaps and bounds.

Many residents of OSBR were drawn to Baton Rouge by opportunities offered by Standard Oil which in turn provided blacks with much sought after steady, well paid employment that permitted home ownership to become the norm in the neighborhood in the 1920s. The growth of the neighborhood can be directly linked to these emerging employment opportunities at the plant.

While Standard Oil was pivotal to the eventual growth of Old South Baton Rouge, at the turn of the century Baton Rouge was still transitioning from a country town to a modern city. The 1899 *Baton Rouge City Directory* reflects this initial growth. In that year the population of Baton Rouge was 12,951. The directory described the growing city, "The staple crops, such as cane, cotton, maize and potatoes, are most generally raised, not because they are the most lucrative products, but from the effect of routine, and the commercial conditions which make these crops almost the sole basis of agricultural credits."

Although the city's economy remained a rural one, small industries as described earlier were beginning to develop. Many of these were concentrated in the western section of the newly designed Suburb Swart (see Chapter II). While Swart was a neighborhood in which both blacks and whites lived, the emerging suburbs south of Terrace were heavily African American.

As the effects of racial supremacy increasingly restricted the lives of rural agricultural workers and share croppers, new waves of African Americans moved into the community. The first church to locate in OSBR was the Freewill Baptist at 107 Fannie (now Eddie Robinson). There had been eight black churches in downtown Baton Rouge in 1899, and some of these also began to make the move into South Baton Rouge. While churches served the spiritual needs of blacks, they were also critical to education. While the Progressive Era (1900-1920) was ushering in modest advances in education for white children throughout the South, its black children were being left behind. According to McMillen, "by limiting the quality and the extent of black education, the white minority could hope to cramp black political aspirations, inhibit black ability to compete economically and assure an adequate supply of low-wage menial black labor" (1989:73). The burden for educating its youth fell on the local churches and on the private schools established by blacks. Mt. Zion and Methodist both used their churches simultaneously as places of worship, but also as schools in which blacks of all ages were taught the basics of reading and writing.

The Negro Baptists of the Fourth District Missionary Baptist Association of Louisiana had organized a private secondary school called the Baton Rouge Academy. Founded in 1875, it was located on St. Louis in downtown Baton Rouge in a wooden frame building **(Fig. 3.4)**. It served not only blacks from Baton Rouge, but also the parishes of West Baton Rouge, East Feliciana, West Feliciana, Pointe Coupée, and Iberville. All teachers had baccalaureate degrees, and it was the only school in the state, outside of New Orleans, that provided a "normal course" for teacher training. In 1901, J.S. Clark (future president of Southern University) would become principal. At this time the Academy had an enrollment of 200 students with four faculty members. A fire destroyed the original building and in 1906-7, the school reopened in a modern three-story building with a new name, the Baton Rouge College; it was located on 16th Street in the heart of Old South Baton

Fig. 3.4. The Baton Rouge Academy—a private school for African American children in Baton Rouge. Courtesy of LSU Special Collections.

Rouge. It served as the only high school for blacks in Baton Rouge until 1916, when it moved to Plaquemine.

The first school actually founded for blacks within OSBR was the Live Oak School on South Boulevard just east of Fannie (on the current site of the Purple Circle Social Club).[3] This school was established by two white missionaries from New York State, Mrs. Ada C. Pollock-Blundon and Frank Blundon, who served as its principal. They called it the Live Oak School because it was in operation throughout the calendar year. The school served both elementary and secondary students, with an industrial department that gave instruction to both boys and girls in the practical arts of home. Prominent members of the community, like Leo Butler, attended school here and with the aid of the Blundons were able to facilitate scholarships to black colleges. The only other private school for blacks was the Catholic school founded in 1895 by the Sisters of the Holy Family, the all-black order of nuns founded by Henriette Delille in New Orleans in 1842. It was located downtown on the site of the present-day post office. The sisters eventually moved the school and convent to St. Francis Xavier Church which was built by black Catholics in Old South Baton Rouge in 1916.

These private schools were critical since before 1906 there was little or no public education available to blacks. While public schooling was available to whites, there was only one public school for blacks in East Baton Rouge Parish, the Hickory Street School. Originally located on the corner of St. Ferdinand and Africa (now Louisiana) streets, this building was torn down and rebuilt on Hickory Street, where it served colored children for twenty-three years. Of the 1,624 "negro educables" in Baton Rouge in 1908, only forty-nine were enrolled in public school (Frazier 1937). According to J.M. Frazier, the schools were in such deplorable condition that black parents preferred to pay tuition and send their children to private schools. This meant of course that they were "second-taxing themselves" by paying regular public school taxes as well as the tuition for private schools.

While private education was the norm in OSBR at the turn of the century, a group of black educational leaders emerged who saw public education as key to the racial "uplift" of all blacks. They focused on building black institutions of learning that reflected self-help and racial solidarity. Simultaneously whites, concerned with the growing independence of black private schools were ready to join forces with black educators to support public schools for blacks since this provided some control over education. This included limits on funding for black staff and students and most importantly limitations on an academic curriculum. In 1906, the new parish Superintendent Strickland, whose commitment was to encouraging Negro public education, hired J.M Frazier and four new staff as the teachers of a newly renovated Hickory School. By 1913, the school was bursting at the seams due to much needed improvements and the leadership of Frazier. With the aid of a colored committee made up of OSBR civic leaders including B.V. Baranco, Sr., H.R. Baranco, Mike Winfield, Thomas Smiler, and Henry Andrews, Frazier was able to work with Mayor Roux and the city council to secure a bond issue of $25,000 for the building of the "first modern brick school building for Negro children at public expense in the entire state of Louisiana" (Frazier 1937:77). Perkins Street School, located in the heart of OSBR on 16th Street, was a three story building containing a large auditorium on the third floor, twelve classrooms, a principal's office, and the latest type of

Perkins Street School
1914

Fig. 3.5. The Perkins Street School in 1914. First McKinley High School yearbook, 1928.

school furniture (**Fig. 3.5**). According to Frazier, this "new building had an electric effect upon the general attitude of Negroes in Baton Rouge in respect to public education" (1937:77). Within a short time there was demand for high school classes and by 1916 the first four high school students were graduated. At a time when the majority of blacks did not receive public secondary schooling, and would not until after World War II, this early development of public education for blacks in Baton Rouge was the exception and drew blacks to Baton Rouge from outlying areas.

The early part of the twentieth century also saw the growth of business and residences in OSBR. The first African American business was Mitchell Connor Cotton Gin Repair, located on the corner of South Boulevard and St. Joseph. The 1899 city directory noted that three black carpenters, Thomas, Warren, and William Cotton lived at 708 S. Boulevard. The residential addresses listed there clearly indicate that African Americans lived in the South Boulevard area. The corner of East Boulevard (Thomas Delpit) and Railroad (Myrtle) was densely populated. Several of the colored inhabitants and their occupations included the following LSU employees: Henry Benton, laborer; Monroe Butler, laborer; William Butler, laborer; Sarah Knox, laundry; and Ada Lancaster, laundry. Several African Americans lived on the corner of Julia and East Boulevard and its residents included: Eli Washington, laborer; Richard Williams, laborer; William Pickett, porter; and Daniel Rogers, laborer. African Americans also began moving onto the corner of Reddy (Terrace) and Fannie (Eddie Robinson). Although the number of black residents coming into OSBR began to increase around the turn of the century, a majority still lived in downtown Baton Rouge.[4] Most African Americans men living in OSBR worked as laborers. However, black residents also worked as cooks (specifically at Posey's Hotel and the Grand Hotel), carpenters, porters, waiters, laundry workers, and employees of the Baton Rouge Lumber Yard.

By 1910, the city map of Baton Rouge officially marked Reddy Street (Terrace) as the southern city limit, and the total population had reached 14,897 (**Map 2.11a**). The 1911 Sanborn Map extended the southern boundary to Reddy Street and the eastern one as far as Perkins Road. South Boulevard was 128 feet wide and still unpaved. Residential development grew steadily, but most blocks were not fully occupied and generally were less than 50 percent developed. The types of residences in OSBR were mixed with most blocks containing both shotgun houses and some larger bungalow-type structures. While attending separate schools and churches, the residential patterns suggest that blacks and whites both lived side by side in the "first" suburb of Baton Rouge. This pattern was to change dramatically as social and political forces sought to implement strict segregation.

Knowing One's Place: Race and Segregation

As the OSBR black community increased at the turn of the twentieth century, African American expectations for political, educational, and economic rights grew. Rising expectations coincided with one of the most savage periods of white repression in the history of the South. Whites strove to ensure white supremacy through segregation, disenfranchisement, and racial violence. The period is sometimes misleadingly labeled with the supposedly benign term of "Jim Crow." Racial separation did not "spring forth fully developed" (Lofgern 1987: 7). In the quarter century following the Civil War, racial separation was "incomplete and the color line remained curiously irregular down through the turn of the century" (McMillen 1989:5). "Capitulation to racism," as described by Woodward, was born in large part in the agricultural depression of the 1880s and 1890s, and in the resultant rise of Populism that threatened white cohesion and stimulated renewed black political organization (1951). White leaders stripped blacks of the political rights they had gained following the Civil War. Louisiana enacted laws in 1890 and 1894 which required segregated railroad cars (Lofgren 1987). In 1896, *Plessy v. Ferguson* made "separate but equal" the law. The Louisiana Constitution of 1898 stripped blacks of all political influence by making property

Fig. 3.6. Beverley V. Baranco, Sr. *Sepia Socialite*, 1942.

ownership and literacy requirements for enfranchisement (Fairclough 1999). The number of black voters fell from 130,344 to 5,320; by 1904; after the implementation of the poll tax, it fell to 1,342.[5] In 1910, the state legislature solidified racial classifications by abolishing the distinction between dark-skinned blacks and light-skinned people of color (locally called Creoles) and established a clear caste system in which no favor was to be given to people of mixed racial ancestry (Fairclough 1999). For all practical purposes, these factors eliminated meaningful black political participation until the 1960s.

Although it upheld the tenants of Jim Crow, Baton Rouge's political culture differed significantly from that of the rest of the state. It was shaped by a growing number of white business progressives and a small middle-class professional black population that made up the heart of Old South Baton Rouge. The desire of Baton Rouge to "progress" and the ability of this black middle class to negotiate with the city's white politicians in order that both could achieve their goals resulted in unique alliances which Mary J. Hebert (1999) describes as a form of racial diplomacy.

Black Republicans, who were the inheritors of the legacy of Reconstruction, struggled to keep alive the "party's original ideals of citizenship and democracy" (Fairclough 1999:10). One member of the African American OSBR community exemplified this commitment- B.V. Baranco, Sr. (1869-1933). His skilled leadership furthered the educational, political, and economic rights of blacks in Baton Rouge.[6] Black Republicans like Baranco, who were active in the Black and Tan faction of the Republican Party, worked with white officials and other black Republicans like Walter Cohen of New Orleans, to mediate and advance the rights of blacks.[7] In a political order that was governed by the principles of white supremacy, black disenfranchisement and one-party Democratic rule, the "Black and Tans" sought to work at the national level with the Republican party as well as on the local level to promote civic engagement.

Fig. 3.7. J.S. Clark, Principal of the Baton Rouge Academy until 1911.

Fig. 3.8. J.M. Frazier, *Sepia Socialite*, 1942

Beverly V. Baranco, Sr. joined a growing number of black civic leaders (**Fig.3.6**). These included J.S. Clark who was principal of the Baton Rouge Academy until 1911 (and later president of Southern University; **Fig. 3.7**); James Monroe Frazier, who after graduating from Leland College in New Orleans and establishing himself as an educator, was recruited in 1908 by Superintendent H.K. Strickland of the East Baton Rouge (EBR) School Board as an administrator to direct the growth of public schools for Negroes in Baton Rouge (**Fig.3.8**); and, finally, H.J. Allen and W.H. Wethers, who served on the Colored Building Committees for the East Baton Rouge Parish Schools (McKinley High School Yearbook).

Another advancement in the education of blacks for Louisiana, put particularly residents of OSBR, was the move of Southern University from New Orleans to Baton Rouge in 1914.[8] The first president became J.S. Clark, whose greatest task was to "win the good will and sentiment favorable toward the idea of black education" (Vincent 1981:76). Many high school graduates from OSBR now had the opportunity to attend college locally and before long Southern also opened a laboratory school which some residents of OSBR chose to attend. In 1915, J.S. Clark and Beverly V. Baranco, Sr. brought Booker T. Washington to address the students and faculty at Southern University (**Figs. 3.9**). After addressing the university community, Washington spoke to a crowd of approximately 5,000 blacks and whites in downtown Baton Rouge regarding the equalization of public education and reduction of racial violence. These OSBR civic leaders did not let racial segregation or prejudice impede their vision of equal education for blacks.

In 1910, the census indicated that almost 49 percent of "Negroes in Louisiana were illiterate as opposed to 14 percent of whites" (Lovell, 1961). In 1915, fewer than half of Louisiana's black children were enrolled in schools, but 79 percent of white children were enrolled (Fairclough 1999). Pat Baranco, the granddaughter of Beverly V. Baranco, Sr. recalled, her family believed that "education was the great equalizer" (2005). According to James Monroe Frazier, "The school year 1908-1909, may well be styled the 'turning point' in public education for Negroes in the city of Baton Rouge" (1937:71). With his leadership, Frazier mustered support for public schools for blacks, and within ten years the EBR school board had built three schools, Hickory Street School (a renovation) in

Fig. 3.9. Booker T. Washington (first row, fourth from left) visits Baton Rouge in 1915.

Fig. 3.10. The Reddy Street School (1917) as seen in the 1930s. The Carver Library stands on this location today. First McKinley High School yearbook, 1928.

1909, Perkins Street School in 1914, and Reddy Street School in 1917 (on the present site of the new EBR Carver library; **Fig 3.10**).[9]

By the dawn of the century's second decade OSBR not only had one elementary school, Hickory, grades one through six, but two brick schools. The Perkins Street School accommodated the upper elementary and the high school grades. It soon after became known as Baton Rouge Colored High School. Reddy Street School took over the classes from Hickory (which closed) in 1917 and taught grades one through seven. These new schools were a vast improvement over the overcrowded conditions that had forced platooning of teachers and students in the primary grades (Gaston, 1971). These up-to-date educational facilities clearly attracted blacks to OSBR, and this led to further development of OSBR in the 1920s. Inez Chrisentery, born in Port Allen in 1910, recalled that her mother said she wasn't going to stay in Port Allen any longer because we had to have an education. She said, "If it takes crossing the river that is what we will do." School in Port Allen convened only three months a year, whereas schools in OSBR were in session nine months and provided a far superior education.[10] The family moved to OSBR so that they could take advantage of the superior education offered to blacks and Inez attended Perkins Street School, Baton Rouge Colored High School (later McKinley) and then Southern University.[11] She went on to become a life long educator teaching in OSBR.

Growth and Segregation—The 1920s

World War I had little effect on Baton Rouge, but an economic upturn for the city followed the war. The oil industry provided 3,000 jobs in 1917. The boll weevil epidemic that impacted black cotton farmers in 1915 and an economic downturn in New Orleans after World War I, resulted in another wave of migration into Old South Baton Rouge. A burst of growth consequently took place in the 1920s. Residential, as well as commercial sites began to expand between East Boulevard and Highland Road and south to Roosevelt Street. Subdivisions developed during this time included Mrs. Cotton, ca. 1928; Diggs Tract, 1926; and Johnston, ca. 1926. The original Swart subdivision between South Boulevard and Reddy Street was now almost fully developed and occupied. In the 1920s, OSBR became a diverse neighborhood in which African Americans, Italian Americans, German Americans, Creoles, and Chinese lived side by side.[12]

Fig. 3.11a. Joe Ridley, *Sepia Socialite*, 1942.

Fig. 3.11b. Joe Ridley original store, established in 1926.

The 1920s saw the appearance of the many black-owned businesses. Black capitalism "although severely handicapped from the outset by black poverty and dependence . . . represented a promising example of what DuBois called the 'group economy'" (McMillen, 1989:178). Influenced by the growing industrial order, blacks sought to create an exclusively black economy. This separate development reflected the ideals of self-help, group solidarity and black pride. McMillen suggests that "as hope for civil equality dimmed, blacks turned gradually from political to economic arenas where they might, as Booker T. Washington had counseled, 'take advantage of the disadvantages' of Jim Crow" (1989:79). Ironically, segregation led to the development of black professionals and black-owned businesses, including the Joe Ridley Tailor Shop on Highland Road just south of South Boulevard (**Figs. 3.11a, 3.11b**). Established in 1926, Ridley's business employed eight men and five women and got the majority of LSU's trade and "sixty-five percent of the people in the state capitol [*sic*]" (*Sepia Socialite*, 1942:21). Joseph Bernard, a civic and business leader, opened Bernard's Chicken Loaf in 1915 and although located on North Boulevard, his residence eventually became 1203 East Boulevard.

Fig. 3.12 Leo Butler, 1918, WWI.

Several black doctors also established practices in OSBR. Dr. Leo Stanley Butler, born in 1899 in Burtville to sharecroppers, was the youngest of thirteen children. After moving to Baton Rouge he attended school at the Blundon Day School and became the first male graduate of Baton Rouge Colored High School. After serving briefly in the army during World War I (**Fig. 3.12**), he graduated from Howard University in 1922 and returned to Baton Rouge after completing his internship at Freedman's Hospital in Washington, D.C. (**Fig. 3.13**). In 1926, he began to practice medicine and worked out of his residence at 963 Terrace Avenue (**Fig. 3.14**). Dr. Leo Butler became a prominent civic leader, serving as a member of the NAACP and as a polemarch of the New Orleans Alumni Chapter of Kappa Alphi Psi. Butler was also the president of the Keystone Life Insurance Company. His brother George Butler studied pharmacy and chemistry and in 1929 opened a one-room drugstore in OSBR (**Figs. 3.15, 3.16**). This enterprise grew and in 1935 became the Ideal Drug Store, which opened in the new Butler Building on the corner of Louise Street and East Boulevard, where the Ethiopian baseball park was previously located (**Fig.3.29**). The building became one of

Fig. 3.13. Dr. Leo S. Butler. *Sepia Socialite*, 1942.

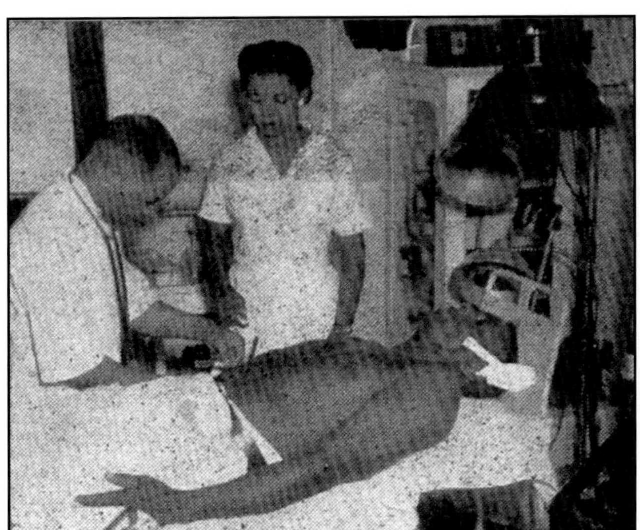

Fig. 3.14. Dr. Butler at work. *Sepia Socialite*, 1942.

Fig. 3.15. George Alson Butler. *Sepia Socialite*, 1942.

Fig. 3.16. South End Drug Store. *Sepia Socialite*, 1942.

the largest all-colored buildings in the state of Louisiana. In addition to the drugstore, it boasted a cafeteria, a post office, a barber shop and Butler's Blue Room.[13]

The growth of commercial enterprises in OSBR can also be attributed to the influx of Italian immigrants during the 1920s. Many Italians immigrated to southern Louisiana between 1880-1910 in response to the need for cheap labor in the Louisiana sugar industry (Gardner 1983; Spitzer 1979:310-13). An economic depression in Italy, combined with problems of land tenure and political oppression, had created a large number of landless farmers, many of whom were encouraged to come to Louisiana by the offer of contracts which paid about three times the prevailing farm labor wage in Italy. In 1890, 7,767 Italians had been recruited for the sugar harvest. They were encouraged to become tenant farmers after their contracts had ended. By 1910, 20,233 Italian immigrants had arrived, and there were 22,678 Italians residing in the state. Because they had taken over the labor previously done by black sharecroppers, their social standing in the established community was low. They were the new slave class, if only temporarily.

The Italians who settled in OSBR came primarily from Sicily. They had worked their way up the Mississippi River from New Orleans. Many took jobs working on former plantations in the parishes between Iberville and Iberia in the west and St. Bernard in the east. Baton Rouge was the closest city for those in Iberville, Ascension and Assumption parishes. Due to the increased mechanization of the sugar industry, many families moved to Baton Rouge, often becoming small merchants.[14]

Fig. 3.17. Bonfanti family portrait.

Joe Bonfanti settled in OSBR in 1924, opening the O.K. Barber Shop. Eventually the family expanded their businesses to include a shoe repair and a grocery (**Fig. 3.17**). The Bonfanti's Friendly Grocery Store at the corner of East Boulevard and Reddy (Terrace) became a fixture in the community for decades (**Fig. 3.18**). In 1920, after his wife died in the Spanish Influenza epidemic, Servio Cascio settled at 1215 East Boulevard with his eight children and worked as a contractor (**Fig. 1.13**). His son Joe Cascio lived next door at 1213 with his wife and two children and operated the general hardware. Joe Delpit, an OSBR resident who grew up on East Boulevard, described the effect that this one man had on the aspirations of many in the black community (refer to quote on p. 6). "While blacks couldn't get their licenses to be plumbers, he would get the permit and let the blacks do the work. It worked out that's how some blacks got to be plumbers."

Fig. 3.18. Friendly Grocery Store, Thomas Delpit Boulevard.

Italian families and their descendants operated businesses on East Boulevard well into the 1970s. In addition, several Italian families also settled on Highland Road (**Fig. 4.39**). The Vicaro family opened Vicaro Grocery at 1631 Highland in the mid-1920s. The Caruso family owned a grocery at the corner of Highland and McKinley in the 1930s. After establishing successful businesses, some of these families relocated within OSBR in the 1950s and '60s to a modern subdivision on Nicholson Drive.

During the late 1920s, WJBO built a radio station in the area and the corridor along Highland began to grow. Although it was still a dirt road, Highland Road became the commercial and entertainment area for LSU students and sports fans. The 1923 Sanborn Map marks Roosevelt Street as the southern boundary of Baton Rouge. According to Robert W. Heck,

> To the south of downtown in the early 1920s, little existed between South Boulevard and the new campus of Louisiana State University. The Negro community occupied only a limited strip between South Boulevard and Terrace Street. Nicholson Drive and the adjoining area was open agricultural land. Few buildings other than the older settlers' houses were in existence. Highland Road was punctuated with these old settlers' houses as was Perkins Road and Old Jefferson Highway (1966:23).

The commercial, residential, and educational growth of OSBR also resulted in the growth of civic and social organizations. As a consequence of segregation, blacks developed their own social clubs. The most prominent of these was the Prince Hall Masonic Temple (at 1335 North Boulevard) built in 1924 as the District Grand Lodge No. 21 of the Grand United Order of Odd Fellows (**Fig. 3.19**). Beverly V. Baranco, Sr., who had been elected in 1915 as the grand master of the Odd Fellows of the State of Louisiana, is credited with directing the construction of this four-story brick and steel building that housed the organization's state offices.[15] Although located in the CBD north of OSBR, this facility became the center of social activities for the black community. In fact, many top black entertainers, including Duke Ellington, B.B. King, Ella Fitzgerald, Louis Armstrong and later Ike and Tina Turner, performed at the Temple Roof garden on the building's top floor (**Figs. 3.20-3.21b**). The dance floor doubled as a basketball court for several semiprofessional teams sponsored by local businesses. There was also a strong link between the Prince Hall

Fig. 3.19. Prince Hall Masonic Temple, *Advocate*.

Fig. 3.20. Louis Armstrong at the Temple Theatre, 1940.

Fig. 3.21a. Dancing at the Temple Theatre.
From the Willie Harris Photographic Collection;
courtesy Mr. James Terry, III..

Fig. 3.21b. A social function at the Temple Theatre.
From the Willie Harris Photographic Collection; courtesy Mr. James Terry, III.

Fig. 3.22b. Dancing at the Purple Circle Social Club
From the Willie Harris Photographic Collection;
courtesy Mr. James Terry, III..

The members of this Club with which it begins its corporate existence are as follows:

Theodore Roosevelt Smith	Clarence Borris
I. C. Lyons	Randolph Chachre
James A. Johnson, Jr.	Robert Monget
C. A. Purnell	Alphonse Boulging
W. S. Barrett	George Purnell
Jonal Hubbard	Armstead Randall
Nuna LeBlanc	Crotol Fleet
David Price	Paul Dornain
Lawrence Benjamin	Ceasar Feast
Shirley Williams	Aldridge Jackson
Neel LeBlanc	Joseph Delooch
Fernan Fitzgerald	B. V. Baranco
Rafe Davison	Jsoeph M. Robinson
Eugene Berryhill	

Fig. 3.22a. Original membership of the Purple Circle Social Club, 1926.

Fig. 3.22c. A Christmas Party at the Purple Circle Social Club.
From the Willie Harris Photographic Collection; courtesy Mr. James Terry, III.

Masons and the NAACP. According to Fairclough, "the Masons provided members and meeting places; they organized voter registration schools; they furnished generous financial support" (1999:70). Huel Perkins, born in 1924 on South Boulevard, recalled, "[the] Masons were big. It was the premier organization to which blacks belonged. And they encouraged blacks to register to vote. Dr. John G. Lewis, Jr. was the Grandmaster and he mobilized the masons, told them to vote and to get registered, told them what they should do in terms of furthering integration" (2006).

A second social club, the Purple Circle Social Club, called OSBR home. Chartered in 1927, it was located on South Boulevard, at the former site of the Live Oak Negro School, and promoted general social interests. Its original charter members included, among others, B.V. Baranco, Sr., George Purnell, Theodore Roosevelt Smith, Numa Le Blanc, Robert Monget, and Joseph M. Robinson (**Fig. 3.22a-3.22c**) The club still exists, making it the oldest operating social club in OSBR.[16] There was also an Italian Club in which weddings and other social event were held for the Italian American community.

Until the 1920s, blacks attending high school did so for the most part at private schools. Later in that decade black, civic leaders continued their push for the expansion of black public education. Overcrowded conditions, due in part to continued black urban migration, necessitated another school in addition to Perkins (Baton Rouge Colored High), Reddy, and the Scott Street schools. Although the majority of the school board members favored an elementary school, William Bass Hatcher, the white superintendant of EBR schools, at the request of James Monroe Frazier, asked that the board open a high school, and the board agreed (Gatson 1971).

In 1927, McKinley High School was built at the cost of $175,000 at the corner of East Boulevard and Louise Street (**Fig 3.23**). According to Gatson, "It was a showplace for Negro schools in the state, and people from Louisiana and the surrounding states came to observe the new school" (1971:82; **Fig. 3.24**).[17] McKinley offered not only vocational training, but also a college-bound curriculum that included Latin, music, math and chemistry (**Fig. 3.25**). McKinley was described as a "splendid two-storey structure, modern in every detail. It [had] twenty classrooms, with laboratories for chemistry, physics, general science, domestic science, shops for manual training, biology, and a library with steel shelves" (Frazier 1937). At the time there were only three other high schools for blacks in the state of Louisiana—New Orleans, Shreveport, and at Southern University (which required tuition). Beyond its pedagogical function, McKinley High School was to become

Fig. 3.23. McKinley High School, built in 1927.

Fig. 3.24. The auditorium at McKinley High School in 1942.

Fig. 3.25. McKinley Laboratory.

in this period an emblem of excellence as the primary institution for African American success and hope for a better future. As the only publicly funded high school in south Louisiana, it drew from throughout the region black students who desired a high school education. Huel Perkins recalled the importance of McKinley:

> To show how important it was, people from all the surrounding towns would move to Baton Rouge so that they could go to school there. People who lived in New Roads, Denham Springs, Zachary, they would move in with relatives and friends. McKinley was central to black education (Perkins 2006).

Even by 1929, only about 8 percent of the black high school age population in Louisiana was enrolled in school.[18] This made McKinley High School an invaluable institution to OSBR residents and to blacks throughout the state who sought to make an education a reality. Although high school education was now available to local blacks, it was not an equal education. In 1934-35 the cumulative educational cost per pupil in EBRP for whites was $56.45, and for blacks $10.95. Average high school teacher salary for whites was $1,179.26 and for blacks, $824.34 (Frazier 1937). Despite these inequities, McKinley High School continued to provide an education that would instill "race pride" and self-determination with the best academic education possible.

Fig. 3.26. Isabelle Morgan Herson. First McKinley High School yearbook, 1928.

McKinley graduates boast about the many excellent and dedicated teachers who served the school. Isabelle Herson, member of the first class of 1928, recalled that "the teachers were hard; they disciplined you . . " (**Fig. 3.26**). Many went on to become the community's first black college graduates. They attended Southern, Xavier, Dillard, Moorehouse and other colleges. Sports were also a highlight at McKinley. Many of the coaches, in particular Coach Kraft, were fondly remembered for furthering sports at a time when few facilities were open to blacks. Various extracurricular activities, including glee club and cheerleading, were also conducted as well as traditional events like homecoming and dances

Fig. 3.27. McKinley Glee Club.

(**Figs. 3.27-3.28**). McKinley High also served as a community center. The auditorium not only held school events but served as a movie theatre on Friday nights, and a venue for live amateur hours. There was a "March Rhetorical" where elementary and middle school students would come from Reddy and Scott Street to recite poems and perform plays. Huel Perkins also remembered the annual "operetta" held at McKinley that was organized by the music teacher A.E. Carter. Clearly, McKinley served as a focal point in the community for creating and promoting a culture that valued education. It became not only a path to a vocation, but it was also central to instilling in young people a sense of confidence and dignity. McKinley was essential to sowing the seeds for the ongoing struggle for equality, despite the separate and "unequal" education that blacks received.

By the close of the 1920s decade OSBR was a growing, multiethnic community. Even within the confines of white supremacy or as W.E.B. Dubois phrased it, "behind the veil," residents had constructed an entire parallel set of institutions—churches, businesses, schools, unions, social and professional organizations. Under the banner of "racial uplift" they organized and enlisted white cooperation and support for ostensibly "nonpolitical" causes like schools and public health (Fairclough 1999).[19] Businesses were growing, children were being educated, and a thriving community life marked a neighborhood that despite segregation had learned to negotiate race relations for its own end. Increasingly, black society was becoming a self-contained world. Residents, who worked outside the neighborhood at Catfish Town, Standard Oil, LSU, or the downtown businesses, left the protected world of OSBR to enter another that sought to maintain racial segregation at all costs.

Fig. 3.28. McKinley Homecoming Queen and Court, 1952.

Commercial Expansion—The 1930s

Baton Rouge was relatively unaffected by the depression of the 1930s. The petro-chemical industry which had built several new plants, created jobs that generated the need for housing, schools, churches and shopping. Although much of this growth was in North Baton Rouge, the relocation of LSU from downtown to its new campus south of Chimes Street between 1926 and 1932 stimulated commercial and residential growth in OSBR.[20] According to Huel Perkins, many of the residents in OSBR were employed in the construction of LSU. They often stayed in the twelve-room boarding house that his grandparents had built on South Boulevard. He recalled, "This was before blacks could stay in hotels. All the carpenters and bricklayers they were from Opelousas and places like that. My grandparents would fix lunches for them and then they'd go home on weekends" (Perkins 2006). While many black laborers helped to build LSU and many residents of OSBR worked there, it was not until the 1950s that the first blacks could attend LSU and then only in its graduate programs. Finally, in the 1960s, LSU accepted black undergraduates for the first time.[21]

Fig. 3.29. The Butler Building on East Boulevard, *Sepia Socialite*, 1942.

Throughout the 1930s OSBR grew steadily. African Americans from surrounding rural areas and New Orleans moved into the neighborhood to take advantage of the educational opportunities that McKinley High School offered as well as the economic opportunities that Baton Rouge presented to black workers who brought to the city their skills as carpenters, masons, and builders. Population growth stimulated the growth of new businesses. East Boulevard developed into a thriving commercial center that was lined with department stores, groceries, drugstores, shoe stores, restaurants and nightclubs. McKinley High School was at the center of this district. Directly across from McKinley was the Butler Building (**Fig. 3.29**). Dr. Butler employed more than fifty people, and by 1940 his gross income totaled $55,000 and his property value was $50,000 (*Sepia Socialite* 1942). In addition to his business enterprises, he continued to serve as group captain of the NAACP, a board member of the Keystone Life Insurance Company, a sponsor of the Junior Hustlers Association designed to encourage young boys to enter business, and a member of the Baton Rouge Colored Civic Association.

Smaller businesses also lined the streets of East Boulevard from Julia Street down to Washington Street. A preponderance of Italian-American stores lined its northern end around the corner of East and Reddy (Terrace). These included Bonfanti's shoe store, DiMattia shoe store, and the General Hardware owned by Joe Cascio, who lived two doors down from his store.[22] The white-owned Allen's Esso Service and Allen's Shopping Center were at the southwest corner of East and Reddy (Terrace), and nearby was the white-owned Earl Langlo's Department Store. Moving south from Reddy were several smaller African American businesses, including Charlie's Cab; Walter Williams' Billards; Nelson Lawrence's Poultry Shop; Mary Lancaster, music teacher; as well as numerous restaurants, shoe shiners, liquor stores, coffee shops and the McKinley Movie Theatre (the only theatre for blacks except for the one at the Prince Hall Masonic Temple).

In 1936, Delpit's Chicken Shack opened on East Boulevard at the corner of Lettsworth and quickly became a hot spot for the neighborhood (**Figs. 1.8, 3.30**).[23] Thomas Henry Delpit (1911-1959) moved to Baton Rouge from New Orleans when he was twenty-one years old. He worked for the LSU Athletic Department, with the food services, and later at Dalton's Green Room in downtown Baton Rouge. According to the *Sepia Socialite*, "The Chicken Shack handles a large white trade and caters to the better element of collegiate and sporting circles" (1942:21). Ray Roy, who worked at his brother's business, Alvin Roy's Gym on Oklahoma Street, remembered eating at the Chicken Shack for lunch. According to Joe Delpit, there were three very popular black-owned eateries in the area, the Chicken Shack, Bernard's Chicken Loaf House, and Percy's

Fig. 3.30. Inside Delpit's Chicken Shack, *Sepia Socialite*, 1942.

Fig. 3.31. The Apex Club Cocktail Lounge, *Sepia Socialite*, 1942.

Bar-B-Que (on Texas Street), at which you had "large number of whites, even though segregation was still in place."

By the late 1930s, OSBR also contained several night clubs and social venues, including the Apex Club owned by Macie Lamott (**Fig. 3.31**). According to the *Sepia Socialite*, the Apex was the "swankiest nite club in Colored America." The lounge, located at the corner of Louisa and Braddock streets, boasted a spacious, art deco dining room, a main dance floor and main bar with beautiful cocktail lounge. Through its doors "only the sophisticated, properly attired can enter" (*Sepia Socialite*, 1942:25). Other establishments included the Club El Morroco on East Boulevard at Alice, which later became the Robin Hood Bar. These social venues, in addition to the Purple Social Club and the Temple Roof Garden at the Prince Hall and the Butler Blue's Room provided sophisticated entertainment venues for African Americans from around the state.

The decades between the wars in OSBR were a time of unparalleled growth of black businesses, advances in education, and the flourishing of civic and social clubs. OSBR entered a period of unprecedented culture growth which exemplified the ability of African Americans to create a unique and healthy set of cultural institutions, by negotiating between the twin patterns of resistance and accommodation. Growth took place despite the ongoing pressures of segregation. Black civic leadership under B.V. Baranco, Sr., Felton Clark, James Monroe Frazier, Thomas Delpit, and Dr. Leo Stanley Butler, among others, worked skillfully to keep alive the original ideals of citizenship and democracy. Delicately navigating the complex terrain of Jim Crow politics they approached white politicians to find intersecting interests that would benefit both races. These men were not militants. As Fairclough suggests, they approached whites as supplicants (1995). Their untiring, small steps were to lay the important groundwork for the sweeping changes to come. By the end of the decade their efforts had paid off in multiple ways: the Baton Rouge NAACP boasted 800 members, the second largest membership in the state; McKinley High School had 976 students, with one-fifth coming from outside of the Baton Rouge area; and job opportunities were expanding. At the same time, the close of the 1930s was a stark reminder of the unchanging nature of race relations in Louisiana. Voting became more difficult for blacks. In 1940, black registration had fallen below 1,000 and represented a miniscule sixteenth of 1 percent of the electorate (Fairclough 1995). In 1940, white supremacy still ruled the day. This was about to change, and OSBR would be at the forefront.

The Winds of Change

> No better argument for the integration of the Negro into the opportunities of American life and democracy can be given than the record of serving his country in a crucial hour as the present one.
>
> Felton G. Clark, President, Southern University, 1941

While unable to partake in many of the rights of democracy, the OSBR community galvanized to support the war effort. One such example was the formation of the Victory Maids by a group of women spearheaded by Mrs. Edmae Delpit, the wife of Thomas Delpit. Victory, represented not only victory abroad, but also victory at home against white supremacy which was described as the domestic version of Nazism. The "Double V" slogan held the promise of long awaited changes

The Paper With A Program For The Race

The Sepia Socialite

The Other Side Of Negro Life

presents

The Negro In Louisiana

Seventy-eight Years Of Progress ....
Fifth Anniversary Edition

Published by The Sepia Socialite Pub Co., 2101 Dryades Street, New Orleans, La. - April, 1942 - Price $1.0

Victory For Democracy

VICTORY Over Race Prejudice In America

VICTORY Over Enemies In Foriegn Fields

61625

Victory For Negro Voters In Louisiana

Fig. 3.32. Double V campaign. *Sepia Socialite*, 1942.

Fig. 3.33. Victory Maids at the Temple Theatre.

(**Fig. 3.32**). The Victory Maids heralded the call by organizing the sale of war bonds at the Temple Theatre (**Fig. 3.33**). Along with the most prominent members of the community, they gave their full support to the war effort. Residents of OSBR, like Dupuy Anderson pictured here, enlisted to serve to fight in the war against Facism (**Fig. 3.34**). Ironically, while blacks fought for democracy abroad, segregation still regulated daily life at home.

Fig. 3.34. Dupuy Anderson, WWII.

By the 1940s, as rural and small town areas were recovering from the depression, Baton Rouge was fully engaged in the war effort. Many blacks had left Louisiana during the "Great Migration," but many others had chosen to stay in the South and move to urban areas. Three-quarters of the jobs in agriculture in Louisiana held by blacks paid less than $1.00 per day in 1940, but they fared better in the cities (Neyland 1958:25). Like all populations, blacks went where the jobs were and by 1940, even in the South, that was in urban areas.

The authors are fortunately able to paint a portrait of Old South Baton Rouge at the outbreak of the war due a survey study that was conducted by a sociology class at Louisiana State University in 1940. While the survey included all blacks in Baton Rouge, OSBR clearly was the largest black neighborhood at the time, and it was its most affluent. Consequently, the figures discussed below need to be interpreted as approximations, rather than absolute indicators of conditions in OSBR. This portrait provides insights into a community that sacrificed for the war effort while experiencing the contradictions of job and housing discrimination.

In 1940, the population of Baton Rouge was 33,719; 33.5 percent, or 11,624, were black. Not all blacks lived in OSBR. Other black communities included Scotlandville, surrounding Southern University, and the emerging Eden and Valley Park areas. However, OSBR was, according to Gwen Hamilton, the focal point for shopping, entertainment, medical care, and church worship.

The black working population in Baton Rouge was divided roughly into three socioeconomic classes. A small professional class (5 percent) included doctors, nurses, dentists, a notary public, Southern University professors, school administrators, and ministers (**Fig. 3.35a-c).** An interviewer reported that "all showed a high degree of culture and refinement" (Louisiana State University 1940:35). This was the group most actively engaged not only in pursuing professions but also in building civic and social organizations that focused on the support of black people locally, and also on strengthening American democracy. This is evidenced by newly formed support organizations

Fig. 3.35a. Butler and Baranco Families.

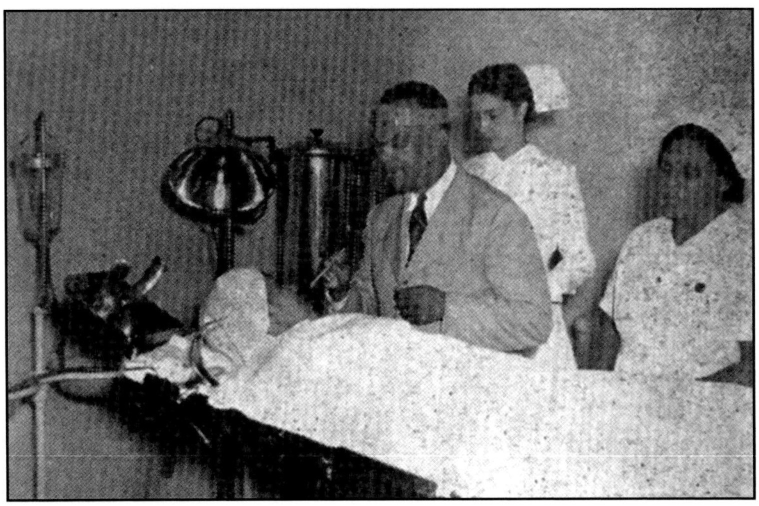

Fig. 3.35b. Dr. R.M. Baranco.

Fig. 3.35c. Peoples Life Insurance, Co., Board of Directors.

like the Victory Maids, but also the continuing efforts of local businessmen and black civic organizations promoting both direct and indirect participation in the war effort.

An intermediate class of skilled workers comprised about 15 percent of the population. Skilled jobs included, store and filling station owners, hotel and café operators, two theater managers, and newspapermen employed by the Associated Negro Press (**Fig. 3.36**). There were barbers including Henry Webb, mortician John Daigre, plasterers including Paul LeBlanc and Clarence Boyd, construction superintendent Link Bryant, brick layers Manuel Roque, Alfred Perkins, and Joe Fields, painters Monroe Green and Joseph Shelvin, and a construction company supervisor Marshall Smith. Skilled jobs in the building trades paid about the same as they did for whites, and there was not too much segregation there. Blacks made up 68 percent of the plasterers and cement finishers in the city, and 42 percent of the masons and stone cutters. There were also many carpenters and house builders. Standard Oil paid black bricklayers $1.25 per hour, a decent wage for that period. On the other hand, there were no black electricians, machinists, or printing craftsmen. Compared to most cities in Louisiana, Baton Rouge provided more job opportunities and better paying jobs; however, blacks were legally restricted to certain occupations because they were not provided licenses or certifications. They were always the first fired and generally never made salaries equal to their white counterparts. Musicians also made up part of this skilled working class. They included George Williams, Tabbie Thomas, Bob Johnson (Big Band), Buddy Guy, Joe Tex, Felix Martin, Buddy Stewart, Henry Batiste, Doc Robinson, and vocalist Lionell Purcell.

The remaining 80 percent of the working population was employed in unskilled labor. Laborers worked in the chemical industries, specifically Standard Oil and Ethyl (701 employees), in the building and construction trades (335), in wholesale and retail (305), in agriculture (120), and in lumber mills (118; Louisiana State University 1940:31). In addition they worked at Kaiser Aluminum, the Baton Rouge Water Works, and in service industries. LSU and the hotels hired cooks, janitors, cleaners, grounds keepers, unskilled construction workers

Fig. 3.36. Esso Gas Station, Horatio Thompson. *Sepia Socialite*, 1942.

Fig. 3.37. A Spanish Moss Factory.

and chauffeurs. Many women were hired to work in the Spanish moss factory (auto seat stuffing), located off of Nicholson Drive (Carleton 1981:180; **Fig. 3.37**). Though not having the advantage of formal education, they worked hard and provided much of the labor in wartime industries.

About 95 percent of black families had at least one adult female who worked outside the home.[24] While some women worked as teachers, the majority of jobs for women were unskilled. In Baton Rouge, the greatest number of jobs available for poorly educated female workers was in domestic service. Of the 5,814 Negroes officially employed in Baton Rouge, 2,251 women reported working as maids, nannies, and housekeepers, and 167 worked in hotels and restaurants. Few skilled jobs were available except for beauticians, bookkeepers, and nurses. "My mother had to hold two jobs some of the time. She worked as a maid, taught at the orphanage home and then went to night school to try and get a better job. All that just to put us through school" (Brown 1969:42).

Housing

In May 1940, the Federal Housing Authority conducted a survey of housing and sanitary conditions in Baton Rouge. The survey reflected the trends in housing.

> Observation shows that the Negroes of Baton Rouge have been, as a rule, pushed by economic forces to the less desirable lowland areas. In many places over the city Negroes originally settled in areas that, due to the growth of the city, subsequently become desirable to the white home builders. In such a situation the Negro houses are gradually eliminated and replaced by white homes (Louisiana State University 1940:47).

The area called "the Bottom" in OSBR is one of those areas referred to. Home ownership in OSBR in 1940 was high. Indeed, 83 percent of resident families owned their own home, indicating that OSBR was more of a middle class community than most. Some excellent housing was available to African Americans. Professional and business people lived in larger, well appointed houses in

Fig. 3.38. Children at Smith House, Lettsworth, ca. 1950.

this period. Most middle and upper class black housing was clustered in the Swart neighborhood. It was, however, a minority of the total population of the area.[25]

Poor sanitary conditions were in part a product of poverty, but also of lack of services provided to black communities. Sewage pipes, electricity, paved roads and other services were reserved for white communities. Lack of basic services severely impacted the health of black residents. The greatest killer was tuberculosis, followed by pneumonia and influenza (Leyland 1958:18-19). Males died at a much higher rate than women. In 1940, the average death rate for whites in Baton Rouge was 11.7 per thousand, and for blacks 17.9 per thousand. But for black males, the death rate was 20.7 per thousand—almost double the white rate.

In 1940, Old South Baton Rouge was a pedestrian community. Children played mostly in and around their houses and those of their friends (**Fig 3.38**). The vast majority of children played in or near their own house or a nearby playground. Street corner culture was not yet highly developed. Most children played with members of their own race, but despite segregation almost 11 percent of the high schoolers reported playing with whites on a regular basis.

Schooling, so important to the future of each child, was a luxury for many. Poverty necessitated that children work rather than go to school. Most children attended one of the four segregated elementary schools available to black children: Scott Elementary (917 pupils), Reddy Street Elementary (988 pupils), Perkins Road Elementary (654 pupils) or Eden Park Elementary (194 pupils).[26] Almost 30 percent of these children advanced to McKinley High School the only black secondary school in Baton Rouge. While this might seem like a small number, it was significantly higher than the rest of the state. In 1940, less than 18 percent of Louisiana's black population was enrolled in a public high school, roughly average for the South (Anderson 1988:237). That year McKinley had 976 pupils, one-fifth of whom came from outside of the Baton Rouge area. A total of 1,444 African Americans graduated from high school in Louisiana in 1940; close to one-sixth of those graduated from McKinley.

The emphasis in black secondary education in Louisiana was on industrial education. African Americans were trained to find jobs in the existing job market, so special training was given in the industrial arts (shop), home economics and vocational agriculture (though at McKinley there was no practice or field experience available in agriculture). Female high school students were trained in food preparation, sewing, and maid service. Many McKinley students received academic training. Perhaps the single most telling statistic about black education in 1940 is found in the cost per student. Louisiana annually spent an average of $58.28 per student on the education of its white students. The equivalent for black students was $13.51. In other words, for every dollar spent on educating a black child, $4.40 was spent on a white, and a large proportion of the funds spend on black education came from the federal government. By the 1950s, education in the state overall had not seen much improvement. In 1950, 23 percent of white children graduated from high school in Louisiana, while only 4 percent of black school children graduated from high school (Bankston and Caldas 2002:30).[27]

African American educators worked under other disadvantages as well. At this time there was only one public park for blacks—Progress Park on North 13th Street (Rodrieguez and Philips 2006:49). Blacks were permitted to rent the facilities of the Baton Rouge city parks for high school football games. They paid 10 percent of the gate fees to the park association. Concession stands cost $10.00. City Park, which bordered the community on its eastern side, was for "whites only." Black children were completely forbidden from using the golfing or swimming facilities of the public parks. All sports were segregated. Black high schools maintained inter-school contests such as basketball, football, tennis, track, and volleyball. This meant that the teams and their supporters traveled as far as Shreveport and Lake Charles to play regular games at other black schools. "Great impetus has been given to athletics by a volunteer organization of colored citizens of the city, known as the McKinley Boosters Club" (Frazier 1937:87).

As World War II came to an end while segregation persisted, it was clear that the war had "placed every facet of the South's racial system under pressure" (Fairclough 1995:75). In cities like Baton Rouge, blacks and whites had worked in factories that supported the war effort—Standard Oil, the Aluminum Company of America, and the Ethyl Gasoline Company. The war put people in new situations and the certainty of the color line came into question. In the summer of 1944, Old South Baton Rouge initiated a push for voter registration. Supported by Gardner C. Taylor (discussed in Chapter V), a minister at Shiloh Baptist Church, the registration drive was conducted by the NAACP, the People's Defense League, the CIO's Political Action Committee, the Prince Hall Masons, and the Knights of Peter Claver. Rev. Gardner Taylor joined with New Orleans minister L.L. Haynes to form a new organization, the Louisiana Progressive Voters League, to coordinate the voter registration (Fairclough 1995). While blacks in OSBR navigated Jim Crow and quietly organized to engage their civil rights, it was the returning soldiers who realized how little had changed on the home front while they had been fighting for democracy around the world. This was about to change. OSBR would be a catalyst for one of the most sweeping changes of the twentieth century.

Old Ways No More—The 1950s

By the 1950s OSBR was a thriving multiethnic community. In addition to the East Boulevard commercial district, two other areas were growing. The Highland Road corridor between downtown and LSU emerged as a commercial area (**Fig. 3.39**). It became the site of many boarding houses, a bowling alley, drugstores, and other retail shops that served the growing LSU student population. Further north, between McKinley and Washington, was the Cotton Club, a bar that was the popular gathering spot for LSU football fans before and after games. There were also several Italian groceries, Highland Cleaners, Streamline Grocery, and service stations. The former WJBO radio station was located near the corner of Highland and Oklahoma. In 1947 Alvin Roy bought the building and opened Alvin's Gym and Slenderizing Studio. Roy opened the gym to women in the morning

Fig. 3.39. North Gate at LSU.

and to men beginning at noon. It was a popular locale for downtown businessmen. Alvin Roy went on to become nationally famous as an early proponent of strength training. His advertisements for a mail-order course appeared in magazines and comic books throughout the country. They particularly appealed to sports-minded youth growing up in the post-World War II suburbs. Roy trained Heisman Trophy winner Billy Cannon, the Istrouma High School football team which won a state championship, and LSU's 1958 national football championship team.[28]

The other commercial area to develop was the Fannie Street corridor (Eddie Robinson) between South Boulevard and Washington. As early as the 1920s, the corner of South and Fannie was the site of several commercial enterprises, including a drugstore and the Bake House next to the Purple Social Club. In 1950, the hub of this corner became the Lincoln Theatre built by Dr. A.L. Chapman, a local physician (who had also built the Lincoln Hotel on Government Street). The Lincoln was a movie theatre and site for black entertainers. It also had a barber shop which is still operating as of this writing. The Lincoln is notable as a meeting place for civil rights activities (**Fig. 1.24**).

The last major commercial area to be developed was a small strip on Washington between Fannie and Napoleon. Green-Ups gas station, the Bakery, and several groceries lined Washington, which was the thoroughfare that connected the community to City Park. Sections of the area south of Washington Street were still sparsely developed with low-lying city blocks containing only a few homes. Part of this area was still being used as a garbage dump. It continued to develop as a residential area in the 1950s and 1960s and eventually became the home of the new McKinley High School.

OSBR continued to function as a self-contained community in which black-owned businesses, clubs, schools, and churches prospered (**Appendix IV**). In part, the success of the African American community resulted because of segregation. Although blacks could shop downtown at Dalton's, Kress's and Rosenfields', segregation limited their use of these businesses. Mrs. Olivia Huey remembered, "Piccadilly was the main store downtown that you could work at, but not eat in at that time. It was disheartening, but at the time, there was nothing you could do about it. You lived with it." Bathrooms, water fountains and changing rooms were all segregated. The buses on which they rode downtown were segregated as well as the lunch counters and restaurants. Rather than endure these dehumanizing laws, African Americans opted to support their own businesses and to remain within the self-enclosed world of OSBR (*Sepia Socialite* 1942). African American taxis, and even a black bus company served the area.

Fig. 3.40. A multiethnic community in the Swart neighborhood, East Boulevard. (Thomas Delpit), 1950s.

Within the boundaries of OSBR, African Americans could maintain the dignity of life in a minimally segregated community. Here, geographic segregation was less apparent. Well into the early 1960s, African Americans, German Americans, Italian Americans and other Euro-Americans lived side by side (**Fig. 3.40**). In some cases they intermarried, defying the norms of the segregated society. Although Italian Catholics lived across the street from African American Catholics, they did not attend the same church, and their children did not attend the same school; yet they might have had daily interaction. According to Kathy Wink, the daughter of Frank Cascio (Cascio's Hardware), when she was six or seven years old she often played with Dr. Leo Butler's daughter and considered Hedi Butler to be one of her closest friends (Wink 2005; **Fig. 3.41**). As a close neighbor she went around the corner to play, but the Butler daughters never went to her house, nor did they participate in other social activities with her. This illustrates some of the ironies and nuances of inter-racial mores of the period.

Fig. 3.41. Hedi Butler and Kathy Cacsio Wink, 1950s.

Oral histories with many OSBR residents describe the community as one where everyone got along, and blacks and whites lived next door to each other. While they resided in the same neighborhood, social segregation regulated aspects of their lives. Even many Italian-Americans were subjected to discrimination and segregation. Virginia Pinnoci (maiden name Caruso), remembered her painful memories of growing up Italian in OSBR. She recalled:

> They were very prejudiced in this town against Italians. My brothers could not work at the Louisiana Creamery, which was *the* creamery then. My brother Vince was the first Italian that ever went to work for Gulf States. They couldn't drive a city bus. They wouldn't allow the Italians in the sororities and fraternities. And they'd make fun of you (Pinnoci 2005).

Prejudice was not an exclusively black and white issue.[29] Divisive constructs of race and ethnicity shaped the complex and contradictory nature of race relations. Even within a climate of legal segregation and prejudice, whites and blacks worked together. Blacks prospered, voted, and they negotiated the intricacies of the racial mores to work with city government officials to slowly but surely attain equal rights, but in the climate of the 1950s, this was not enough.

Increasingly, strategies of resistance and confrontation were added to the tactics of accommodation. The first large scale example of the new militancy was dramatically revealed in the Baton Rouge Bus Boycott of 1953 (**Fig. 3.42**). In the spring of that year, Rev. T.J. Jemison, the recently arrived pastor at Mt. Zion Church, went to the City-Parish Council to complain about bus fare increases and the fact that blacks had to stand in the back of the bus while empty seats remained in the white section. The City-Parish Council agreed with him and approved Ordinance 222, which stated

Fig. 3.42. Leaders of the 1953 Baton Rouge Bus Boycott, including Rev. T.J. Jemison, Fred Matthews, Acie Belton, Gus Young, Victoria Young, Rev. Frank O'Connor, and Robert Gerney.
From the Willie Harris Photographic Collection; courtesy Mr. James Terry, III.

Fig. 3.43. The Baton Rouge Bus Boycott, 1953. Courtesy of Ernest Ritchie, photographer.

that blacks could fill up the bus from the back to the front and whites could fill the bus from the front to back on a first-come-first-served basis. In effect, the ordinance abolished reserved seating for blacks and whites and implemented a more fluid form of segregation. On June 14, bus company officials suspended two white bus drivers for not complying with the ordinance. In response the drivers went on strike. At that point Louisiana Att. Gen. Fred LeBlanc declared that Ordinance 222 violated the state's segregation laws. Four days later in response to the ruling, 200 African Americans formed the United Defense League and announced a boycott of the buses. Boycott organizers created a free ride system that immediately went into effect (**Fig. 3.43**). Rev. T.J. Jemison recalled that: "Nobody rode the bus during the strike. There were about eight people who didn't hear the call that night and they rode to work. But by afternoon there was nobody riding the bus. For days not a Negro rode the bus." On June 24, the city-council passed Ordinance 251 which in effect was a compromise. The new law reserved the first two bus seats for white riders and the last two seats for black riders. Blacks would fill the bus from the back to front and whites front to back. OSBR African American activists including Johnnie Jones, Willis Reed, Dupuy Anderson, and Joe Howard objected to the compromise because it left segregation intact. While falling short of dismantling segregation, it represented a vast improvement over the old arrangement. Most importantly, the Baton Rouge bus boycott "showed that even in the Deep South blacks were ready to openly protest, en masse, against the segregated status quo. "An entire community had been speedily mobilized and effectively organized" (Fairclough 1999:162).[30] Baton Rouge buses were not integrated until 1962 (**Fig. 5.34**).

The success in pushing back the boundaries of segregation grew out of a strong sense of activism that had been operating in the community for several decades. The NAACP chapter had become increasingly active since the 1920s. In Louisiana, only Baton Rouge and Monroe had successful and dynamic chapters (Fairclough 1999). The Bus Boycott was just the beginning of a relentless battle for civil rights in OSBR. In 1954 the landmark Supreme Court case, *Brown v. Board of Education*, legally desegregated all public schools. At the beginning of the 1954-55 school year, attorneys Alex Pitcher and Johnnie Jones accompanied about thirty black children to the gates of a white elementary school and attempted to enroll them. They were unsuccessful. Clearly, legal pressure alone would not bring about the equality that blacks desired. Activists like Pitcher and Jones believed that more direct pressure and radical action was necessary to dismantle segregation, but this represented the views of only a part of the black community. Many, including the state officers of the NAACP, did little to encourage more radical strategies. They feared that civil disobedience would only result in a backlash against all blacks and erode the racial diplomacy that they had worked for decades to achieve. OSBR stood at a decisive historical moment when the unified strategies of the black community began to unravel in the face of the persistent and unyielding segregationist hegemony.

Members of the Baton Rouge African American community continued to push for the integration of the City Park golf course (1953), the City Park pool (1963), and the lunch counter at Kress's on Third Street (1960). In 1964, the first African American undergraduates enrolled at LSU. That same year, the Supreme Court declared segregated public parks to be unconstitutional. Rather than integrate its public parks, Baton Rouge closed its public swimming pools. The late '60s and early '70s saw racial tensions increase as resistance to integration increased. In 1963, the Citizens Council put pressure on the registrar to place a ceiling on black voter registration. Simultaneously, the desegregation of the schools was impeded by general sentiments, including Gov. Jimmie Davis, who had "vowed to prevent any African American student from ever attending school with a white child" (Parent 2004:108). Baton Rouge eventually became embroiled in one of the longest court-ordered school desegregation suits in the country, with several of the plaintiffs coming from Old South Baton Rouge. Although they were clearly central to the fight for civil rights, Baton Rouge's contributions to the Civil Rights Movement have been overshadowed by those in Selma and Montgomery. Success was not complete at the legal level until 1972, when the state legislature expunged all its Jim Crow laws.

Voices of Old South Baton Rouge:

Integration

Joe Delpit:

Integration coming—to be frank with you—it had a tremendous impact on our community. A lot of people felt they had the money, they'll go were they want to go, and they forgot about the businesses in their own neighborhood. Therefore people in the neighborhood weren't making any money so they couldn't put money back into their business to keep them up. I know in the milder incidents with the Chicken Shack, we just saw the business getting bad and getting worse and worse. And then there were problems with the purse snatching and things like that. And people would be afraid to come out at night . . .

Reverend Lionel Lee:

African American businesses in this community didn't necessarily move, they went out of business. Now one of the weaknesses of African Americans still is that when one generation of business people pass on the youngsters don't carry on, they close up. That's the weaknesses. I can't think of one right now except for Joe Delpit that followed his father. Well I can think of two, Darensbourg Shoe Shop . . . that was a shoe shop on Government and South Eighteenth. But the rest of them in that time have passed, they closed business, they had no interest. And that's one of the weaknesses of blacks to not carry on the traditions of their forefathers. So it wasn't voluntarily, it was done because of lack of interest.

Peggy Goods:

Integration is probably one of the worst things that has ever happened to black people. They fanned us out to schools where we didn't want to be, they closed our schools. That was the end of the neighborhood schools which was to me an absolute disaster. We grew up where we could walk to school. We walked to school everyday. [In] nineteen sixty-five they bused us to Lee High and that was a miserable experience. I remember recollect ions of the first day they took us out. We of course had to go to school with police and it was such a hostile environment. You never understand why people could hate so much people they don't even know. And so I think after the loss of the neighborhood school that did not help the community because then people started moving away, [there was] a flight from the community, and that was a decline.

Alton Ingram:

The major changes that I see in the community are that a lot of people who went off to college got degrees and some moved out of state, some got jobs in the local plants and other places. Since things started opening up for blacks a bit after the desegregation . . . some of the job markets started opening up and hired blacks [like] police departments and some of the government. And blacks could afford better homes because they had better jobs making more money. So then we had a black flight out the neighborhood. Of course that left people who were low income or no income living in this area and it started to just go down. That is why the businesses suffered because people did not have money to spend in the neighborhood and the people who had the good jobs moved out the neighborhood and they were spending money elsewhere.

Reverend Charles T. Smith:

Primarily [black businesses] went out of existence because of integration. At the time that these businesses flourished everything was strongly segregated on the basis of race. Once integration came these businesses found themselves competing not just against each other but against better financed white business establishments, and eventually they succumbed to that competition. Integration was not readily accepted and of course a number of black businesses did survive even after legal integration came into being because black people didn't feel too welcome in a lot of the integrated business places. But as they became more welcome there and they frequented them more, this eventually lead to the demise of more and more black businesses.

Fred C. Matthews, Jr.:

One of the things that happened, and unfortunately happened, [is] that the fast food restaurants have virtually put black businesses out of business. What I mean is it's unfortunate because if black people who are operating restaurants and cafes at that time had expanded and proved their business they had a good chance of being top people in Baton Rouge as far as serving food is concerned, but they let go and they didn't improve. And so these fast food restaurants like the McDonald's, and Burger King, and Piccadilly, and all those places, they just put us out of business. They didn't necessarily have to put us out of business, but we went to sleep on the job. When they started the nonviolent movement in fifty-four . . . a lot of people had a different notion about what integration was going to be all about. But integration wasn't what a lot of people thought.

A Community in Transition

> Negroes were served without incident Tuesday afternoon at lunch counters in twelve major stores throughout Baton Rouge.
>
> *Morning Advocate,* 1963

Ironically, the end of segregation in Baton Rouge, while bringing political and civic advances for African Americans, adversely impacted the basis of their economic independence—black-owned businesses. Access to formerly all white restaurants and stores meant a decline in the traditional African American businesses that had been the heart of the thriving East Boulevard commercial district (**Figs. 3.44, 3.45**).

Fig. 3.44. East Boulevard (Thomas Delpit), looking north from McKinley High School, 1950 by Chester Beaty. Courtesy of LSU Special Collections.

The late 1960s and following years witnessed a drastic economic decline in OSBR. Simultaneously, there was a virtual exodus of established families who now sought more modern dwellings and a different life style in the new suburbs of Baton Rouge. The younger generation, many of whom were college educated, sought better opportunities in other cities. But perhaps the most dramatic factor in the economic decline of the neighborhood was the construction of I-10 through the neighborhood in 1965. As described in the previous chapter the construction divided and crippled the community economically. Court-ordered school desegregation in the early 1970s further robbed it of its youth through busing. It resulted in the eventual closure of important community-based schools, and most notably and symbolically, McKinley High School.

Despite the economic decline of the neighborhood, OSBR remains a strong community in several ways. Elderly community residents have chosen to stay, and they provide a stabilizing factor. The homes in the neighborhood provide rich examples of Louisiana's vernacular architecture and contain some of the earliest suburbs in Baton Rouge. The churches (over forty in total) remain active and provide a sense of community. The Leo S. Butler Center and the new community center at the resurrected McKinley High School preserve not only the history of the community, but are vital to providing social, economic and public services. The new Carver Branch Library and McKinley Middle Magnet School signal new growth and a renewed commitment to invest in OSBR. Entire neighborhoods of HUD-sponsored single and duplex houses are springing up along East Boulevard and on E. Polk Street. New commercial growth at the North gates of LSU and on Nicholson Drive will also hopefully have a positive impact.

Fig. 3.45. Thomas Delpit, looking north from the same location, 2006.

Yet, perhaps one of the greatest strengths of this community is the pride of its residents. In spite of economic decay, increased crime and poverty, residents still see this as a community where everyone knows each other and is willing to help their neighbor. There is a sense of a shared history, of a community that was strong, successful and proud despite the injustices of racial oppression. In oral history interviews, community residents point to the many successful African Americans who had their start in this neighborhood.[31] OSBR is a community with a rich history, one which has not been clearly articulated or documented. Important themes in American history are revealed by the changes and social events which occurred here. These historical events and processes, including segregation, desegregation, urbanization, the impact of national policies and global events, and cultural creolization, have all been pivotal in shaping the character of OSBR. Processes of creolization are dramatically stamped onto the cultural landscape, and it is to this topic that we turn to in the next two chapters.

Notes

[1] It is reported that Hart transferred much of this property to African Americans, including to Belle McTier and her daughter Robertine Edmund, who lived in OSBR.

[2] Other employers of African Americans in the late nineteenth century included: Standard Box Company, Louisiana State University, local railroad companies, E. Schloss Gin, Schloss Moss Factory, Lake Brick Company, Grouchy Hotel and the Istrouma Hotel.

[3] The school also appears on the 1911 Sanborn maps and is noted as "colored school—private." This school is still in existence today and is called the Blundon School. It is located on West McKinley.

[4] The areas of concentration for African Americans are in Beauregard Town, particularly on Royal, St. Napoleon and along Government, and also in Spanish Town, where Mt. Zion church was located (on Spanish Town Road).

[5] The poll tax also disenfranchised poor white voters.

[6] B.V. Baranco, born and raised in Baton Rouge to Beverly V. Baranco and Sarah Gordon (a teacher), received his early education in private colored schools in Baton Rouge and attended Straight College (now Dillard) in New Orleans. After working in New Orleans for several years, he returned to Baton Rouge and entered the barber business. In 1915 he was elected grand master of the Odd Fellows (a fraternal order) of the State of Louisiana (*Sepia Socialite*, April 1942).

[7] Although most whites professed loyalty to the Democratic Party, the remaining Louisiana Republicans gave blacks indirect access to white officials. The "Black and Tan" faction was the African American segment of the Republican Party who had a history of political activity following the Civil War.

[8] Southern had originally been founded in New Orleans in 1879 as the first state-funded university for African Americans in Louisiana.

[9] The funding for the Perkins Street School was secured by a committee made up of Fraizer, B.V. Baranco, H.R. Baranco, Mike Winfield, Thomas Smiler, and Henry Andrews. The group met with Mayor Jules Roux and the city council in 1913 to describe the inadequacy of the colored public schools.

[10] James Anderson reports that most blacks in the 1920s went to school fewer months out of the year than whites.

[11] Inez Chrisentery also received a Masters in Education from LSU in 1955; she was one of the first blacks to receive an advanced degree at LSU.

[12] At least one family, Mattie Chin is residing at 905 Terrace in 1927.

[13] This was the first post office in the state of Louisiana to have a black postmaster.

[14] The strength of "Louisiana" folk religious customs such as St. Joseph Day altars is directly attributable to the Sicilian presence in southern Louisiana.

[15] The history of the Prince Hall Masons dated from 1842, when free blacks formed the first of several lodges in New Orleans. Although it was forced to go underground during the 1850s, it reemerged during Reconstruction and was linked to the Republican Party (Fairclough 1999).

[16] Refer to Chapter V, pp. 124-25.

[17] The previous year the school board approved the construction of Baton Rouge High School on Government Avenue with approved contracts totaling $510,243. This school was designed for 1,200 students, whereas McKinley had 456 and 630 in the 1935 school year.

[18] In the South in 1930, 38 percent of white children were enrolled in high school compared to the rest of the nation where enrollment was 47 percent (Anderson).

[19] Fairclough argues that, unable to attack segregation head-on, blacks adopted tactics of indirection. Without abandoning the ultimate goal of full citizenship, they worked for short-term improvements within their segregated sphere (2001).

[20] The first Baton Rouge home of LSU was in the quarters of the Institute for the Deaf, Dumb and Blind. In 1886, the federal garrison grounds (now the site of the state capitol) were formally declared the domicile of the University. Land for the present campus was purchased in 1918, construction started in 1922, and the move began in 1925; it was not, however, until 1932 that the move was finally completed. Formal dedication of the present campus took place on April 30, 1926.

[21] Pat Smith recalled that the first residents of OSBR to attend LSU were Milton Wicks, Donald Griffin, Aaron Hardnett, Larry Fields, and Veronica Bajoie—all attended, but did not finish.

[22] Joe Cascio's daughter, Kathy Wink, was interviewed for this report. She was born in OSBR in 1944 and lived at 1213 East Boulevard. Like most of the Italian children in the neighborhood she attended St. Agnes School and later attended Baton Rouge High School. The family moved to the Garden District when she was seven, but the family-owned business, General Hardware, remained in OSBR. Her grandfather Servio continued to live in his home at 1215 East Boulevard until his death.

[23] From oral history interview with Joseph Delpit, 1996, LSU T. Harry Williams Center for Oral History.

[24] The sex ratio of blacks in Baton Rouge was unusual, illustrating the unique economic and standard of living pressures the community suffered under. It was 78.1. In other words, in 1940 there were almost four females for every three males. However, in the 35-64 age group where male jobs were available, males outnumbered females.

[25] The survey selected a number of areas of the city with the greatest housing problems. Of 3,335 houses surveyed in these mostly minority areas, 88 percent of the houses were owned or occupied by blacks. For homeowners, the average white house had five rooms and the average black house had four rooms. For those who rented, the average black house had three rooms while the average white rental had four rooms. Only 16 percent of the black-occupied houses in the depressed areas were recognized as being in good repair. Forty percent of blacks in these areas owned their own homes. While home ownership was common, the housing condition for blacks, as well as for many whites, was well below national standards for the time. A substantial proportion of the residents of OSBR were relatively impoverished and unable to purchase what by that year had become basic middle class amenities for their houses. Many people did not have indoor toilets, showers, hot water, electricity or refrigeration, glass windows or telephones (**See Appendixes I, II**).

[26] LSU, Sociology 204 1940:78-79. The section of this report entitled "Negro Education in the City of Baton Rouge, Louisiana," was written by J.E Cladwell.

[27] A survey of McKinley reported that the furniture was old and in fair condition. Movable furniture such as tables was scarce, and lighting was inadequate. The school library was poor, and black students were not permitted to use the Baton Rouge public library. The blackboards were also in a bad state of repair, though the building was well maintained, being clean and presentable. There were still only twenty teachers, resulting in a teaching ratio of forty-nine students per teacher. All of the teachers held A.B. degrees. Most had been trained at Southern University. Nevertheless, this resource-starved high school attracted black students from around the entire state of Louisiana.

[28] See oral history interview with Ray Roy (June 14, 2005) at the T. Harry Williams Center for Oral History at LSU, Baton Rouge, for further information about Alvin Roy.

[29] In fact, Italians had been lynched in New Orleans in the early part of the century (Fairclough 1999).

[30] An interactive presentation on the bus boycott was prepared the LSU Special Collections and T. Harry Williams Center for Oral History at LSU; as well, a full length documentary on the Baton Rouge Bus Boycott has also been produced.

[31] See Appendix V, *One Square Mile*, which lists the accomplished men and women of the neighborhood.

Chapter Four

The Architectural Character

My father was a carpenter. He went to work every morning with his hammer and his saw and his nail apron . . . . He built our house since he didn't have any money.

~Josephine Bonfani

Architecture is like a window into the soul of a community. With some practice, it is possible to read an historic community through an examination of its architecture in much the same the way a psychologist reads one's personality through the use of projective tests. Many details of daily life reveal themselves through the kinds of architecture which people select for themselves. A couple of brief examples may illustrate the point: Identity is intimately reflected in one's home. Whether a house is owned or rented, over the years each family modifies its residence and its surroundings according to personal tastes and values. One's ethnic and class allegiances and one's commitment to a particular socially established way of life may be read directly from the type of house and the relative amount of care lavished upon it. Each house may also be read as a kind of social map of the family. A principal function of architecture is to wall off and separate groups and individuals into socially established functional spaces. Who "owns" the kitchen or the living room, where do children play and sleep, and how and where guests are entertained—these and many other questions are answered by a close examination of the socio-spatial practices of a culture or social group.

Many of the cultural practices surrounding the design, use and decoration of houses in OSBR grow out of the processes of creolization which were discussed in Chapter I. The character of major portions of the architecture of this community illustrates almost chaotic levels of culture blending of African, Caribbean, French Creole and Anglo architectural traditions. For example, we will discuss the exceptionally high occurrence of front porches and their distinctive uses. The uses of colors and decorations reflect non-European stylistic sensibilities revealing a higher value placed on personal expression and individuality than is found in many of the more stylistically conformative suburbs of Baton Rouge. These same values also extend into the layout of landscapes and the values placed on distinctive patterns of gardening. Though stamped into the material heritage of the community, these culture patterns represent a fast-disappearing component of the historical patrimony of Baton Rouge.

The Old South Baton Rouge community is, at its heart, a working-class community of the 1930s decade, but its character is more complex. This large area is divided between industrial, commercial, and residential zones, with the latter dominating more than half of the total land area.

Industrial Zones

The zones of heavy industry are located mostly along the river between old Highland Road and the batture (**Figs. 2.3-2.4, 2.8 upper left hand corner**). As we have seen, even before the year 1900 the area south of Catfish Town had developed into an area of heavy industry coupled with residential districts constructed for the workers in those industries. Industries included brick and lumber yards, several oil terminals, other heavy industries, and the old city docks. A zone of foundries and machine shops extended beneath what is now the eastern approach of the I-10 bridge

Fig. 4.1. McKinley High School building on Thomas Delpit, now a community center following its restoration in 2005.

between the old Natchez Street Railroad line and Nicholson Drive. An area of lighter industry also soon developed along the Louisiana and Arkansas (IGC) railroad right of way between 15th and 16th streets.

Commercial Zones

As described in Chapter II above, the area between Terrace Boulevard and the LSU campus was laid out in sections, beginning in the north in the 1920s and moving towards the south in the 1930s and early 1940s. In conjunction with this urbanization, commercial zones grew up along two thoroughfares running north-south—East Boulevard (Thomas Delpit), and Highland Road. In both places a combination of Italian grocery and dry goods stores and African American owned specialty businesses such as Joe Ridley's tailor shop, flourished (**Fig. 3.11b**). East Boulevard became the social core of the community and the principal commercial strip. Besides McKinley High School (1927; **Fig. 3.23, 4.1**) and several service organizations, it included grocery and dry goods stories, clothing and shoe shops, bars and clubs, a movie theater, drug stores, fast food restaurants and other commercial outlets (**Figs. 3.16, 3.18, 3.29, 3.43-3.45**). Photos of the period reveal that much of the clientele consisted of foot traffic. Few automobiles clogged the streets, and people walked from their houses to the stores (**Fig. 3.43**). The area south of Reddy Street (Terrace Boulevard) was populated primarily by African Americans. This zone remained the social and commercial heart of the OSBR community until the combined impacts of racial desegregation and the construction of I-10 in the early 1960s dealt a severe blow to its commercial viability.

Following the collapse of local commerce in the late 1960s, there was little commerce in the entire neighborhood for many years. The principal exception was businesses which arose to service the LSU community. Most of these were crowded along Highland Road and Chimes Street, but bars, apartments and rooming houses stretched out along Highland Road as far north as the terraces (Washington Street). Recently, there have been dramatic changes in this area, with an old shopping center being razed, and large scale apartment and condominium complexes springing up along both sides of Highland Road (**Fig. 6.8**).

Residential Sections

The residential section of OSBR is best thought of as two different zones. The earlier settled zone is the Swart neighborhood, originally planned in 1899. Railroad Avenue (Myrtle Street) was being constructed as early as 1909, and Reddy was in place the following year. Swart is bordered by South Boulevard, Reddy (Terrace Boulevard), Highland Road, and S. 15th Street. This is an area three blocks in depth (north to south) and twelve blocks running east to west. It was originally an extension of Beauregard Town towards the south. Much like Beauregard Town and the contiguous Garden District bordering Park Boulevard to the immediate east, Swart was established as a neighborhood for business and professional-class families, together with working-class African American families who served their domestic needs (**Map 2.14**). Even as late as 1950, it was a strongly mixed neighborhood **(Map 4.1).** The pressures of residential segregation eventually rendered it largely black.

Map 4.1. A section of the Swart Neighborhood bounded by: South, Terrace, Highland Road and Maxmillian–color coded by ethnicity, and illustrating the diversity of house and business ownership in 1950. Orange = white; Green = black.

The architecture of the old Swart neighborhood was originally bungalows and Queen Anne-style houses, with smaller shotgun and other more modest houses surrounding them. Shotguns were sometimes crowded shoulder to shoulder on narrow lots. The racial character of the area was mixed black, Anglo white, and Italian American (**Fig. 3.40**). Since the mid-1930s, some of these older blocks have undergone renovation, with older houses replaced by sections of more modern dwellings, often still in the shotgun or bungalow style.

The southern section of OSBR is primarily a series of subdivisions of relatively narrow lots laid out for and settled by working-class people. The houses were typically modest wooden structures of 400 to 1,800 square feet. Wooden bungalows, shotgun houses, and cottages dominate the area (**Map 4.2; Figs. 2.6-2.7, 4.18**). This area was laid out in the 1920s.

Larger and more modern houses do exist. Middle class and even upper-middle class subdivisions exist within this zone as well (notably Lake Crest west of Dalrymple Drive, and Nicholson Drive Estates east of Magnolia Mound Plantation).

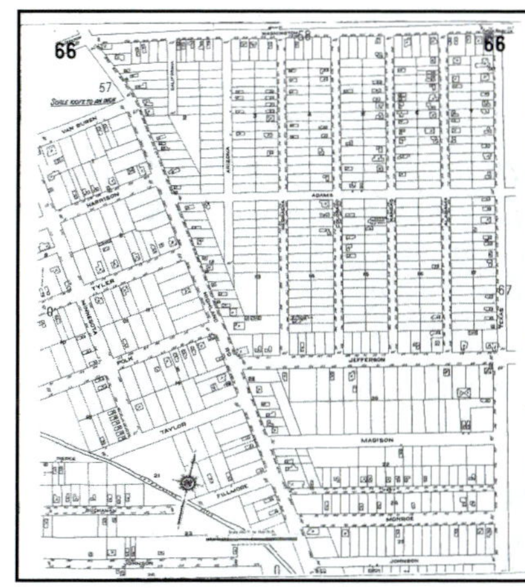

Map 4.2. A portion of OSBR east of Highland Road, between Louise and East Washington streets, illustrating typical narrow lots with shotgun houses and bungalow types.

The Cultural Landscape

Landscape surveys of OSBR reveal a neighborhood with a certain level of historical integrity and with its own individual character. The neighborhood was laid out at a time when pedestrian traffic was more important than automobile traffic. Although older houses in the Swart neighborhood sit on medium-sized urban lots 60 by 120 feet in size or larger, most residences are crowded together on forty-foot or thirty-foot wide lots. Both resident-owned houses and rental properties are commonplace. Landscaping represents both more traditional values and newer technologies and materials which became popular after World War II.

Front yards are typically small. Many houses are set back ten to fifteen feet from the street (Alomar 1994:84, 88). African American urban neighborhoods in the South are not dramatically distinct from those of other

Fig. 4.2. A kitchen garden on Julia Street, 2005.

Fig. 4.3. Terrace Street bungalow with chairs on the gallery.

Fig. 4.4. Bungalows along Julia Street.

Fig. 4.5. A shotgun with decorated yard, Kentucky Street.

ethnic groups of similar socioeconomic standing. They do, however, have a special character worthy of note. Cultural geographer Richard Westmacott, studying rural African American neighborhoods in Georgia noted four basic functions of the house-yard complex (1991; 1992). They were divided into zones of subsistence (kitchen gardens, fruit trees), ornament and display (decorative objects, found objects, flower beds), extensions of the kitchen (tables, chairs, food preparation equipment, barbecues), and leisure zones in which people gathered to socialize or to play. He might have added a fifth function of vehicle storage (driveways, carports, repair zones).

In urban settings with small yards, certain modifications of this pattern are seen. Although kitchen gardens still occur occasionally in the area, they are often located on vacant lots, either adjacent to the house or separated from it (**Fig. 4.2**) With the exception of barbecue pits, food preparation areas are uncommon. Typical of the house-yard complexes of OSBR are the following: Most houses have front galleries or porches where potted plants are placed and where chairs or benches are common (**Figs. 4.3-4.4**). Large shade trees are less common in front yards (**Fig. 4.5**). Yards are planted with an ornamental, rather than a spatial patterning in mind. Placement is often improvisational (Alomar 1994:90; **Fig. 4.6**). Decorative flowering plants are placed mostly close to the house (**Figs. 1.17, 4.7**). Red, pink, yellow, and white flowering plants are favored (**Fig. 4.8**). Potted plants and understory-sized plants are common decorative features, while full-sized trees are less common. Ligustrum, crape myrtle, camellia, azaleas, elephant ears, philodendron, Pittosporum, pecans, plums, cherries and Southern raintrees are popular (**Fig. 4.9**). Small front lawns are common, but African-style scraped yards are present minimally.

Yards are commonly surrounded by cyclone fences. Their beds and walks may be bordered with bricks or cinder blocks, but less commonly with the border (Liriope-monkey) grass, so common in the white suburbs (**Fig. 4.10**). Found objects may be placed in the yard (**Fig. 4.11**). Icons (grottos) of the Virgin Mary are proudly displayed in the yards of Catholics (**Fig. 4.12**).

Social use of the public areas in front of the house is significant and distinctive in OSBR. People use their front yards and porches often. They even function as a substitute for house interiors, being commonly used for hospitable social intercourse. Intense interaction with neighbors and other pedestrians is a characteristic of African American neighborhoods in general. High levels

Fig. 4.16. Bungalow style combined with bungalow type: a Swart bungalow with wooden pillars set on masonry bases, Maximillian Street.

floorplan consisting of two shotgun house plans placed side by side and with doors interconnecting the two sides and covered by a single roof with its ridge running perpendicular to the front and the street (**Fig. 4.15**). A full-width front porch spanned the front of the house. If the two sides of the house did not interconnect, the building might be used as a duplex and was referred to as a "double shotgun." In either case, it was very common in Louisiana in this period to decorate such vernacular buildings with the trappings of the Greene and Greene style, particularly the battered pillars so popular in the numerous pattern books (**Fig. 4.16**). Thus, although residents linked their traditional type houses with the new popular style through the addition of stylistic adornments, Kniffen borrowed the name to refer to the geometry of the regionally popular plan—the distinguishing feature of the house *type* in his system of architectural classification. In discussing the houses of this period, we must carefully distinguish between the bungalow style and the bungalow type. They are genetically unrelated architectural patterns, though, through historical coincidence in Louisiana, they are conjoined in many individual houses of the 1920s and 1930s, particularly in OSBR.

The Shotgun House Family

Perhaps, the most elaborate and productive family of vernacular house types in Louisiana is that generally referred to as the shotgun family. The shotgun form was named by Fred Kniffen in 1936 in his paper on Louisiana House types. The same house form was also popularly known by a wide variety of other names, including the "New Orleans Cottage" and the "Raised Victorian Cottage." Shotguns were introduced into New Orleans at about the time of the Louisiana Purchase (1803). They had been used as a common rural folk house type in southern Saint Domingue/Haiti in the years before the Haitian revolution (1791-1803), and appear to have been carried in very simple forms to those places where free people of color and African slaves fled after the beginning of the revolution (Edwards 2009). Between the 1790s and 1810, they were carried by French and mulatto

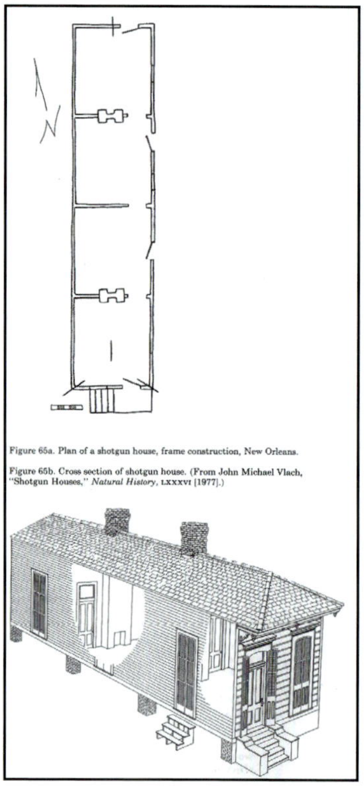

Fig. 4.17. Plan of one New Orleans shotgun and cut-away elevation of another, by John Vlach.

refugees into Cuba and the New Orleans area (compare **Figs. 1.15-1.17**). Surveyor's plot maps show that they are already fairly abundant by 1806. Ironically, about one-third of the 30,000 French speaking Haitian refugees in Cuba were expelled after 1808. Many arrived in New Orleans in 1809-10, further expanding the popularity of Creolized West Indian vernacular building forms.

Shotguns are distinctive in that they are based upon a single line of rooms, usually of equal size, running from front to rear. Whatever the specific form of the shotgun, there is almost always a sitting porch or gallery on the front, and the building is generally raised upon pillars about a foot or two. These features are also common to indigenous domestic forms from coastal West Africa and from colonial Haiti (**Figs. 1-15–1.17**). John Vlach has pointed out that another feature shared by folk shotgun houses in these widely separated places is the preference for small rooms, averaging about 10' by 10' in both Africa and Haiti (Vlach 1986:42-47). Many shotguns with nearly identical dimensional preferences were also constructed of board and batten or clapboard-covered frame in rural Louisiana in the nineteenth century (**Fig. 4.17**).

A large number of shotgun houses were constructed for laborers' families in OSBR. Some were ordered as partially prefabricated kits sold by Steam, Sash, and Blind companies throughout Louisiana and beyond in the late nineteenth and early twentieth centuries. These were purchased and erected in groups by industries such as the Pearce Foundry and Machine works (next to South Boulevard between Brickyard and St. Phillip) and probably the Texas Oil Refinery (houses between Terrace and Oklahoma west of Nicholson; **Map 2.10; Fig. 2.8, upper left corner**). South of Terrace and east of Highland, the neighborhoods were laid out with long, narrow lots roughly thirty-five by ninety feet (**Map 4.2**). Many are still in use today, though it is getting increasingly harder to find an intact row of shotgun houses. Until recently, some of the best surviving shotgun rows were as follows (**Fig. 4.18**):

1. 13th Street between South and Myrtle.
2. 11th Street between South and Myrtle.
3. 10th Street between South and Julia.
4. Lehman Street between 16th and 17th.
5. Howard and Alice between Thomas Delpit and Braddock.
6. Terrace between 17th and 18th.
7. Alice between Napoleon and Highland.
8. 17th between Julia and Matilda (two blocks).
9. Matilda between 15th and 17th.
10. 18th north of Terrace.
11. South side of Fig Street between Thomas Delpit and Braddock.

Fig. 4.18. Shotgun row, 200 Block Tyler.

12. Julia between Thomas Delpit and 11th, south side.
13. Tennessee between Washington and Harrison, west side.
14. Myrtle between St. Joseph and Maximillian.
15. South side Margaret between Highland and Napoleon.[1]

Fig. 4.19. Shotgun house 661 Lettsworth, west of Thomas Delpit, 2005.

Beginning, probably in the late teens of the nineteenth century, timber frame shotguns with brick infill were constructed around the fringes of settlement in New Orleans, particularly in Faubourgs Tremé and Marigny. The first shotgun houses were very small, running only about ten to twelve feet wide in the Afro-Caribbean style, and extending two or three rooms deep. In the 1830s and 1840s the shotgun form was expanded in width and in length. It became popular among developers as speculation housing for laboring class people in the rapidly developing suburbs of New Orleans. Larger versions were built in the Vieux Carré and Marigny, often in rows, as they could be set onto lots only fifteen or twenty feet wide. Later, the shotgun was sold as a partially prefabricated "bundled house," and was shipped to both planters and urban developers via steamboat along the entire Mississippi River waterway system.

The principal difficulty with the single shotgun form is the rather considerable lack of privacy which it affords its residents (**Figs. 2.6-2.7, 4.19**). To move from the front of the house to the kitchen in the rear, one must pass through every bedroom. Residents raised in shotguns are of two minds concerning this. Some prefer a lifestyle in which everyone knows everyone else's business in the family, while others desire more privacy and find life in a shotgun house discomforting. Both before and after the Civil War builders began to experiment with the shotgun form and to stretch it outwards in several ways in order to ameliorate its limitations. They created a number of more or less standardized variants which are widespread in southern Louisiana and in OSBR.

The Side Hall and Side Gallery Shotgun

This is a shotgun with either an open gallery or an enclosed hall running down the entire length of one side. As such, its facade contains three fenestration bays. This form permits more privacy as the front and rear service rooms generally open onto the side hall (**Fig. 4.20**). The North Shore house was surrounded on two or three sides by an open gallery. It had a "L" or "T" expansion in the rear. Doors, rather than windows, ran along the flanks as well as the front (**Fig. 4.21**).

Fig. 4.20. Fieldworker Sylvia Mince in front of a side hall shotgun house, the last of many in this area, 215 Terrace Street, 2005.

Fig. 4.21. A North Shore type shotgun house from Sunshine, Iberville Parish. Sketch by Charles Funderburk after a photo by Jay Edwards, ca. 1970.

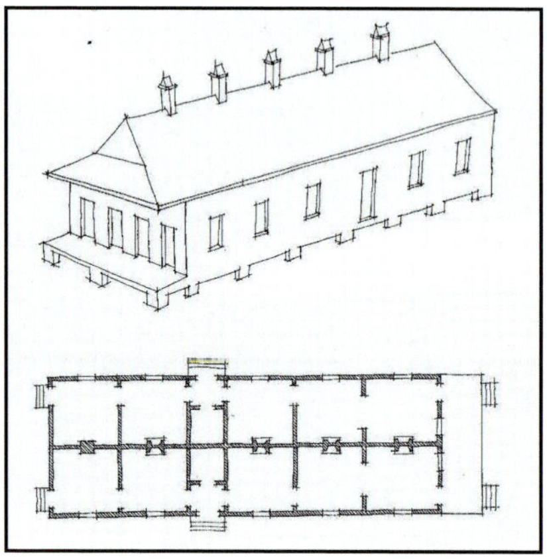

Fig. 4.22. Sketch of a New Orleans double shotgun by Lloyd Vogt, 2002.

Fig. 4.23. Double shotgun house on 1800 block of Thomas Delpit Avenue, 2005.

This form also appears also to be historically derived from Haiti where it is still found today. In Louisiana it is found principally on the north shore of Lake Pontchartrain, where it was used as summer vacation housing by those wishing to escape the heat and epidemics of New Orleans, beginning in the 1840s. The house in **Fig. 4.20** bears a close resemblance to this house type, once common in African American communities along the east bank of the Mississippi between Baton Rouge and St. Gabriel, indicating that this may be a house type carried into OSBR from African American quarters lanes along the Mississippi River

The Double (Shotgun)

This is a duplex divided by a wall running lengthwise which separates two shotgun plans—the entire building being covered by a single roof with its ridge running perpendicular to the front and the street (**Figs. 4.22-4.23**).

The Bungalow (type)

This is a double shotgun built as single family residence. The central wall is penetrated by several doors permitting a free flow of movement between the two sides. In effect, the owner resides in side-by-side shotgun houses. One side may be used for access, permitting privacy in the other.

Fig. 4.24. This bungalow type on Johnson Street sits atop the Magnolia Mound terrace, 2005.

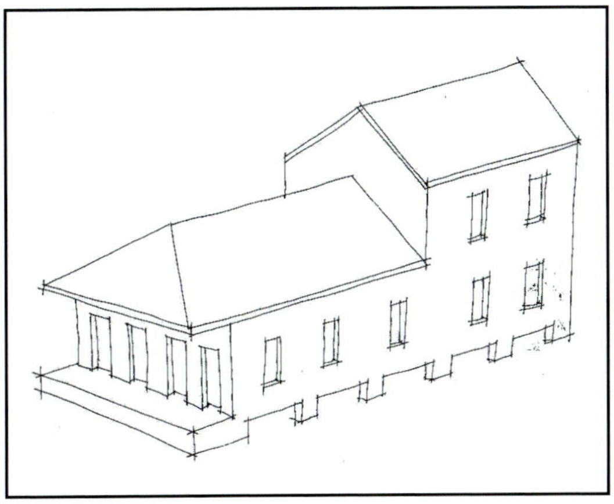

Fig. 4.25. Sketch of a camelback double shotgun by Lloyd Vogt, 2002.

Fig. 4.26. A camelback house on Royal Street, 2005.

This houseform became popular in New Orleans in the 1840s, if not earlier. The bungalow is, perhaps, the most common type of house in Old South Baton Rouge, following the single shotgun, which is fast disappearing (**Fig. 4.24**).

The Camelback

This house has a two-story tall expansion at the rear only. It is said that the camelback was invented in order to escape the additional property taxes levied upon a two story house, but interviews with long-time residents of shotgun houses in New Orleans reveal a better explanation. The camelback form permits the addition of a master bedroom where the parents may seek some measure of privacy (Edwards 2009; **Figs. 4.25-4.26**).

The Baton Rouge Bungalow

Beginning in the 1920s, a somewhat different form of bungalow house became popular in Baton Rouge. As the Standard Oil refinery expanded and required hundreds of new workers, developers began to construct entire subdivisions of bungalow-type houses along Scenic Highway to accommodate them. Based, probably, on a bungalow pattern book plan popular in that decade, they built a distinctive type of bungalow with one front room pushed forward about five feet, while the other remained recessed. The side without the expansion retained a front porch across that half of the house only. Doors from the porch entered both the side of the forward-projecting living room, and the front wall of the room

Fig. 4.27. A Baton Rouge bungalow, 15th Street, 2005.

on the porch side of the house (**Fig. 4.27**). The expansion on one side was the result of the insertion of an interior bathroom near the rear of the house. Baton Rouge bungalows were the first small laborer's houses built in large numbers with the convenience of interior plumbing. Many hundreds of these houses were constructed in Baton Rouge, and although they occur wherever pattern book houses were popular, they are most highly concentrated in this southern city.

Fig. 4.28. A two-story shotgun house on Matilda Street, 2005.

The Two-story Shotgun

Most unusual among the shotgun family of houses is the two-story shotgun. It was once fairly popular in the early nineteenth century in New Orleans, and it remains popular throughout central and southern Haiti, but it is now an endangered species in southern Louisiana (**Fig. 4.28**).

New Orleans Style Raised Shotgun

Although the shotgun family of house types originated in New Orleans in the 1803-30 period, most of the bungalows and other shotgun family buildings of OSBR do not closely resemble their New Orleans counterparts. New Orleans shotguns and bungalows are often more ornately decorated with wooden gingerbread ornament, with brackets and Eastlake decor. There are, however, some buildings in OSBR which closely resemble their New Orleans counterparts in form, if not as much in decoration. One of these is the raised shotgun and the raised bungalow, common to North Carrolton and the area around City Park (**Fig. 4.29**).

Mid-Century Style

Ranch and other single story houses, constructed on a slab, became popular about 1950. Many of the grander houses of Baton Rouge were designed by professional architects. Because of limitations of capital, most of the houses of OSBR were not in this category, but a few are. One notable section is an area of upper-middle and upper class homes immediately to the northeast and east of Magnolia Mound Plantation on a short, disconnected section of Iowa Street connecting with Duncan Drive. Some of these houses appear to have been built in the 1950s and may soon be eligible for nomination to the National Register of Historic Places (**See map insert**; **Figs. 4.30-4.31**).

Fig. 4.29. A New Orleans style raised double shotgun house, Eddie Robinson Street, 2005.

Fig. 4.30. A modern style "ranch" house on Iowa Street, 2005.

Fig. 4.31. A smaller ranch style house, Terrace Street, 2005.

Queen Anne Revival, 1880-1910

Few styled historic houses of the late nineteenth and early twentieth centuries survive in Old South Baton Rouge. Queen Anne Revival houses are one of the best candidates. These buildings were popular throughout the South immediately following the waning of the Victorian era. Many were built along the up-scale residential streets of Southern cities. Although Baton Rouge had a considerable number of Queen Anne houses, apparently few were built in OSBR (**Fig. 4.32**).

Builder Tudor Eclectic

Between 1890 and 1940, a number of eclectic colonial revival houses became popular in the developing middle and upper-middle class suburbs of American cities. One such house is referred to as "Tudor," though in style it has come a long way from its original namesake. Tudoresque houses generally expressed only vague allusions to Elizabethan England. The roofs were steeply pitched with multiple gables often facing in different directions. Chimneys were set outside the walls in prominent locations—even in the front of the house. American Tudoresque employed a variety of wall materials, but stucco cladding was very prominent, with brick coming in a close second. Door and/or window openings were often arched, and sometimes windows were multiple small panes in diamond or other shapes. OSBR boasts a number of these suburban-style buildings (**Figs. 4.33-4.34**).

Fig. 4.32. Queen Anne Revival house, St. Joseph Street, 2005.

Fig. 4.33. Large brick Builder Tudor eclectic house, Julia Street, 2005.

Fig. 4.34. Stuccoed Builder Tudor eclectic house, Louise Street, 2005.

Creole Architecture

Louisiana's Creole architecture may be divided between two types—Anglo-Creole and French Creole. Creole architecture finds its origins and inspiration from the early West Indian colonies of the Spanish, French, and English. One principal difference between French and English Creole lies in the floorplans. Although both styles of architecture are adapted to tropical life and include amenities such as full length or surrounding galleries (piazzas, verandas), smaller open-sided loggias, and cabinet rooms, the internal plans of the two varieties of Creole architecture differ. Anglo Creole architecture is common to the British settled parishes of Louisiana, particularly those east of the Mississippi River between West Feliciana and Assumption parishes, including East Baton Rouge.

Anglo Creole Architecture

One distinctive local example of this style was the Bluffland House. LSU Geography Professors Fred Kniffen and Milton Newton identified a popular local house form in the classical mode from East Baton Rouge and adjoining parishes (1985). Kniffen named the house type because it was found along the bluffs of the east bank of the Mississippi River, between Ascension Parish and the Felicianas (**Fig. 4.35**).

These houses were based upon an Anglo vernacular form with a gable roof. A broad inset gallery spanned the front of the house. The front door generally had side lights and a transom. It was flanked by a pair of very tall windows on either side of the symmetrical tripartite facade. The plan was that of a central hall house with two sets of rooms on either side in the fashion referred to as "semi-double" in Louisiana. That is, the rear rooms were less deep than the front rooms. Bluffland houses were adorned with shouldered chimneys in the Carolina Tidewater fashion. These were set outside of the gabled ends of the building. Decorated Bluffland houses had pedimented dormers and cornice returns. The cornices were bracketed in the Italianate style. A rear "L" contained the kitchen and dining room, and perhaps a separate bedroom for a servant. Bluffland houses were popular in Baton Rouge, particularly along the old wagon roads including Airline and Scenic highways. They were typical farm houses of the 1840 to 1900 period, and they have essentially disappeared from the city of Baton Rouge. While no classic Bluffland houses were located in OSBR, several close cousins were (**Fig. 4.36**). Urban examples differ in that the chimneys are inside, rather than outside on the ends. These houses also lack the Italianate decor of their rural cousins.

Fig. 4.35. A Bluffland house on Plank Road, North Baton Rouge, 1971.

Fig. 4.36. An Anglo-Creole house, St. Joseph Street, 2005.

French Creole Architecture

Far more common in south Louisiana than the Anglo-Creole form are a variety of house types which are collectively referred to as French Creole. They derive from the earliest days of the Louisiana colony, and may be found in both large raised plantation house forms such as Magnolia Mound Plantation house, and smaller Creole cottages such as Cajun cottages (**Figs. 4.37-4.38**). One principal difference between Anglo Creole and French Creole plans is that the French variety is hall-less, the encircling galleries substituting for circulation passages. Although OSBR was settled in the twentieth century when Creole architecture had been long out of style, nevertheless, several smaller Creole forms were located, widely scattered among the more recent house types.

Classical Mode

In his 1970 report *Historic Baton Rouge*, LSU Professor of Architecture Robert Heck refers to smaller residences which imitate in some way the mansions of the Roman and Greek Revival style (1820-1860) as houses in the "Classical Mode" (1970:39). Depending on the wealth of the owner, such buildings might receive relatively elaborate decorative treatments, or they might be almost unadorned, with only the slightest references to the architectural decor of the Greek Revival or Antebellum periods. A nearly unadorned vernacular farm house with a roof cornice which returns (cuts back) at the eaves of the gable, would, in this sense, be included in the classical mode (**Figs. 4.39-4.40**). Classical mode houses continued, with diminishing popularity, to be constructed throughout the nineteenth century and into the first decade of the twentieth.

Fig. 4.37. Magnolia Mound Plantation house on Nicholson Drive, ca. 1791, as rebuilt ca. 1812, 2006.

Fig. 4.38. A smaller Creole house, Tyler Street, 2005.

Fig. 4.39. The Vicaro house on Highland Road, a modest vernacular farmhouse in the Classical mode, 2005.

Fig. 4.40. The Carr house in the Classical mode, Terrace. This building was used as a recreation center by the Progressive Baptist Church, 2005.

Fig. 4.41. A double pen style house with a full front porch, 2005.

The Double Pen

The typical laborer's house of the Louisiana plantation was the double pen cabin. It consisted of two rooms set side by side, each room having a front door. These small abodes often had an inset front gallery, and a rear shed which was used for a kitchen and dining area. Double pen buildings were popular with both French and English planters, and they continued to be built of frame construction after the Civil War. The double pen cabin evolved naturally into a two-room laborers house in the early twentieth century (**Fig. 4.41**). In Baton Rouge, they were constructed around industrial sites such as brick foundries and saw mills, located along the river south of the city. Expanded and decorated to resemble other urban house forms, they remain popular in Old South Baton Rouge.

The Quonset Hut

This is a lightweight, partially prefabricated structure of corrugated iron having a semicircular cross section. The design was based on the Nissen hut developed by the British during World War I. In 1941, the American navy needed an all-purpose, lightweight building that could be shipped anywhere and assembled without skilled labor. The George A. Fuller Construction Company was selected to manufacture them. The first was produced within sixty days of contract award. Several are to be seen in OSBR (**Fig. 4.42**).

The sides were corrugated steel sheets. The two ends were covered with plywood, which had doors and windows. The interior was insulated and had pressed wood lining and a wood floor. The building could be placed on concrete, on pilings, or directly on the ground with a wood floor. The flexible interior space was open, allowing for different program spaces required by the military: barracks, latrines, offices, warehouses, medical or dental offices, isolation wards, housing, and bakeries. Later designs created a standard size of twenty-foot x forty-eight-foot with ten-foot radius, allowing 720 square feet of usable floor space. Other sizes were developed, included twenty-foot x forty-foot, twenty-foot by fifty-six-foot, and forty-foot by 100-foot warehouse models. 170,000 Quonset huts were manufactured during World War II. After the war, the U.S. military sold the surplus Quonset huts to the public for $1,000 each. Many are still standing throughout the United States (the Free Dictionary 2005). Several of these now historic structures are to be found in OSBR. They function as both industrial and commercial buildings.

Fig. 4.42. Industrial Quonset hut by the rail line between 14th and 15th streets, 2005.

Conclusion

This summary of the vernacular architecture of OSBR provides only a brief glimpse of the diversity and complexity of its cultural landscape. We must remember that much, perhaps most, of these valuable cultural assets were constructed by the owners themselves together with the aid of their friends and relatives. We see in their architecture a more direct reflection of the tastes and values of the people of their community than we find in the suburban landscapes of the typical middle-class and affluent neighborhoods. While the original homeowners in those neighborhoods sketched or simply selected the plans which appealed—plans then "perfected" by designers and professional architects—the people of OSBR were deeply and directly involved in the design process. They were the creators of a handmade cityscape. This is the character of vernacular architecture. But as the vernacular neighborhoods from the first decades of the twentieth century rapidly disappear, it is worth pondering their value as reminders of an increasingly remote time when people and communities accomplished so much with such limited resources. As these neighborhoods dissolve under the bulldozer's blades, we find ourselves faced with hard decisions. This, after all, was the real America of the early twentieth century. As it is expunged in favor of developers' visions of the future, a way of life is vanishing forever. How much of that history is worth fighting for?

The cultural patrimony of OSBR is far deeper than its built environments. It is reflected in the folklife of its people. But as the family system has changed in the late twentieth century, and as young people have turned their attention and energies to new technologies and new pursuits, other kinds of traditions are also rapidly passing away. In the following chapter, community folklorist and LSU English Professor Carolyn Ware, with Elecia Lathon and Dorian McCoy, explore the cultural traditions, social organization, and folk practices of early-mid twentieth century OSBR.

Notes

[1] Survey information gathered by LSU Geography Graduate Student Sylvia Mince, June 2005.

The Places
of Old South Baton Rouge

PHOTOS BY JAMES W. TERRY, III

HOTEL
LINCOLN
400

HOTEL
LINCOLN

POSITIVELY
NO LOITERING

NO LOITERING
NO DRINKING
OF THE PREMISE
LA. STATE

BROOKS PARK

BROOKS PARK
EAST BATON ROUGE PARISH
RECREATION AND PARK COMMISSION
BREC
WWW.BREC.ORG

Chapter Five

Creating Culture and Community

Well, [while] I lived here, the neighborhood was lively. We didn't have these places to go like parks, museums, play-stations, and computers, so we mostly did things with people in the neighborhood, and the church was our primary focus.

~Welhelmenia G. Thompson

A variety of cultural institutions, traditions, and creative individuals have shaped everyday life in Old South Baton Rouge from its earliest years to the present. Drawing on historical sources and oral histories, this chapter explores the neighborhood's cultural life as an expression of residents' deeply rooted, shared values, beliefs, and aesthetics. It traces the importance of sacred and secular organizations—churches, benevolent societies, and social clubs—and the activities centered around them. As their secrets unfold, we witness both continuity and change in community life during the twentieth century. In addition, we introduce four notable present-day artists whose work draws on community aesthetics and contributes to the character and richness of neighborhood life.

For Catholics and Protestants alike, churches have long played a pivotal role in local life. As William Wiggins noted, the church is "the central institution in the lives of many Afro-Americans" (1983:145). According to Southern social historian Leon Litwack, "while fulfilling its role as a spiritual agency, the church took on broader responsibilities as the traditional center and unifying institution in the black community. Viewed by many of its members as an extension of the family, the church served as a school, a lecture hall, a social and recreational center, a meeting place for an assortment of groups, and a source of information" (1998:379). For many OSBR residents, the history of local churches *is* the history of the neighborhood. Churches are significant not only as places of worship, but also as centers of social life. Their rituals, music, and fellowship are part of the neighborhood's cultural glue.

In the years before integration, secular places and organizations also played a crucial part in maintaining community ties. Neighborhood social clubs, benevolent societies, fraternities, and sororities were focal points of local life, as were juke joints, hang-outs like the now-defunct Chicken Shack, barbershops, and theaters such as the Lincoln and the Temple (which had a dance floor on its roof). Social clubs held dances and served as a place for members to get together, cook, and feast on pork chops or fried fish, and entertain each other by telling "lies" (tall tales). Some of these places have disappeared from the neighborhood, but others continue to serve many of the same functions they did fifty years ago.

Then as now, OSBR was home to many musicians, folk craftspeople, painters, and sculptors. The late Emerson Bell, born in the neighborhood in the early 1930s, remembered it as a "Mecca for the arts" in his youth, a "haven for great knowledge in my day." These artists and their work both reflected and shaped community life, providing an example of continuity, creativity, and change over the years. All of these together contributed to the distinctive lifeways and unique aesthetics of the OSBR community.

Fig. 5.1. Star of Bethlehem Baptist Church, St. Joseph and Julia Street.

Fig. 5.2. St. Francis Xavier Catholic Church at Julia and 11th streets, 1943.

Fig. 5.3. The Islamic Center on Thomas Delpit and Washington, 2006.

"Amazing Grace in the Bottom:" The Role of Religion in African American Life

On almost every street corner in Old South Baton Rouge are churches, the heart of the OSBR community. The church was, and continues to be, the primary focus for community identity. So strong is the hold of these institutions that, although many residents moved out of the community in the 1960s and 1970s, they drive back to attend church in OSBR. Beryl McGhee, a member of Bethel A.M.E., reflected that, "Well, sometimes location hurts, because a lot of people look at the area and decide they don't want to come down there. But, I don't know that it would make any difference because a lot of the members, [a] majority of the members, live away from the area, and they drive in every Sunday" (McGee 1997). The churches—all forty-three of them—continue to play a vital role in community life. In many suburbs, churches are miles apart from one another, but in OSBR you only have to ride a block or two to see multiple religious institutions at work in the community. The neighborhood is home to several different denominations: Baptist, Catholic, Methodist, and the Nation of Islam, among others (**Figs. 5.1-5.3**). Despite denominational differences, the overarching mission of the religious institutions is the same: to serve God and God's people.

Commentators often note that African Americans are a strongly religious group. According to Edward Queen, "While African religiosity rarely survived intact in the United States, cultural elements from Africa did remain and shaped how slaves interpreted and presented the Christian message" (1996:9). There is abundant evidence that African religious beliefs and behaviors survived enslavement and were reinterpreted and revitalized under Christianity in the Americas. Hazel Freeman, a member of Mt. Zion Baptist Church and life long educator, explained to an interviewer:

> The black church's legacy came out of slavery. The people had no other hope but the church. Think about all of the hymns that blacks sing, 'Steal Away Home to Jesus.' When they would say, 'steal away home from Jesus,' they would sing that on the farm and when the other slaves would hear it they knew there was going to be a meeting. And at night when everybody was gone to sleep and the master was at his mansion they would probably go down in the forest and they would have a meeting to try to plan how they would stick together and how they would survive. Now this was the church (Freeman 1997).

For African Americans, religion served as a primary source of independence, allowing them to create a viable society within the system of slavery. African Americans used this source of freedom as an opportunity to express their understandings of spirituality and to empower themselves in spite of the dehumanization of slavery.

Religious-based institutions played a pivotal role in African Americans becoming engaged in the political activities of the community, city, and state (Harris 1994; Matthews & Prothro 1966; Peterson 1992; Arp and Boeckelman 1997). Many of the over 200 slave rebellions in the United States occurred because of religion. This is an historical precursor to the black church's involvement in the civil rights movement and in every important facet of black life. The independent black church was born due to the desire of blacks to be independent of white authority (Wingfield 1988). Religion unified African Americans, allowing them to begin to create a viable society.

Through encouragement and influence from the church, citizens of Old South Baton Rouge created an independent society, one that unified African Americans, resisted racist religious practices, and empowered African Americans to become agents of change and make a difference in their own communities. Jennifer Jones, an assistant pastor at Shiloh, stated "religion is what nobody can take away from us." Hazel Freeman says, "The church has provided me with a spiritual and a social education, as it was the only place to learn how to interact and intermingle for Blacks when I was growing up." She continued by saying that she credits Rev. T.J. Jemison, pastor of Mt. Zion Baptist Church, with "changing the face of Baton Rouge, by starting the Bus Boycott of 1953." Echoing Ms. Freeman's comments, Frederick Harris held that the racially segregated black church may have planted the seeds for the destruction of segregation by organizing the political efforts of Southern Blacks (1994:45). Churches in Old South Baton Rouge have played foundational roles in the community: spiritual, political, educational, and social. They also serve to connect members of the community to their past—their African roots, slave history and long struggle for emancipation. The churches and religious life of OSBR are briefly summarized below.

History of Old South Baton Rouge Churches

Enslaved Africans brought with them their religious belief systems. In Louisiana under French and Spanish rule, slave owners were required by the *Code Noir* to baptize enslaved persons as well as provide them with a religious education. Records at the Catholic archives in Baton Rouge attest to the fact that most enslaved persons were baptized by priests who went from plantation to plantation. Catholicism to some degree had features that overlapped with traditional African beliefs, including a correlation between African gods and Catholic saints, female deities as well as blessed icons, gestures, and prayers that played a role in rituals and rites (Porche-Frilot 2006).

Atypical of most of the south, the Catholic Church predominated in Baton Rouge and southern Louisiana in general. The first church in Baton Rouge to open its doors in 1792 was St. Joseph's Church on Main Street. African American Catholics, both enslaved and free, belonged to its congregation. In 1847, with the establishment of St. Mary's Academy (on the corner of Florida and 4th, then Church Street), the sisters began a Sunday morning catechism school for white girls and one on Sunday evening for slaves (Uter 1992). In 1867, the Christian Brothers Institute was established in downtown Baton Rouge, and, by its fourth year in operation, it had an enrollment of 286 boys, including seventy blacks. Although African American girls had been taking religion classes at the newly established St. Joseph Academy (1870), there was no full Catholic education available to them until the Sisters of the Holy Family (the black order of nuns founded by Henriette Delille in 1842 in New Orleans) opened St. Mary's School and orphanage for blacks in 1881 on Florida Boulevard about eight blocks from the river (Deggs 2001). The school suffered under the growing racial prejudice that emerged after the Civil War. The Sisters of St. Joseph were forced to take over the

Fig. 5.4. The Old St. Francis Xavier School in 1920.

school until 1895, when Mother Katherine Drexel aided the Sisters of the Holy Family in returning to Baton Rouge where their school became known as the Holy Family Academy. In 1919, the academy and convent was moved to the corner of South 11th and Julia Street in the heart of OSBR. The name of the school was changed to St. Francis Xavier (**Fig. 5.4**).

After the Civil War, many African Franco-Catholic families, including Ricard, LeBlanc, DeCuir, Bajoie, Bienville, Patin, Baranco, LeDuff, Franklin, Sibrie, Domino, and Allain, migrated from Pointe Coupée and the Felicianas to Old South Baton Rouge (**Fig. 5.5**). They walked the more than two miles each way from Baton Rouge's "colored" settlement each Sunday to St. Joseph's Church. As racial unrest and separation of the races increased under Jim Crow, the Catholic Church sought to establish a separate church for blacks. In 1912, as plans were being made for the construction for St. Agnes on East Boulevard and Government on Swart Hill, it was decided that this would function as a "mixed" congregation with Italian and African American Catholics on one side, while white Catholics sat on the other. While this was to be a "mixed" church, African American Catholics in OSBR experienced many forms of racial segregation. Sadie Keel recalled that: "We didn't have a church of our own until we got St. Francis [Xavier]. We lived in the St. Agnes area, so we went there on Sundays, but it was a white church. At the time there was a certain mass said for black Catholics."

As a consequence, a group of African Americans, led by Dr. Raymond Baranco and his sister Sara Leone, spearheaded a fund-raising campaign for an all-black Catholic church. In 1918, after two years of fundraising, the Josephite Father Joseph Dubé arrived and conducted separate services for the black members at St. Agnes until the final completion of St. Francis Xavier Church on the corner of Julia and South 11th streets. The church was built by many parishioners most of whom were skilled craftsmen. In 1920, with the help of the Sisters of the Holy Family, the school and convent were built, giving St. Francis Xavier the distinction of having the first parish school in the Diocese of Baton Rouge. The church and the school drew Catholics from all over the parish since they were the only all black Catholic institutions. In 1940 it had a membership of 1,700 with an average Sunday attendance for three masses of 1,100. Its very active organizations included the Knights of Peter Claver (men), the Ladies of the Auxilliary of Peter Claver, the St. Francis Xavier Ladies' Circle, the Children of Mary (young women), as well as two boy scout and two girl scout troops, and a PTA organization. The school continues to be run by the Sisters of the Holy Family today and is a clear link to the rich history of African-French Catholic life in Louisiana.

While Catholicism was the primary religion during the French and Spanish rule, by the Louisiana Purchase (1803), the influx of Americans resulted in the introduction of several other religious denominations that shaped African American religious life and resulted in the formation of African

American churches in Baton Rouge. The first church was Mt. Zion Baptist Church, established in 1858 on the corner of Spain and East Boulevard. However, the church's organization was not actually finalized until January 1859 by the Reverend A. Palmer, a black minister and the Reverend John Bundy, a white minister. Eventually the church was able to purchase an entire block of East Boulevard where the church now resides at No. 356. The church has only had seven pastors during its long, eventful history. Several of these pastors have distinguished themselves nationally. Gardner Calvin Taylor, born in 1918 in Baton Rouge, was a graduate of Leland College and Oberlin Graduate School of Theology. In 1943, he returned to Baton Rouge to become pastor of Mt. Zion until he left in 1948 for Concord Church in Brooklyn New York. Noted for his preaching style that "includes a sort of grand nineteenth century Victorian style, the richness of the African American folk tradition, and a unique interpretation of modern homiletical theory, the richness of his words and sermon design are legendary" (Taylor 2000). He has lectured at Yale, and was honored by *Newsweek* as one of the twelve greatest preachers in the English-speaking world. Mt. Zion is the oldest African American church in East Baton Rouge Parish, and, by 1940, it was the largest single Protestant church, with 800 members. Average attendance on Sunday was about 450, and at Sunday school, about 125. Mt. Zion became known for its political activism during the fifties under the leadership of Rev. T.J. Jemison, who led the first bus boycott in OSBR. Pastor T.J. Jemison holds the longest pastorate.

Fig. 5.5. The August and Corrine Hebert Bajoie family.

In 1866, the first black Methodist church opened its doors. Wesley United Methodist Church now located at 544 Government Street began serving the African Methodist community in the first Methodist Church (white) on the corner of Laurel and 4th Streets. The pioneers of Wesley were Ruben Jordan, Mother Sarah Gordon, Martha Morris, Mother Hester Williams, Hannah Dalsamoor, Beverly Salla, Maria Andrews, Emma Thomas, Margaret Andrews, Fanny Pinkney, Emma Green, Louise Holt, Mary Jennings, Aaron Lee, Louise Houston, and Harriett Heron. Mt. Zion and Wesley are the two oldest Protestant churches in Baton Rouge to serve African Americans, and, although they are located just north of South Boulevard, their parishioners are predominately from OSBR.

A year later, in 1867, another Methodist church called Bethel A.M.E. was founded by the Reverend George Gordon and a small number of followers. It was in the years after the Civil War that many African Americans decided to follow the spirit of free Methodism that was being practiced by a number of congregations across the country. It was originally located downtown on St. Hypolite between Laurel and Florida, around the corner from the Jewish Synagogue and two blocks from the convent of the Sisters of the Holy Family. Today Bethel A.M.E. is still a thriving church located at 1358 South Boulevard.

Fig. 5.6. Portrait of the Rev. George Byrd of the Shiloh Baptist Church, 1902.

Shiloh Baptist, founded in 1872, was originally located at 317 Spanish Town Road, and is now located at 185 Eddie Robinson Drive. Rev. George Byrd, a native of Virginia was the founder and served faithfully for thirty-four years (**Fig. 5.6**). Mt. Gillion Baptist Church was founded four years later at its current site, 346 East Buchanan Street. These faith-based institutions represent the beginning of organized religious life in OSBR.

Although these were the first churches of OSBR, by the 1920s and '30s churches began to proliferate as the community began to expand and grow. Churches were erected by local craftsmen and masons. Most congregations raised their own money in order to build their church. Rosella Williams, a member of Israelite Baptist Church before converting to Catholicism, recalled how churches in the community raised money.

> Suppers started on Thursday and they would sell supper dinners until Sunday. On Sundays they would have what is called a tea. A tea was really another party because they would sell hot sausages and fish sandwiches. They served alcoholic beverages to make money for the church. The suppers and teas were not held at the church. They were held in the homes of the members so they could raise money to build the structure.

Pew rallies, church bazaars and other activities were held to raise money for the many churches that sprang up in OSBR.

Today there are approximately forty-three churches throughout the community for residents to attend and to participate in the worship experience. Despite obvious denominational differences, most OSBR churches have several features in common: the role of music, the distinctive role of women, and an emphasis on community outreach. Central to this worship experience is the music that exemplifies the spirit of the churches.

Singing on Sunday Morning—A Song in My Heart

> I got religion in 1931 on August 16. I even know what the man was singing. "Swing low chariot, let's take a ride," that's what he was singing. When I came out, when I came back, I was a new person. The world didn't look the same and I didn't feel the same and people didn't look the same. I'm born again. I didn't make no mistakes, I can feel it all in me. I got Jesus in my life. I'm satisfied. I'm going home.
>
> Annie Kimble, 1997

The people of OSBR are no strangers to music. On Sunday morning the piano, organ and drums can be heard playing in church sanctuaries throughout the community. If someone were to ask most people from here about music and the church, they would readily tell you about their musical experiences during a Sunday morning service. Betty Parker exclaimed, "I always have a song in my heart, you know I keep a song in my heart." Keeping a song in their hearts was how many survived difficult times while living in OSBR. If you knew God, you knew a song that could help you sing your way through your troubles. Black people were able to face their situations and to articulate their troubles, hopes, solutions and protests in song.

Spirituals like "Swing Low, Sweet Chariot" were sung by slaves working in the fields to maintain hope, but were also used to carry messages that the overseers could not understand. Eula Mae Hatter of New Prospect Baptist Church recalled:

> We didn't know gospel when I was a youth. . . . First there were spirituals, Negro spirituals, and then came blues, and then jazz and then gospel. I say that gospel is the word of God put to music. Spirituals came from the cotton fields. These are the songs that our fore-parents sung when they were picking cotton or raising gardens. They sang spiritual songs. Songs without [instrumental] music (Hatter 1997).

These spirituals embodied many African traditions. Spirituals eventually gave away to more modern gospel music, although traditional spirituals are still sometimes performed in rural African American churches and on special occasions.

Throughout the South during Jim Crow, churches were meeting places where African Americans could come together to discuss the injustices, trials, and tribulations of their day. Old South Baton Rouge was no different. The church as a meeting place was at the forefront of change for African Americans; it provided an avenue for them to voice their concerns and dissatisfaction with traditional practices of their day. According to Flake, "during the civil rights movement of the 1960s, the church arose as a meeting place to strategize, sing and pray. Unlike many songs in the nineteenth century freedom movement, songs of protest were sung openly in the black church. The lyrics no longer contained double meanings to keep whites ignorant, but were direct, clear of purpose and filled with a spirit of discontent" (Flake 1997:2). Many songs were probably sung at Mt. Zion in Old South Baton Rouge as Dr. T.J. Jemison, a well known leader and pastor of Mt. Zion Baptist Church, led the first bus boycott. Songs were created and adapted to a variety of circumstances and situations facing the black community. God was ever present in the black church and God was a friend who would help the Black community fight their battles.

Some of the more familiar songs are sung still today in the black church. One particular favorite entitled "I Want Jesus to Walk With Me" can still be heard at a Sunday morning service in Old South Baton Rouge. As Beryl McGhee, a member of Bethel A.M.E., says, "Music plays a very big part in any service. The music is basically the Chancel Choir, traditional anthems and music. The Gospel Choir sings, the Youth Choir sings, and it is very upbeat, up-tempo. You leave different from the way you came in, and the music, and the sermon, everything plays a part in it" (1997).

Mother Sarah Jones of the Magnolia Baptist Church reflected on the "old meter" hymns (sometimes called "long meter" hymns) sung in the church many years ago (**Fig. 5.7**). She recalled,

> The preacher would give out this *old meter*. You know the preacher would do that: "Guide me over great Jehovah," that's when you open the church. The preacher would do that. But now, we all sing that song together when we open church on Sunday morning. And now I notice that the choir sometimes don't sing *old meters*. They'll just sing *I Surrender All* . . . you know, for the opening song when they get ready to pray. But years back, they would sing that *old meter*.

Fig. 5.7. Mother Sarah Jones, Magnolia Baptist Church, 1997.

It seems that as the churches of OSBR have grown and changed, so has the music. Still, music continues to be a powerful force in the church. Even though they no longer sing meters, the songs that are chosen still give glory to God and the people still seek God's guidance and help through song just as they did centuries ago.

The influence of music has not been limited to church services themselves. Several choirs have emerged from OSBR and are known throughout the larger community. The "Voices of Zion," begun in the 1960s by Paul Simon, Edward Gaines and Leo Perkins, combined singers from OSBR and the Scotlandville area and made several recordings.

Who Can Find a Virtuous Woman? (Proverbs 31:10) The Role of Women in the Church in OSBR

The Bible asks "Who can find a virtuous woman, for her price is far above rubies and riches." In Old South Baton Rouge it is not hard to find a virtuous woman in the church serving God and her fellow man. Townes maintained that at the beginning of the nineteenth century, worship and spirituality were expressed in groups as people gathered to worship in a form that blended African traditions and white evangelical Christianity (1993). Biblical women became role models for black women. According to Brooks, "The mother[s] of Isaac, Moses, Samson, and others gave black women a view of women as more than bodily receptacles through whom great men were born. They saw these mothers as being responsible for raising sons who would deliver Israel from its oppressors" (1984:146). African American women compared themselves to the women in the Bible; biblical identification appeared to have helped black women journey through their own difficult lands.

By embracing biblical examples, African American women found the strength to cope with the stresses and outrages of their lives. Townes opined:

> African American women did not break from the orthodoxy of the Black church, but restated that orthodoxy in what Evelyn Brooks characterizes as a "progressive and liberating" language for women. Black women took the roles of sister, wife, daughter, and mother, combined them with a personal spiritual experience of God in Christ and understood themselves to be ministers in their homes (1993:83).

By doing this, black women shifted from positions of being homemakers and domestic servants to a higher calling by God. Hazel Freemen, born in 1914 on Highland Road, recalled that when she was a child, "the women would read their Bibles and say their prayers just as the first evening star came out of the sky. As the men would return from the fields, they would join their wives and children in prayer and Bible reading." This was how her childhood church, Evening Star, was founded and named by her grandparents. Today she attends Mt. Zion Baptist where she has been active in the church and a community activist. She feels strongly that "the church has provided me with a spiritual and social education, as it was the only place to learn how to interact and intermingle for blacks when we were growing up" (1997).

Women were not readily accepted into the black church as leaders or legitimate ministers, due to traditional religious views. They continued to battle exclusion even in the black church. Women like Almenia Williams of Calvary III Baptist Church and Ida Mae Whiten of St. Joseph Baptist Church echo these thoughts. In her 1997 interview Williams said, "Calvary III has grown quite a bit because [when I was] a child, women were not allowed in the pulpit. They could only fix communion—women were allowed to break the cracker and pour the wine in the glasses and put them on the trays and cover it and that was it." Whiten noted, "Back then they didn't have women preaching but now they do." Women were usually found serving as the deaconess, teachers or ushers. Annie Mae Holmes of Fairview Baptist Church shared her thoughts on deaconess in the church. She said, "A deaconess is one who is being set aside to be able to help the deacons. Just like if someone is sick—maybe it's a lady that's sick and the deacons going to see about her—they won't approach the house because we never know if she is in there by herself. The ladies go ahead of the deacons and see the situation of the home before they let them come in" (Holmes 1997). Beryl McGhee had a different take on women in OSBR. She held that, "If you are in a church where there are no men, somebody have to do it, and women always no matter what, women always step up to the plate and do whatever is necessary. Women are compassionate, they are spiritual. And I think the A.M.E. Church has not held women back as much as some other denominations, you know, and I think denominations, we get caught up in traps, in saying that you can't do certain things. I think the A.M.E. church has allowed women greater freedom to move into the ministry, because we have quite a few" (McGhee 1997).

Catholic women, primarily nuns, played the biggest role in the Catholic church. Sadie Keel, a member of the St. Francis Xavier Catholic Church, made her first communion at age twelve in 1926; "It was the nuns that trained them about their roles as Christians" (Keel 1997). The Sisters of the Holy Family, who had been in Baton Rouge since the 1890s, ran St. Francis Xavier School and were also responsible for much of the religious education (**Fig. 5.8**). She recalled:

> The nuns taught us how to go to communion. You would walk up in orderly fashion. We had kneelers all around the rail, you knelt there until the priest came to you. After you received communion, you got up and went back and someone else in line took your place. I'm remembering a linen cloth which was all the way around the rail. You had to keep your hands under because you were not allowed to touch the host. Should it fall it had the linen cloth there to catch it (Keel 1997).

In addition to religious education, the Sisters of the Holy Family ran the school and lived on the second floor. Sadie recalled vividly the nuns:

> During that time you never saw their hair. They wore long black robes that touched the floor. They wore long black stockings, and black shoes. They had a white, very stiff head-piece, that went around the head and which held the black veil that they wore. They wore a long rosary which hung almost down to the waist with a large cross. In the wintertime they had a long black cape that they threw around their shoulders. The children dearly loved and respected them (Keel 1997).

Today, while not under the instruction of the nuns, the St. Francis Xavier School continues to educate black Catholics. Since Hurricane Katrina a small group of Sisters of the Holy Family who were displaced from the convent in New Orleans now reside at St. Francis Xavier. In addition to the role of the nuns, women at St. Francis Xavier played a large role in social functions and outreach through the St. Francis Xavier Ladies' Auxiliary and the Children of Mary.

While Catholic women religious ran institutions and to some degree led independent lives free of the bonds of marriage, Protestant women's roles in the church were shaped more by traditional gender roles. Protestant women played an important, but limited, role in the church. As Emilie

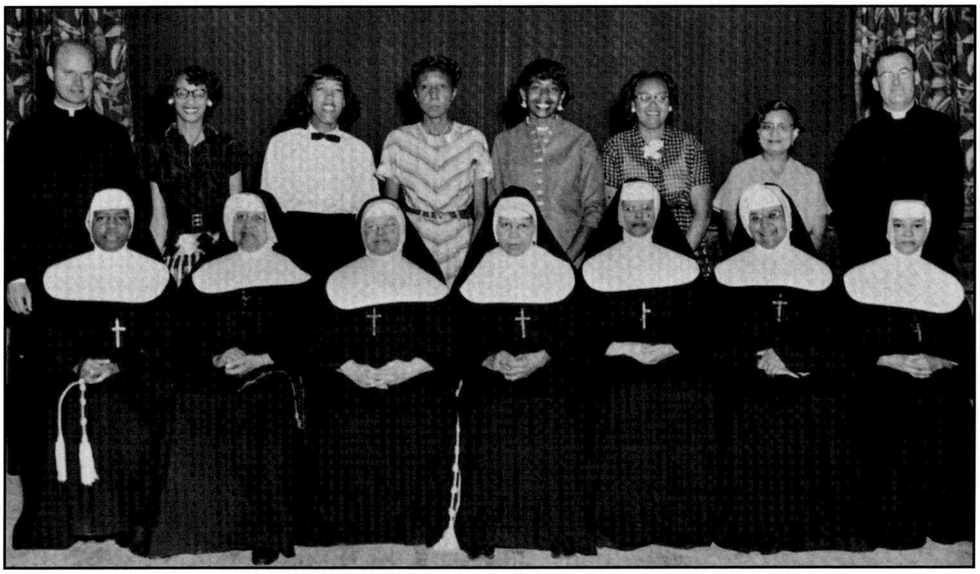

Fig. 5.8. St. Francis Xavier school teachers and staff.

Townes asserted, over time, "They were able to accept the traditional roles handed to them, yet shape and bend them to reflect their understandings of their ultimate relationship to God" (1997). One role women have adopted in the church is that of "mother." According to Annie Mae Holmes, who migrated to OSBR in 1943, the mother of the church "is supposed to be set aside to be able to talk to the children, pastor, whoever in the church. They are like a mother of the house" (1997).

Women's organizations within the churches also play a strong role in shaping community. Shiloh has a ministry for the female members of the congregation called the "Sisterhood" which meets on the first Saturday of every month. Claryce Minor explained that the goal of this ministry is for women "to get to know each other because going to church is not enough. By being a member of the Sisterhood you have as many as fifty friends to call on." One of the many activities the sisterhood engages in every year is reading and discussing a book together. They have also formed "cluster prayer groups" so that members could hear themselves pray (1997).

"Said I wasn't gon' tell nobody, but I couldn't keep it to myself." Sharing the Goodness of God with Others

First Sunday morning or whatever day has been set aside for testimony, you can find the many members of churches in OSBR talking about the goodness of God—how good God has been to them. This practice is known today as "testimony," or as most know it, "speak meeting" and, for some, "tell your determination." Referring to testimony as your "determination" is not used as much as is was many years ago. However, Mother Sarah Jones of the Magnolia Baptist Church remembers telling her determination on Friday night. She says,

> We use to have a Friday night—that we use to call: "tell your determination." You know when you say I'm determined to go to heaven. There is a difference between testimony and telling your determination. When members would tell their determination they would say something like, "My determination is heaven and I'm going to watch, fight and pray until I die so that heaven might be my home."

When testifying, members would actually share stories and things that had happened in their lives that God brought them through. In articulating one's determination, there was a pretty standard response at most churches and in testifying members of each congregation had an opportunity to "testify" and share how God has blessed their life. Sometimes people just stand and simply say, "Thank you, Jesus!" For most African Americans testifying and sharing the goodness of God is what every member should do on a daily basis. In most cases old meter hymns were sung as each person got up and shared their determination or testimony. Afterwards some people would walk around and shake hands with the deacons and deaconesses. This was a common practice that has changed over the time, but the overall goal was still to give God glory for all that he had done in the lives of his people and to help others see that the same was available for them.

At Shiloh, testifying is done on the first Sunday night of each month. During these "speaking meetings," members are encouraged to take turns standing up and testifying. Another form of testifying occurs during such practices as the Midnight Watch. From 10:00 to midnight on New Year's Eve, there is a service that prepares one for the upcoming year. Isaac Patterson values Midnight Watch because he has found it better to be "on my knees at New Year's rather than at someone's party with a drink in my hand."

"Just having church praising the Lord" — Community Outreach

It is clear that the church had a great impact on the lives of those living in OSBR during the early twentieth century, but what about today? According to Mother Jones, "It's so important for me to go to church. Because that's all . . . Mmmm, I love church. I love people. I love the Lord.

And that is my greatest pleasure that I have. And it's from growing up." The churches of OSBR have a tremendous impact on the lives of those living in OSBR, not only on Sunday mornings, but the whole week long. Most of the churches provide a variety of services to serve not only their congregations, but the community at large. These services range from daycare centers, youth organizations, financial aid, social activities, education, housing and prison ministry. There is no aspect of life that the churches leave untouched.

Brenda Patterson, a member of Shiloh Baptist Church, says she sees Shiloh as meeting "the needs of the whole person" and making "you feel like you belong" (1997). Isaac Patterson agrees, "Shiloh meets the needs—educational, economical, social, whatever background you come from. There is a place for you at Shiloh." Claryce Minor says, "Shiloh's doors are open . . . very receptive to anybody." She continues, "What Shiloh has to offer is wide enough to reach everybody that has a need." Shiloh currently has a daycare center open to the community, summer youth enrichment programs, a federal credit union, social services, prison ministry, street ministry, Project Lifeline, and a scholarship program that annually awards scholarships to members of their church family and the community. The Sisterhood, youth ministry and family ministry are for members only. Shiloh is one of the larger, if not the largest, church in the community with a membership of approximately 3,500 members. They are able to provide such services because as Minister Jennifer Jones of Shiloh Baptist Church puts it, "Ministry is the church serving the people" and serving the people is what they do. Jones feels, "This type of church work change[s] people's lives and [helps them] hold on in the midst of the struggle. The A.M.E. church has a mission and that is to clothe, feed, and to improve the quality of life, to make a difference in the community in which the church is located" (Jones 1997). Shiloh has been called a "24 hour/7 day a week church."

Youth ministry at Shiloh is a constant focus. The youth members are called the "Circle of the Chosen." Several programs focus on youth including: summer youth enrichment program, True Love Waits, the youth ministry, the Baptist youth encampment, the scholarship program, and vacation Bible school. The summer enrichment program is one in which youth are mentored in professions they are interested in. The "True Love Waits" is a voluntary youth group in which youth commit themselves to abstinence from sex until after marriage. Special praise and attention is given these youth because the commitment is not an easy one. Young ladies are also introduced into the Christian society in the Christian Debutante Program. Bethel A.M.E. also has a Miss Christian Teen—a debutante presentation of all the teenagers.

A primary focus of youth ministry in OSBR is education. The churches of OSBR are no strangers to studying the word of God. Sunday school, vacation Bible school, and Bible study are three activities that take place in the churches of OSBR to help members of the churches become knowledgeable about God and their role as disciples for God. Sunday school is held on Sunday mornings at the church. Some churches even refer to Sunday school as church school. Classes are typically available for all ages. The children are usually separated from the adults. Vacation Bible school is usually held for one or two weeks during the summer months. There are classes for all ages and children can learn about God and also engage in crafts and music. Bible study takes place once a week usually in the evenings for most churches in OSBR. After Bible study, or sometimes before Bible study prayer meeting is held. This is a time where members of the congregation are able to sing a favorite hymn and pray aloud while others listen and pray silently with them. Members take turns thanking God and calling on Him for help and guidance as they travel along their pilgrim journey. Ministers of OSBR believe that their members must attend Bible study, Sunday school and vacation Bible school in order to be fed the word of God. Rev. Charles T. Smith holds that, "The church is an agency of nurture, and an agency of discipleship. Uniquely, we are also an agency of ministry. And when I say uniquely an agency of ministry, because we are primarily African American and African American people have unique needs, we're dedicated to addressing those needs. Through Sunday school, Bible study and vacation Bible study those unique needs are addressed" (Smith 1996).

The Scott-Gilchrist Quality of Life Center at Bethel A.M.E. also provides a variety of outreach programs. Each weekend hot meals are provided on Saturdays. Groceries and clothing are provided for the needy. For the youth, there is the Governors After School Drug Program and the State Saturday Tutorial Program and the Tutorial Academy in the summer months. Bethel A.M.E. also sponsors "Juneteenth Day," which is celebrated by the entire community in commemoration of the emancipation proclamation (McKinley High School Oral History Project 1997). The members of the church provide barbecue and there is music in tents.

Many of the small churches in the community can offer only that which is most important, the word of God. However, from time to time churches work together to host different events such as revival, Martin Luther King Day services and festivities, vacation Bible school and summer programs for children and youth in the community to restore unity and to influence change in the community. Six years ago, the South Baton Rouge Ministers Coalition was formed, and each Friday the churches have what is called the "Noon Hour of Power," a prayer service where all the churches get together during the noon hour. Although things have changed in the community over the last few decades, one thing remains constant—the love, hope and commitment to the Old South Baton Rouge community lives on in the hearts and minds of those who are a part of the OSBR community, more affectionately known as "the Bottom."

Churches and Community Life: Special Events

Churches have always been lively centers of community life, strengthening community ties as well as spiritual ones. Older residents have vivid memories of weeks-long revivals, river baptisms, church anniversaries, and homecomings, all pivotal events in community life. Many of these occasions and events are shared by other African American communities in the South, revealing OSBR's cultural and historical links with a wider, regional way of life.

A variety of religious dramas, part of what William Wiggins calls a long "tradition of black religious folk drama," provided entertainment for community members and elevated "worship to the aesthetic level of theater drama" (1983:149). Some churches, for example, produced special Easter and Christmas plays. Other kinds of folk dramas, entertainments, and social events were periodically staged to raise funds for the church. OSBR resident and member of Shiloh Baptist Church Jennifer Jones explains, "For years in our churches most of what we did centered around fund raising, to get the bills paid and the lights on and the building up where it could be some place to come to. . . . So they did fund raisers such as pew rallies, car washes, suppers, fashion shows, and the Zodiac Club party. We had fundraisers because we are there to serve others, and not necessarily to be served."

Almenia Williams, raised in Calvary III Church, remembers "devil's funerals" as a favorite form of fundraiser at Calvary. She says:

> Once a year, somebody in the church would contact a local funeral home and get a coffin and bring the coffin into the church and they would keep it closed until the end of [the evening]. And then they would have somebody in the church to be the deacons and somebody else to be the ushers, and somebody else to be the preacher. And they would have like a mock funeral for the devil and a portion of the services, and they'd have candles lit and turn the lights out. And then at the end, they'd let everybody walk around and look at the casket . . . and they would have a mirror in it. So when you looked there, you saw yourself (Williams 1997).

People "used to pay big money to come to that," Mrs. Williams says, and the church was usually packed for a devil's funeral. One church might hold a mock funeral one month, another church the next month. Mrs. Williams says, "It was a type of entertainment. . . . Back during segregated times, there were not a lot of places for black people to go for entertainment, so the church became a source of entertainment too."

Calvary and other OSBR churches also hosted Tom Thumb weddings as fundraisers—another widespread form of entertainment. A young woman and man were chosen to dress as bride and groom, and "then they'd have a bride and groom of little kids," Mrs. Williams explains. Both sets of brides and grooms "would have all the attendants and the ring bearer and the little flower girls and they would wed, like a mock wedding. They would wed, each of the little kids, and the parents would be proud and all that. And people paid money to come see it, and parents would spend lots of money on making wedding dresses for these girls, and it was really nice."

Churches also held pew rallies (sometimes simply called "rallies") at certain times of the year, a tradition some churches still carry on. Mrs. Williams says that "back in the old days" church members were assigned pews to fill up with friends and other "outsiders." The person who brought the most guests won a ribbon or a small plaque. Anna Williams recalls that at her church, members brought food to the rallies; after the church service, everyone sat outside and ate at tables under the trees, a custom often called "dinner on the ground." Although pew rallies, Tom Thumb weddings, and devil's funerals were social occasions, they were ultimately aimed at increasing membership and raising money. Church bazaars were another form of fundraising, as members sold homemade food and raffled off donated goods.

During the summer, Protestant churches held annual revivals that often lasted a week or two, with nightly services. A young girl moved to "confess Christ" during revival would tie a white fabric band around her head; a young man might tie a similar band around his arm. They wore these until they were baptized so "the whole world would know she's been saved," Almenia Williams says. She recalls that "when kids were ready to confess Christ, they had to sit on a mourner's bench.[1] And sometimes you sat there for summer after summer after summer" (Williams 1997).

Revivals and the renewal of faith they inspired were often followed by group baptisms. Baptism remains one of the most important rites of passage for young African American Baptists in the South (Jackson 1997; Staten and Roach 1997; Wiggins 1983). As a "symbolic ritual of purification and initiation," it changes a person's social and religious status (Jackson 1997:29). Years ago, before most Baptist churches in the South built indoor baptismal pools, baptisms were performed outside, in lakes and rivers (**Fig. 5.9**). According to Joyce Jackson, "As late as the 1950s, river submersion was common in both African American and Anglo-American churches," but today the custom "continues today primarily among African Americans." The symbolic roots of river baptisms lay in the Biblical example of John the Baptist baptizing Christ in the Jordan River, but Jackson suggests that similar African religious rituals of immersion in water may add another traditional layer of meaning (Jackson 1997:29; see also Staten and Roach 1997).

In OSBR, outdoor baptisms took place in local creeks, the Mississippi River, or the LSU Lakes. They usually happened during the

Fig. 5.9. An outdoor baptism at a local lake, 1958.
From the Willie Harris Photographic Collection; courtesy Mr. James Terry, III.

Fig. 5.10. Baptismal font and background scene with Jesus in the new Shiloh Baptist Church.

summer months (when revivals were generally held); the water was too chilly in the winter. Here as elsewhere, baptisms were significant not only for the individuals being baptized but for the whole church community. Almenia Freeman recalls that she was baptized in a local "creek in the woods" when she was about thirteen, and a "majority of the [church] members were there." Girls wore loose-fitting white gowns, tied with two or three bands of fabric so they wouldn't float up. Boys wore white garments or white fabric around their arms.

The procession to the creek or river was a joyful one, with congregants singing hymns as they walked. The late Rev. Lionel Lee remembered that in his parents' day, river baptisms "were very much enjoyed by African Americans during that time. . . . They used to walk for miles in the street—there were not many cars then—just singing hymns until they get to the river, and then they baptized. Great time back in that day" (Lee 1997). Deacons staked out a safe place in the water in advance, and then one by one, initiates were led waist-deep into the muddy water and immersed.

Baptisms were often followed by an evening church service, after newly baptized members dried off and changed clothes. Girls usually changed into a white Sunday dress. Almenia Williams says, "They take you to somebody's house and dress you and take you on to the church with your white dress on, you had revival and you sit on [the] mourner's bench and you pray and all that kind of stuff" (Williams 1997).

Ida Mae Whiten remembers her "old fashioned" baptism and the spirited service that followed:

> The year I was baptized they must have had about twelve of us and I was the last one to go in the water, which was a hallelujah time. It's different. It's different from baptisms now. Back then that feeling was like, 'Oh Lord.' I just can't describe it to you. I mean the church would rock. I mean the singing and jumping and the noise, but now there is silence (Whitten 1997).

River baptisms are rare today; most churches now have indoor baptismal pools instead—some with mirrors so the entire congregation can clearly see the ritual (**Fig. 5.10**). Donald R. Sterling says, "My mother and them say they baptized in the river. But we've graduated from that now. We baptize in the pool in the church." However, river baptisms remain symbolically important as a link to the past, and Mr. Sterling says, "We have a picture on the wall up there of the old time baptism" (Sterling 1997). Baptism's significance as a rite of passage is unchanged. Eddie Johnson of New Sunlight Baptist Church explained to interviewers, "Baptism is an outward showing of people that you know you have accepted Christ. And we believe in the full baptism, so that means you are going to merge into water . . . And once you are baptized and you take your first communion you are accepted into church" (Johnson 1997).

Fig. 5.11. St. Francis Xavier Girls' marching band. Courtesy of Pat Smith.

If baptisms represented spiritual rebirth, funerals were rites of passage that marked departure from this life and entry to the afterlife. Bodies were usually laid out at home—typically in the living room—by women from the church, and family and friends came in to view the body. Almenia Freeman says:

> I remember when they took the bodies to the house because when I first joined that church my mother, if someone would die they would tell her to come lay the person. They didn't have embalming back then. They would put you on a

> cooling board and lay you out. My grandfather used to make caskets and put you in the casket then put you in a wagon and take you to the graveyard (Freeman 1997).

Once the body was laid out, a wake took place. Wakes were held at home and usually included singing, food, and good times. Donald Sterling explains that when he was a boy, "they used to have wakes. They used to bring people back to their houses. I guess it was an old African tradition. They would bring the body back to the house and have the wake that night and the next day they would bring it to the church." He continues, "They would have a lot of food and people would eat and drink and just have fun. And the next day they would have the funeral" at the church. Sterling remembers that funerals were always held in the daytime, never at night.

Older residents recall that you could often tell which church the deceased belonged to by which church bells were tolling. Sadie Keel says that St. Francis Cathedral's bell was rung "if a member happened to die. The fellow who kept the building up would toll . . . the bell. Everybody in the community knew something had happened in the church and perhaps a death had taken place" (Keel 1997). Some older residents comment that although funerals in general haven't changed greatly, people today "don't cry and wail like they used to" in the old days.

Catholic residents also had their religious rites of passage, including baptisms, first communions, and funerals, among others. For Catholics, St. Francis Xavier Church was a center of community and social life (**Fig. 5.11**). Before Xavier was built, however, Creole Catholic families usually held christenings at St. Joseph's Cathedral. First communions marked an important transition for Catholic boys and girls much like baptism did for Baptists. Sadie Keel remembers that at twelve,

Fig. 5.12. First Communion girls, St. Francis Xavier Church.

> I made my communion and confirmation at the same time. I remember my first communion dress, the veil and everything, how it was designed. . . . The nuns had purchased little wreaths for all the little girls, little candles, the prayer books and beads. Everybody was given a saint's name. I think mine was St. Ann. (Keel 1997; **Fig. 5.12**).

The church's annual fair was a social highlight for parishioners. Bridget Jackson Brister remembers attending the fair as a girl:

Fig. 5.13. St. Francis Xavier Church, 2009.

> There was no way you could do anything other than go to a St. Francis Xavier Bazaar. And they used to have rides, the Ferris wheel, the tilt-a-whirl, fun stuff, you know. And then the parishioners would get together from the parish. And, oh, the food was just incredible, from the chicken dinner to the gumbo on Saturdays, to the pralines or as we call them, the pecan candy [to the] homemade cakes. You name it, it was there.

Girls competed in ball tosses and other games to win dolls wearing hand-sewn clothes (1997).

After the interstate split OSBR in two (**Fig. 5.13**), Bridget Brister's family began attending a different Catholic church, but as an adult she returned to St. Francis Xavier, in large part because of what she calls "the camaraderie of the people." The parish, she says, has "a strong sense of family . . . So many people were grown up in that parish that it's an integral part of their lives in some way or other." Numerous organizations including the Knights of Peter

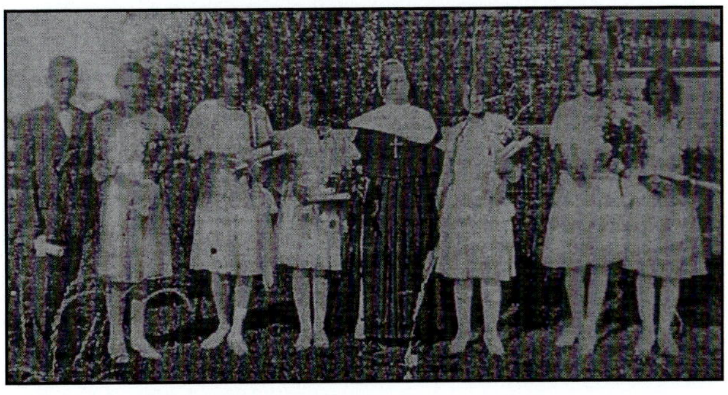

Fig. 5.14. Friends of St. Francis Xavier Church.

Claver, Children of Mary, and Ladies Auxiliary, contributed to building this sense of community (**Fig. 5.14**).

Social Clubs and Organizations

> The rituals, titles and uniforms that characterized the fraternal orders gave members a welcome respite from their daily routines and made them feel like somebody in a society that insisted they were nobody.
>
> Leon Litwack, *Trouble in Mind*, 1998:375

Social clubs and organizations are an integral part of the Old South Baton Rouge community. The scope of these clubs and organizations ranges from fraternal (Odd Fellows, Masons, etc.) to social (Purple Circle Social Club, Clovers) to the historically black Greek-letter organizations (National Pan-Hellenic Council fraternities and sororities). In their own way, the members of each of these clubs and organizations have contributed to the history of Old South Baton Rouge. Social clubs and organizations fostered pride and provided the camaraderie and social interaction denied black men and women in the larger society (Litwack 1998). The hallmarks of these organizations have been their commitments to serving the community, civic engagement, and providing social outlets for their members. Members remain connected and committed to the community through their involvement in these social clubs and organizations. Edmae Delpit Butler, who resided on St. Joseph Street as a child during the 1920s and owned the Chicken Shack with her husband Thomas Delpit, defined the importance of the social clubs and organizations to the Old South Baton Rouge community, "Social organizations are for the betterment of the community. Anything that is constructive, well, that's positive" (2002).

Odd Fellows and Prince Hall Masons

According to Butler, outside of churches, fraternal and benevolent societies are the largest and most durable organizations in the black community. The fraternal organizations were often influential in their communities because they "emphasized truth, light, charity, and a brotherhood of builders or leaders working together to form strong communities" (Butler 2005:74). They also put into practice a mutual self-help ideology that enabled their members to set aside modest savings that would cover the cost of burials and hospitalization and provide members with support in hard times (Litwack 1998). Prior to black insurance companies and social services, it was the Grand United Order of Odd Fellows (or Odd Fellows) and the Prince Hall Masons (Masons) that were the cornerstones of the community during the early and mid-twentieth century.

The Odd Fellows (Knox Enterprise Lodge No. 9949) was one of the first fraternal organizations established in Baton Rouge for African Americans. Although the Prince Hall Masons are recognized as the oldest fraternal organization for African American males, it was not until 1906 that a lodge (Blazing Star Lodge #114) was permanently established in Baton Rouge. This occurred almost 125 years after the first Prince Hall Lodge, African Lodge No. 459, was established in Boston, Massachusetts. A hallmark of the Odd Fellows and Masons has been the benevolent and charitable contributions these fraternal organizations make to the sick and distressed members of their organizations. This benevolence began prior to Social Security and Medicare being established and during the height of segregation.

Beverly V. Baranco, Sr., who served as Grand Master of the Grand United Odd Fellows of the State of Louisiana, was instrumental in getting what is now the Prince Hall Masonic Temple built in 1924 (**Fig. 3.19**). The Temple Building was originally built as the District Grand Lodge No.

21 of the Grand United Order of Odd Fellows and housed numerous businesses, including a theater and a barbershop. The building was designed by white architects Wogan & Bernard and built by African American general contractors Conner, Bryant, and Bell (*Advocate*, December 29, 1997). In 1948, it was purchased by the Most Worshipful Prince Hall Grand Lodge of Free and Accepted Masons for the State of Louisiana.

The Temple Building (1335 North Boulevard), though not within the geographical boundaries of OSBR, became the hub of social life for the black community. The Roof Garden located on the fourth floor, hosted many of the major African American entertainers of the twentieth century. Entertainers that performed there included Cab Calloway, Duke Ellington, B.B. King, Ella Fitzgerald, Louis Armstrong, the Ink Spots, King Oliver, Louis Jordan, and, later, Ike and Tina Turner. The Temple Roof Garden was also used for basketball tournaments because blacks had no gymnasium in the city. These tournaments were often sponsored by the Baton Rouge Negro Basketball Conference (B.R.N.B.C; **Fig. 5.15**). Several semi-professional teams, sponsored by major black businesses, many from OSBR, competed in the building, including the Chicken Shack Pirates, sponsored by Thomas Delpit; the Commodores, sponsored by Macie Lamotte of the Apex Lounge; and the Catholic Youth Organization Team, sponsored by St. Francis Xavier Catholic Church.

Fig. 5.15. Basketball program at the Temple, 1942.

Under the guidance of Grandmaster Dr. John G. Lewis, Jr., who served as grandmaster from 1941-79, the Prince Masons of Louisiana would become highly visible and involved in both the state and local communities. The masons were committed to developing strong social ties among their members, assisting their members and members' families when in need, and improving the black community as a whole. Individually and as a grand lodge, the Masons were actively involved in the Civil Rights Movement. Regular donations were made to the NAACP Legal Research Fund (Walkes 1986). Masons in local lodges were encouraged to register to vote and to assist in the fight against segregation.

Fig. 5.16. Masons on parade, OSBR, ca. 1950.

The Prince Hall Grand Lodge of Louisiana was also instrumental in funding an annual leadership conference at Southern University (Baton Rouge) during the 1950s. The leadership conference was established to educate African American civic and political leaders in "such diverse subjects as constitutional law; principles and techniques of leadership, state and local government, production, distribution and consumption, political processes, etc." (Walkes 1986:230).

Fig. 5.17. A Masons' meeting, ca. 1950.

Huel Perkins, a retired faculty member and administrator at both Southern University and Louisiana State University, who was a member of Blazing Star #114, commented on the significance of the Masons in the Old South Baton Rouge Community, "[The] Masons were big.... It was the premier organization to which Blacks belonged" (**Figs. 5.16-5.17**). Isadore E. Tansil, Sr., who was born in West Baton Rouge Parish, but lived in Old South Baton Rouge and graduated

Fig. 5.18. A Masons' youth camp poster.

from McKinley High School, realized that as a Mason his character would be emulated by others, particularly the youth. He stated, "Well it [being a Mason] made me tell myself, that each time that I walked out of my house; eyes were on me to see what my actions would be. So, I had to tell myself to walk upright so that if a child came behind me, he would see the right image on which to build himself" (2002).

The Masons also served as mentors and assisted in the development of their younger members. Charles A. Jones, Sr., who grew up on Howard Street during the 1930s and '40s and was a cook at LSU, commented on the importance of masonry in his life: "when I was given an opportunity to join the Prince Hall Masons that was a great turning point in my life because like children, men need mentors too. It [Masonry] has really shaped my life. I have done things I thought I would never do (2002)."

The Masons were also committed to the education and development of the youth in the OSBR community. The Prince Hall Masons owned and operated Camp Chicota in St. Landry Parish, Louisiana (**Fig. 5.18**). During the summer, the Masons and their sister organization, the Order of the Eastern Star, would transport members of their youth organizations (the Knights of Pythagoras and Youth Fraternity Chapters) from the OSBR community to Camp Chicota. At the camp the youth would participate in leadership development programs, outdoor activities, and athletic competitions. Charles A. Jones, Sr. described the need for the Masons to continue to be involved in the development of the community's youth: "It's in our areas, like here [in Baton Rouge], that we have the hardest time with [raising] these children and putting them on the right track. We teach the children, just like we teach the Masons" (Jones 2002).

Social Clubs

There are numerous clubs and organizations that are indigenous to the OSBR community. The social clubs and organizations that are a part of Old South Baton Rouge were also committed to philanthropy, civic engagement, and improving the social life of their members. Some of the clubs and organizations were established for purely social reasons such as the Progressive Matrons. Social clubs in the OSBR community included, but are not limited to, the Junior Matrons (est. 1941), the Clovers Social Club (est. 1960), the Diamond Social Club, the Golden Gophers, the Purple Circle Social Club (est. 1926), the Bonanza Club, and the Victory Maids.

These organizations have often encouraged their members to become actively involved in community and local politics. Many of the organizations have sponsored voter registration drives and supported legislation that would improve the Old South Baton Rouge community. Other activist efforts have included food drives, clothing drives, and sponsoring programs for youth in the community. The focus on getting community members to register to vote has been significant. Edmae Delpit Butler recalled registering to vote: "Yes, I do remember when I registered [to vote]. I registered as a Republican because Blacks could not register as Democrats at [that] time" (2002). J.W. Vaughn, who grew up near Bynum and 17th Street, stated, "It wasn't necessarily the organization that impacted the community but the members of the organization that lived in the community. These individuals took the initiative to give back to the community in which they had grown up" (2002).

Dr. Barbara Carpenter, who lived on Nebraska Street and is a Southern University administrator, recalled the importance of being involved in the community: "I grew up in a household where parents were community activists, particularly in the South Baton Rouge area because my grandfather was a Baptist minister. So we were accustomed to being servants of the community" (2002).

One of the oldest social clubs in Old South Baton Rouge is the Purple Circle Social Club, located at 1352 South Boulevard (**Figs. 5.19-5.20**). Established in 1926 with twenty-three charter members, the Purple Circle Social Club is an all-male organization that has been actively involved in the social and civic life of Old South Baton Rouge. The group's formation occurred in 1925, when a group of the Knights of the Loyal Seven decided to secede and organize the "The Knights of Collegiate's;" the remaining Loyal Seven became the Purple Circle Social Club. The original members were mostly craftsmen—cement finishers, plasterers, bricklayers and carpenters. Its members are expected to be of good character and applications for membership must be endorsed by two members prior to being approved by the entire membership. New initiates, who are blind-folded, take part in a ceremony of vows and prayers. The Purple Circle Social Club has sponsored youth football and baseball teams, clothes drives, and has provided financial assistance to its members when they were sick. Once a year, it has a Founders Day Celebration in June, and throughout the year there are several dances including the King and Queen Dance (**Figs. 1.4, 5.21**). Among the organization's charter members were B.V. Baranco, Sr., Theodore Roosevelt Smith, and Joseph M. Robinson. In the past, the club was also frequently a site for political stump speeches. "Before integration they used to call this place 'politic hill,'" said Louis Hall (*Advocate* 2006, 3H). Mr. Hall continued, "This is where the politicians would come. It could be 1,000 strong when they did politicking around here" (2006).

Another organization that has been in existence for almost fifty years is The Clovers. The Clovers were established on January 15, 1960 by twelve ladies who lived in Old South Baton Rouge. Harriet Jones, a retired food line supervisor who was living on Taylor Street in 1960, described the Clovers as group of young mothers with nothing to do, "so we decided we would get a club together" (2002). The Clovers are involved in numerous charitable activities, such as food drives, and continue to sponsor an annual ball.

Many of the social clubs focused on programs and activities for youths and young adults. Organizations such as the Golden Gophers and Pirates often coordinated with Thomas Buffington on scheduling "big-named" bands to perform at the Temple Building. In addition, athletic teams were sponsored by numerous businesses in the Old South Baton Rouge community.

National Pan-Hellenic Council Fraternities and Sororities

Other organizations represented in the Old South Baton Rouge community include the member organizations (e.g., Alpha Phi Alpha, Fraternity, Inc.; Zeta

Fig. 5.19. Purple Circle Social Club membership, ca. 1930.

Fig. 5.20. Membership of the Purple Circle Social Club.

Fig. 5.21. Night in June, Purple Circle Social Club, 1940s.

Fig. 5.22. Delta Sigma Theta Sorority meeting in OSBR, ca. 1940s.

Phi Beta Sorority, Inc.) of the National Pan-Hellenic Council (NPHC). These black Greek-letter fraternities and sororities were established "for the good of the race" (Harper Dickinson, 2005:12). The first of these organizations, Alpha Phi Alpha Fraternity, was founded in 1906 at Cornell University in Ithaca, New York. The first NPHC Greek-letter organization to be established in the Baton Rouge area was the Rho Chapter of Phi Beta Sigma, Fraternity, Inc. at Southern University in 1923. In 1932, the first NPHC sorority to be established in the Baton Rouge area was the Beta Alpha Chapter of Zeta Phi Beta Sorority, Inc. at Southern University. Numerous residents of the OSBR community would eventually join these and other fraternities and sororities upon enrolling at Southern University and colleges and universities throughout the United States. The Greek-letter organizations were committed to community service/activism, educational advancement, political involvement, and fostering a sense of brother- or sisterhood among its members.

Isabelle Herson, who grew up in OSBR and is a retired educator, was the first president of the Zeta Phi Beta Chapter at Southern University. She recalled the importance of developing a sisterly bond among the members of the sorority:

> I was very proud that they [the sorority members] elected me for the first president [of the chapter]; but we had to learn together because we didn't know what sororities were all about. But I stressed sisterly love because I have always believed that with a strong bond of love and family it will make for a successful life (2002).

Established in the early twentieth century, the black Greek-letter organizations were all committed to the uplift of the black community. They would become involved in the Civil Rights Movement, social activism, and the promotion of scholarly achievement (Washington & Nunez 2005). Alpha Phi Alpha often sponsored voter registration drives to encourage African Americans to vote. Huel Perkins, who grew up on South Boulevard in OSBR and is a member of Alpha Phi Alpha, recalled during the Civil Rights Movement, that one of the fraternity's civic mottos was "a voteless people is a hopeless people" (2006).

Jean Myles, who was born in raised in New Orleans but visited relatives in OSBR every summer from early childhood until she graduated from college, is a member of Delta Sigma Theta Sorority, Inc. (**Fig. 5.22**). Her sorority has a five-point program that focuses on economic development, educational development, international awareness and involvement, physical and mental health, and political awareness and involvement. Mrs. Myles commented on the importance of Delta Sigma Theta being involved in the local community, "We have worked with [the local] government in trying to improve the laws that affect blacks. We get involved in community affairs" (2002). Dr. Barbara Carpenter, who has served as International Basileus (president) for her sorority, Zeta Phi Beta added, "We are to provide service to the community—community service and scholarships" (2002).

Pat Baranco, a member of Deltas, remembers fundraisers called "Jabberwocks." Another manifestation of the group's civic work is their organization of debutante events. Mrs. Baranco told an interviewer in 2005, "Delta Sigma Theta, Baton Rouge Chapter, has the oldest black debutante function in Baton Rouge. And so we're very proud of that. And each year we try to enlighten young ladies. . . . We want to reinforce the social training of, making a debut and becoming a young lady and being useful to society."

She also recalls social functions such as dances during the Christmas and Mardi Gras seasons. The Bonanza Ball, she says, is "a Christmas dance that many of the prominent people belong to today. . . . And the men wear full tails. And the women wear formals." In the days before African Americans could hold their social functions at hotels, these galas were held on the dance floor atop the Temple Theater.

Community Artists

Prior to being transported to the Americas, "Nearly every member of an African community practiced some form of handicraft. Crafts such as those of ironwork or woodcarving were reserved to a favored few because their work was created particularly to serve the royal courts, or for religious ceremonies. Most crafts, however, were practiced by anyone in the community" (Chase 1978:135-36). Imported skills were applied to the manufacture of architectural wrought iron grillwork, latches, and hinges. Chippendale chairs, and other European-style products on the plantations were modified by African skills and sensibilities. Some Africans continued to produce products much like those of their homelands as well, mostly in the decorative arts. Much woodworking was done with an adz, African fashion, rather than with a knife (LeBeuf 1961:172-73; Chase 1978:145). Basketry, fish netting, rope, hats, and fabrics were woven using African skills. Other examples of Africanisms in material culture included grave decorations (Peek 1978:112-13), walking stick carvings (Wahlman 1987), musical instruments (gongs, banjos, trumpets) and effigy jars (Peek 1978:128-28; Edwards 2002:69). Enslaved Africans had played a particularly important role in their contributions to agriculture, animal husbandry, and handicrafts. Rice cultivation in South Carolina and along the lower Mississippi had been made possible by Africans familiar with the raising of indigenous "red" rice in West Africa (Carney 2001). Open grazing of cattle was a West African practice, as were the making of split cane or wooden baskets, iron fabrication, hoe agriculture, medicinal practices, cooking with thickened stews, and numerous other practices which persisted in rural life.

Fig. 5.23. Red Sticks quilt by Anna Williams.

OSBR had, and still has today, a wealth of creative artists, including blues and jazz musicians, traditional (folk) craftspeople, self-taught artists, and formally trained painters, sculptors, actors, and singers. A number of well-known performers have ties to Baton Rouge's vital music scene. Blues great Buddy Guy, born George Guy in the Louisiana countryside in 1936, began playing South Baton Rouge clubs as a teenager before moving to Chicago in the late 1950s. Pianist and singer Bobby Powell, a blind native of Baton Rouge born about 1941, began singing in local churches when he was four years old. He later sang in gospel groups. His soul and blues recordings reflected his early experiences in gospel music, and, in the 1980s, he returned to gospel music. Lenora Lafayette, also once an OSBR resident, became a successful opera singer. The late Valerian Smith, a dentist, composer, and playwright, was another influential figure on the Old South Baton Rouge music scene, forming the Baton Rouge Community Chorus in 1952. His daughter, Lynn Whitfield, is an Emmy-award winning actress.

Fig. 5.24. Detail of a string quilt by Anna Williams.

South Baton Rouge also has an abundance of craftspeople, sculptors, painters, and other material artists. They, like local musicians, demonstrate both individual creativity and links to African American traditions, here and in other parts of the South. Historically, carpentry and other

Fig. 5.25. Anna Williams at work.

building arts, metalwork, and textile work were prominent crafts among nineteenth-century African Americans (Vlach 1981, 1991). Early in the twentieth century, OSBR had its own blacksmith shop, and many of its male residents were bricklayers, plasterers, carpenters, and other masters of the building trades who built many of the churches and clubs still standing (**Fig. 3.1**).

Women in OSBR practiced textile arts such as sewing, crochet, embroidery, and quilting. Residents remember fancy, hand-made "bed dolls" created especially to decorate beds. Often they wore dresses stitched together from layers of felt disks and tied with yarn bows. One of the neighborhood's most skilled seamstresses, though, was a transvestite known as Escarete, who designed and made elaborate costumes and gowns.

Quilting has been a popular folk art for many generations of African American women. Black quilters often use many of the same patterns as Anglo American quilters. However, they bring their own distinctive aesthetics, particularly color and design preferences to the art. In particular, strip or "string" quilts, featuring long strips of fabric, are associated with African American quilters from Maryland to Texas (**Fig. 5.23-5.24**). Folklorist John Vlach, among others, attributes this form to "the widespread African practice of making larger textiles from thin strips on horizontal looms" (Vlach 1991:38. See also Roach-Lankford 1985).

Anna Williams is an acclaimed traditional quilter who moved to OSBR in the early 1950s when she was twenty-five. She learned to quilt as a child on the Kleinpeter Farm near Baton Rouge and

Fig. 5.26. Monkey Wrench for Mr. Al, Anna Williams quilt.

Fig. 5.27. Cotton Patch Paths, by Anna Williams.

made her first baby quilt at the age of nine (**Fig. 5.25**). Women there, like many traditional quilters, worked cooperatively with neighbors on their quilts, and these get-togethers (sometimes called quilting bees) served as welcome social occasions for women (Vlach 1991; Roach-Lankford 1985). Mrs. Williams recalls, "After work we'd come from work [in the fields], we'd go and help our neighbors until we got all out quilts done. . . . You didn't take that long because everybody had a little part, and they quilt on that little part." Quilt tops were pieced together from scraps of worn-out clothes, and the bottoms were made from printed feed sacks.

Fig. 5.28. Emerson Bell, portrait.

In Baton Rouge, Mrs. Williams continued to make quilts in traditional patterns, including log cabin, a triangular pattern she calls "monkey-wrench" (**Fig. 5.26-5.27**), and string quilts. However, in Baton Rouge, she no longer quilted with neighbors. Instead, piecing quilt tops became an individual art she could practice almost any time and any place. She says, "When I go places, I take my pocketbook full [of quilt pieces] and I sit there and sew by hand."

Like many traditional quilters, she finds plenty of room for creativity while working with traditional patterns—in her choice of colors and fabrics, for instance. She says, "Sometimes at night when I'm laying down and resting, something will come into my mind like a figure where I get up and cut it. . . . and fit it on my bed and sometimes I'll sew a little of it together to see what it would look like." Today, people send her scraps of fabric "from all over the world," she says. Her work has received considerable recognition locally and nationally, and has been featured in exhibits and a book (Rabalais and Watts n.d.).

The late Emerson Bell, a well known sculptor and painter, was born in OSBR in the early 1930s, and he spent his early formative years here (**Fig. 5.28**). After traveling the world, he returned to Baton Rouge, where he became a well-loved fixture of the art scene. His art, he said, was influenced strongly by his Baton Rouge experiences, as well as by other places in which he lived as an adult. He remembered the OSBR of his youth as a "very wonderful area. It was very inspiring then . . . Because there was always a lot of talent—great talent—that arose out of South Baton Rouge. Such as musicians and artists, a lot of notable people came from South Baton Rouge." Art and music were an important part of his boyhood—an uncle painted signs and did drafting, for example, and he said that his family first taught him to value the arts. His mother in particular encouraged him to develop his talents.

Fig. 5.29. Emerson Bell painting.

Mr. Bell's first art job as a youth was painting a mural for a small church in South Baton Rouge (now torn down). A "mother of the church" knew he was good at drawing and "so she asked me would I do something for the church," he recalled. A cousin from Texas came to help him, and Mr. Bell says, "I did all the saints, he and I, in fresco. That was my first introduction to doing fresco." Throughout his career, much of his work reflected religious themes and images—icon-like paintings of Black Madonnas (**Fig. 5.29**), angels, Christ-like figures, and a sculpted bust of John the Baptist.

He continued to develop his skills in painting and sculpture through unofficial apprenticeships with master artists. Today, his abstract sculpture "Destiny for Children" stands twenty-six feet high at the intersection of East and South boulevards, eerily reminiscent of the African American sculptures documented by John Vlach in rural Southern cemeteries.

Fig. 5.30. Artist Wayne Jones with his mural of painted soldiers.

Another artist with connections to OSBR is Keith Douglas, better known as "Cartoonman." Raised in New Orleans, Mr. Douglas taught art for nine years at McKinley High School in OSBR, and he maintains ties to the neighborhood. As a child, he says, "I used to draw characters, I used to create always in my head" and draw his own comic strips. He says, "I've always had this creative mind. I would write my own stories." At Xavier University, he studied art with a number of talented teachers. Now, he says, "I do a lot of caricature work, I'm known as a caricatures illustrator." He got his start in making caricatures when a friend who owned a nightclub asked him if he knew how to draw them. "So I said, 'I don't know, give me a week.' So I figured I could learn anything, just give me a book. I read it, look at it, I observe it, I could do it. So what I did, I did thumbnails [sketches] of people in the street. . . . When I drew those people, I went to him that Friday, and I said, "I'm ready." His work was an immediate hit.

Keith Douglas is also known in OSBR for a character he created to entertain at parties. He recalls:

> So I became this character called Marshall Quickdraw. I used to dress in a cowboy hat, I had these chaps made, even created a puppet to come along with me to birthday parties for kids . . . And I would talk to the kids and have my little puppet, which was called Ricochet the Rattlesnake. I was always very creative. And I would draw with the other hand while I had Ricochet looking at the kids. . . . So eventually I became pretty well-known for parties (Douglas 2002).

Fig. 5.31. Carved Angel, Wayne Jones.

Fig. 5.32. Runaway slave mural, Wayne Jones's house.

Fig. 5.33. Wayne Jones's mural of the Bus Boycott on Thomas Delpit Boulevard.

Although he teaches art for a living, Mr. Douglas considers himself an artist first, and a teacher second. He says, "This community supports the arts. . . . In this area, we basically have street [or neighborhood] artists. . . . People who in the community are known . . . like you got Emerson Bell, who is really well known in Baton Rouge." He adds, "I think they are appreciated basically because people know talent." Although OSBR does not have an organized arts scene like New Orleans does, he feels that here "you have a pretty good flourishing area as far as the creative arts community," one that is ripe for promotion and development.

Wayne Jones is another OSBR community artist (**Fig. 5.30**). From his colorful shotgun house (**Frontispiece**), he works in various media including painting, sculpture, jewelry making, and murals (**Fig. 5.31**). He is self-taught, claiming that all of his art work is not his own, but a direct inspiration from God. Some of his murals come with an activist—sometimes almost revolutionary—perspective (**Fig. 5.32**). Mr. Jones's murals enliven the facades of several buildings in the OSBR community (**Fig. 5.33**).

Museums

In addition to the artists described above, the OSBR community is also home to four museums. Museums, like churches and social clubs, play a vital part in community life today. They are means of conserving, celebrating, and educating people about the neighborhood's distinctive cultural heritage.

The Magnolia Mound Museum on Nicholson Drive is home to a plantation home, overseer's house and several slave cabins. The interpretative center of the museum is on the museum grounds. It also includes a tour, Behind the Big House, which focuses on the enslaved workers (**Fig. 5.34**). The Odell S.

Fig. 5.34. Rear view of Magnolia Mound showing kitchen and kitchen garden.

Williams Now and Then Museum run by Sadie Roberts-Joseph on South Boulevard, was designed as a museum to showcase the contribution of African Americans to American history (**Figs. 5.35**). The T.J. Jemison Museum is located on South Boulevard in the former Lincoln Theatre. The exhibit focuses on the role of T.J. Jemison in the 1953 Bus Boycott. The most recent addition to the museums of OSBR is the McKinley High School Alumni Museum which is a museum dedicated to the role of McKinley High School in educating African Americans in OSBR (**Fig. 5.36**). It is located in the newly restored original high school which is a National Historic Site. It traces the history of the high school from 1927 to the present day. These new museums and the growing arts community are examples of the beginnings of revitalization in OSBR.

Notes

[1] According to Joyce Jackson it is called the mourner's bench because this is the area designated for family and friends during a funeral. Before you are baptized you have to sit on the first benches in the front of the church during revival and after. You are usually removed from the mourner's bench after your first communion (personal communication).

Fig. 5.35. Odell S. Williams Museum, South Boulevard.

Fig. 5.36. The New McKinley High School Alumni Museum.

The Churches of Old South Baton Rouge

PHOTOS BY JAMES W. TERRY, III

Bethel African Methodist Episcopal Church

Mount Zion First Baptist Church

Mount Zion First Baptist Church

Shiloh Baptist Church

St. Agnes Catholic Church
Masses
Saturday: 6:00 AM & 8:00 AM, Vigil: 4:00
Sunday: 6:30, 8:00, 9:30 Latin
Monday – Friday: 6:00

Wesley United Methodist Church

Neely United Methodist Church

St Joseph
Baptist Church

Chapter Six

The Power of Place: Community Revitalization

Where I lived, there's nobody there, but a highway. Everybody's gone. Everybody's moved, when they built the highway. It's dead, dead. No groceries, no nothing. No people. They took one side of the street and made us move. A lot of people moved away. Grocery stores and everything, they didn't have them no more. Everything was gone.

~Louise Haynes

> The power of place—the power of ordinary urban landscapes to nurture citizens' public memory, to encompass shared time in the form of shared territory—remains untapped for most working people's neighborhoods in most American cities, and for most ethnic history and most women's history . . . Identity is intimately tied to memory: both our personal memories and the collective or social memories interconnected with the histories of our families, neighbors, fellow workers, and ethnic communities.
>
> Dolores Hayden, 1995: 9

Old South Baton Rouge is clearly significant to the identity of those who call it home as the stories in this book have testified. This is evident in the numerous commemorative acts in which community members have engaged. In 1981, residents worked to have McKinley High School nominated to the National Register of Historic Places. After its designation, it slowly deteriorated, and, in 1998, fire almost destroyed the building. The McKinley High Alumni Association rededicated itself to renovating the building. While no longer a high school, the newly renovated building is a testament to the thousands of black students who gained a public high school education during the height of Jim Crow. One focal point in the newly restored building is the McKinley High School Museum that documents the history of this historic African American High School (**Fig. 5.36**).

On South Boulevard, local activist Sadie Roberts-Joseph has opened the Odell S. Williams Now and Then Museum of African American History (**Fig. 5.35**). In 2005 the museum inaugurated the "Juneteenth Freedom Celebration." According to Roberts-Joseph "It's time for healing to take place in Baton Rouge, because we've not totally healed" (*Advocate* 2005b). The YMCA on Thomas Delpit is adorned with a large mural of B.V. Baranco, Sr. and J.S. Clark, two of the community's leading civic leaders in the early part of the twentieth century (**Figs. 6.1-6.2**). The Leo S. Butler Community Center proudly displays in its showcase pictures of Dr. Butler as well as other leading figures (**Fig. 6.3**). The new Carver Library sits on the site of the Reddy Street School, the elementary school that served this community for generations (**Figs. 6.4, 6.5, 3.10).** It now houses all 230 oral history tapes of the McKinley Oral History Project, which are available to the public (See also **Appendix V**).

These acts of commemoration are occurring within a community that has little resemblance to the thriving 1950s community we have portrayed in this book. As suggested earlier, the impact of building I-10 through the middle of the neighborhood, the loss of community schools through desegregation and busing, and increasing suburbanization and urban flight resulted in the

Fig. 6.1. YMCA wall mural of B.V. Baranco, Sr.

Fig. 6.2. YMCA wall mural of J.S. Clark.

economic decline of this neighborhood. It is a shadow of what it once was. The OSBR community is described in the City of Baton Rouge Office of Community Development Consolidated Plan for 2002-2004 as a severely distressed neighborhood. The 2000 census reports that the total population is 9,620 (7,209 African American, 1,652 white, 22 Native American, 536 Asian, 4 Native Hawaiian or Other Pacific Islander, 65 of other races, 120 of two or more races). The median family income is $15,117.00. Forty percent of the population (3,889 persons) were determined to be below poverty level. While a percentage of the elderly residents live in owner-occupied homes that they have inhabited for numerous years (1,109 persons are 65 years or older), the majority of residents are between the ages of eighteen and thirty-four (3,215), have not completed high school, and are living in rental property. In 1996, over 25 percent of the housing units in the area were vacant (Hurlbert, et. al.1996). Crime, panhandling, and vagrancy are serious problems that make many elderly residents feel like prisoners in their own homes. Alton Ingram, owner of Ingram's Fabricated Filters, Inc., and Ingram's Upholstery, cannot understand why the city can't "expand policing strategies to help fight crime, particularly drug dealing from homes and street corners" (*Advocate* 2005a). Ingram's Upholstery, on Thomas Delpit Drive, is currently one of the oldest businesses in OSBR. Most of the businesses that once lined East Boulevard have long since closed or relocated. There is no grocery store, gas station or drugstore. When the summer afternoon rainstorms bring a downpour, the flooding due to poor drainage is a persistent problem and access into and out of the neighborhood is a problem. On the surface many might say "bulldoze the neighborhood" and start over. Yet many community members hope to "bring back better days" (*Advocate* 2005a).

Fig. 6.3. Dr. Leo Butler.

In spite of persistent problems, members of the community have been determined to revitalize their neighborhood. While poverty and suburban flight contribute to some of the problems the neighborhood is facing, many residents feel that the neighborhood has been neglected by city officials. Robert Ware, who grew up in OSBR, maintains that "We got a great, big ballfield just sitting there, with no lights. There are a lot of things they could do like they do out there in Sherwood Forest (a predominately white suburban neighborhood in BR) and those other places," he continued. "We as black people, don't receive the financial support that we should" (*Advocate* 2005a). Community residents wonder why crime persists, why there isn't better drainage and sewer repair, why the streets are not resurfaced, or

Fig. 6.4. The Carver Library on Terrace Street.

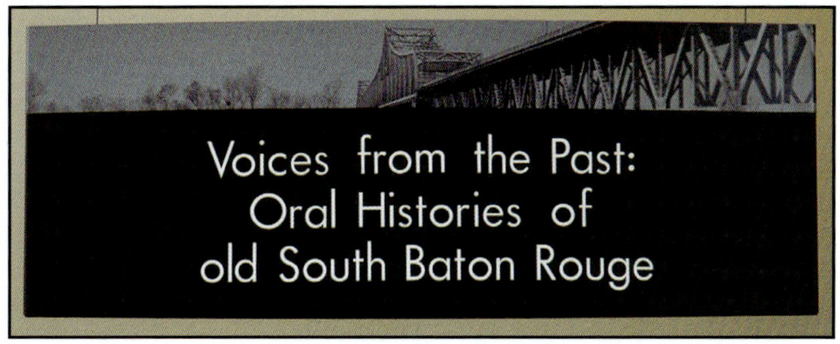

Fig. 6.5. Carver Library Oral History Project sign.

why there aren't more parks for children and young adults to play. David Whitten, who grew up in OSBR, also wonders why more young people don't know about the rich history of OSBR. He claims that "the neighborhood's old history of success stories, such as McKinley basketball coach Carl Stewart as well as McKinley graduate and Grambling football coach Eddie Robinson (**Fig. 6.6**) has been replaced by its more recent history and bad reputation;" children need to know that their "grandparents came out of here and went to college and they can too" (*Advocate* 2005a).

Fig. 6.6. Coach Eddie Robinson.

Residents of the community are ready to revitalize. For many residents this means learning how to get loans to improve their homes, or how to work with police to stop crime, or how to reduce the blight on the many vacant lots that are scattered throughout the neighborhood. Other issues include how to obtain small business loans to start economic enterprises in the neighborhood or how to work with the city to get lights, streets, and sewers repaired. In addition to these basic needs, members of the OSBR community have increasingly been engaged in acts of remembrance that represent the experiences of the struggle for political, economic, and social progress. Despite the many challenges and the changing nature of the neighborhood community, residents have been vigilant in their desire to preserve the history of the neighborhood as well as to "tell others" about the rich history. On April 9, 2006, hundreds of McKinley High School alumni attended a ribbon cutting ceremony to open the newly renovated high school. Brooks Park, the first public park built with a pool for blacks in East Baton Rouge Parish was renovated and rededicated. The all-black "Lutheran" cemetery, in the southern part of the community has been cleaned up and refurbished by a local city council member (**Figs. 1.5, 6.7**). A row of shotgun houses has recently been renovated, rather than torn down, as a reminder of the unique architectural style that characterized many African American neighborhoods at the turn of the century. While these sites might not seem significant to outsiders, the meanings attached to them by community residents are a reminder of a time in which they struggled on a daily basis to defend their dignity and humanity. Because of the unique struggles of African Americans in the era of Jim Crow, these sites of remembrance and preservation represent powerful

Fig. 6.7. The restored Lutheran cemetery.

memories and experiences, yet they have not traditionally been deemed "historically significant" (Grandison 1999:159-68). The community revitalization that is currently taking place must take into account the experiences of previously unrepresented and underrepresented perspectives. What might appear at first to be a jumble of different housing styles could, according to Elizabethe Lyon and Richard C. Cloues represent "an historic multi-use social and economic community shaped by racial segregation" (1999:44). Clearly the unique history and culture of this community as part of the larger story of American history is significant. Yet, the questions remain: "Who decides what is significant?" "How is significance determined?" and "Who decides the nature of revitalization?"

These questions are of urgent concern to community members as the neighborhood has now been targeted for urban revitalization. There are varied positions or approaches being taken to revitalization which reflect the various stakeholders or interest groups that are invested in the community. These can be divided into three major models that we will characterize in terms of the locus of change, in other words, who will direct community redevelopment efforts. We refer to these models as the Community Development Model, the Structural Redevelopment Model, and the Planning Model.

The Community Development Model

This group is characterized by members of the community including the Metropolitan Community and Housing Development Project, the McKinley Alumni Association, and members of the Community University Partnership (CUP). These groups are composed of residents of the OSBR community who have self-organized to address issues of housing, crime, jobs, and urban renewal. They are self-empowered and see themselves as active agents in bringing about change. These community residents and the local city council representatives advocate first and foremost addressing the immediate needs of community residents (housing, jobs, stopping crime). They would like to retain the neighborhood as it is and use state and local funds not necessarily for large-scale projects, but for small-scale projects that will directly support residents and the traditional quality of life of the community. The vision is to "bring back" the vibrant nature of the community and make sure that the elderly can "age in place." One of their greatest fears is the gentrification of the neighborhood as well as the role which LSU plays in the community.

The Structural Redevelopment Model

This position is taken by some community residents who support the use of state and federal funds to address issues of substandard and inadequate housing. This group is composed largely of business and political interests from inside and outside of the community. It has been aided by the LSU School of Social Work. It has obtained federal aid from Housing and Urban Development (HUD), and the city housing authority. This group has been ready to "move forward" and change the physical nature of the neighborhood through tearing down and rebuilding. This type of urban renewal is controlled by governmental agencies and does not necessarily include a large scale plan or coherent vision for urban renewal. It is considered by some to be piecemeal because focusing on new housing developments still does little to address jobs, crime, etc.

The Planning Model

Community residents who support this vision of urban renewal see the use of outside experts in urban planning as central to successful revitalization. The renewal of OSBR must be part of a larger plan for the city of Baton Rouge. This "Smart Growth" strategy is designed to some degree to empower community residents but also relies on "experts." This planning model for urban development has been undertaken by Baton Rouge Area Foundation (BRAF), a non-profit organization. They are invested in a total renovation of the neighborhood that would include some historic preservation, but also new growth that would attract a wider, deeper market by capitalizing on the assets of the area.

While community members have been engaged in local activism since the early 1990s, in 2003 a citywide initiative to revitalize OSBR was undertaken by BRAF, a nonprofit organization that forms partnerships with philanthropists, nonprofit organizations, and other community leaders to implement programs that will have positive, lasting impacts in the Baton Rouge community. Some of the numerous stakeholders involved in this process include OSBR community activists, HUD, CUP, and the City and Parish of Baton Rouge. BRAF serves as the umbrella organization in the development of the Old South Baton Rouge Strategic Plan. This plan is coordinated with a larger development plan for the entire city—Plan Baton Rouge. The Pennington Family Foundation and the East Baton Rouge Mortgage Finance Authority funded Plan Baton Rouge $250,000 to develop the OSBR Strategic Plan. As a first step in 2004 they hired RKG consultants from Alexandria, Virginia to assist in the one year process of developing a revitalization plan. This initiative by Plan Baton Rouge coincided with a number of other initiatives including the emergence of the North Gates Merchants Association, the First Worthing's development of student housing near LSU, and the construction of McKinley Middle School and the Carver branch of the public library.

We cannot possibly represent all voices or perspectives in this redevelopment process. It is a deeply contested issue. Ironically, this community emerged as a consequence of segregation; its historic institutions arose out of the need to create a separate community or place. The strength of these institutions were a consequence of the determination of African Americans to embody the dignity and humanity that they were being denied. It is this historical memory, the significance it plays in the story of African American and Italian American self determination that is at risk of being erased. There is much at stake, not least for many residents who fear that they will lose their homes, and that their neighborhood will change dramatically and no longer be the familiar place that they called home.

Community at a Crossroads

Community Activists

When the urban renewal process began in 1994, it became immediately obvious that while community members had deep personal knowledge of their community, its significance had remained almost completely undocumented. Spanish Town and Beauregard Town were both popularly identified as unique and historic neighborhoods with valuable cultural assets such as historic architecture. Old South Baton Rouge, the first suburb of Baton Rouge, and the first African American community to emerge at the turn of the twentieth century, remained largely invisible. The few published histories of Baton Rouge barely mention the OSBR community, much less any of its substantial contributions to the wider culture of the South (Carleton 1981; Heck 1966, 1970).

It was during the last decade of the twentieth century that grassroots forces within the neighborhood began to gather momentum to organize community improvement projects. "In November, 1993, a group of these community members came together to create an organization which it hoped would address the area's pressing problems. The group was coordinated by the top aid of a state legislator who was raised in the community and is active in numerous civic and religious associations in Baton Rouge" (Livermore and Midgley 1998:126). The Metropolitan Community and Housing Development Organization (MCHDO) addressed numerous issues, including economic development, educational opportunities, physical improvements, and the construction of housing. However, for most of the members, the slogan "take back the community" epitomizes their ideal of reconstructing a vibrant, sustainable neighborhood (Livermore and

Midgley 1998:126). These stakeholders then turned to LSU to invite them to create a partnership that would focus on urban renewal.

The Community University Partnership (CUP)

The urban renewal efforts of the Metropolitan Community and Housing Development Project (MCHDP) coincided with the efforts of LSU to become more publicly engaged in its civic mission under the leadership of the LSU chancellor William Jenkins and the new Associate Vice Chancellor for Research and Economic Development Jim Midgley, and newly hired social work intern Michelle Livermore. Beginning in 1993, LSU began a partnership with the MCHDP that committed it to active participation in the urban renewal process for OSBR. LSU saw as part of its mission not only a civic duty, but also an opportunity to conduct research and to share resources and knowledge with the public. But at the same time, "LSU wished at all costs to prevent the emergence of a paternalistic service approach, and wanted instead to enter into a dynamic dialog about the problems facing the community and the best ways to respond to these problems (Livermore and Midgley 1998:127). As OSBR's neighbor, it was incumbent on LSU to partner with OSBR. This relationship also provided an avenue for LSU's faculty, graduate students and undergraduate students to apply what they were learning in their courses in "real world" situations. These service learning courses and initiatives spanned many disciplines and types of projects. These include the McKinley Oral History Project, clean-up projects, a farmers' market, literacy training, expanded service-learning opportunities, social capital development initiatives, a project relating to improving the physical structures in the community, and a neighborhood beautification project for the development of community gardens and environmental improvements. All of these projects were in partnership with the residents of OSBR and identified by members of the MCHDO and the CUP task force. In addition, CUP and MCHDO began to research productive employment and self-employment in the community through programs such as job links and small business support. All of these CUP projects were based on a community developmental model. This model "rejects the idea that economic growth, alone, can promote the well-being of the population as a whole, and it criticizes traditional social programs for being impractical in times of slow economic growth (Livermore and Midgley 1998:128). This model is holistic in that it addresses social, environmental, and economic concerns.

While significant in contributing to individual projects that addressed immediate issues, many of these service learning projects were short term and residents came to expect that LSU students would come but would not remain on a long-term basis. While the original intent was for CUP to address neighborhood problems through integrated socioeconomic development, high staff turnover, changes in university administration, and lack of funding resulted in lack of systematic long-term plans for the complex problems facing the neighborhood. Many residents welcomed the students and saw hope for increased understandings across the LSU-OSBR divide, but these limited projects would not be sufficient to establish an effective partnership for long-term growth. Throughout the history of CUP, Patricia Smith, a former director, provided the thread that brought continuity to the work between LSU and OSBR that has sustained this collaborative effort.

Several projects conducted by CUP have been embraced by the community including the McKinley High School Oral History Project and the playground installed at Polk Elementary School by an engineering class taught by Mary Beth Lima of LSU, who won national recognition for this project. The Paul Hebert Law Center provided a free legal clinic for OSBR residents working in conjunction with the BR Bar Pro Bono Division and Capitol Area Legal services. OSBR Community Revitalization Corporation received faith-based grants that established a mentoring program between three churches and schools in OSBR using the Kids Hope model. In addition, they were the recipients of a capacity building grant, which was also written by the faculty of LSU's School

Voices of Old South Baton Rouge:

A Community Resident Speaks: Pat Smith

The efforts of LSU CUP that began in the early 1990s have continued through today. CUP officially formed a department in 2001 with the announcement of a $400,000 grant from the HUD's Community Outreach Partnership Center (COPC). Faculty in the School of Social Work along with representatives wrote this grant from the Chancellor's office and those who were already involved in the OSBR outreach activities. Originally, the grant targeted the corridor of Thomas Delpit from West Roosevelt to South Boulevard. With a number of other revitalization projects such as HOPE VI and the OSBR Strategic Plan, CUP expanded its target area to match those efforts.

Keeping a community presence is an important part of the CUP mission. The CUP Advisory Panel was established in 2001 with a purpose of involving residents and stakeholders in decisions on CUP activities, gaining input regarding programs on which CUP should focus and assisting with program implementation. Currently, the make-up of the seventeen member CUP Advisory Panel includes five OSBR residents and three LSU representatives. Those remaining are pastors of churches in OSBR and business owners in OSBR. All are stakeholders in this community. The original CUP faculty task force is no longer functioning. In its place is a faculty advisory group that meets periodically to receive updates on CUP initiatives and provide insight on any future activities. This group also tackles the concern of sustainability of CUP initiatives once funding is no longer available.

of Social Work. CUP also sponsored a grant that allowed BR Green to collaborate with various OSBR groups along with students from LSU and Southern University to landscape and beautify the corridors of Thomas Delpit and East Washington streets inclusive of the Leo S. Butler Center.

The OSBR community and other parts of Baton Rouge now engage over 1,200 students per semester in service-learning activities. Other departments at LSU such as kinesiology have been able to bring their students in for studies dealing with the senior citizen population in the community. The MBA and architecture departments have provided graduate students the opportunity to work with various businesses and churches in OSBR. To date over twenty-five homes of senior citizens have been painted by LSU students and community residents in conjunction with the Center for Community Development on their Saturday-in-service days (<ccell@LSU.edu>).

Many of these projects have contributed to the revitalization of the community. In 2005, CUP received a grant from the U.S. Department of Housing and Urban Development's Office of University Partnerships for $200,000. The grant is part of the Community Outreach Partnership Centers New Directions program. This program provides grants to help colleges and universities establish and operate centers that develop outreach and applied research activities aimed at addressing the problems of urban areas. The activities proposed include providing educational workshops on financial planning and home ownership; developing an employer-assisted, home-ownership pilot program for LSU employees interested in owning homes in the OSBR area; repair and fix-up programs, job training targeted for sixteen-to-twenty-four year olds, and providing young children with programs in the arts and area adults help to finish their high school diplomas.

Community members and LSU students working together has fostered new understandings of each other. LSU students have learned not only more about their disciplines, but have enriched

Fig. 6.8. 2006 construction on Highland Road near State Street, south OSBR.

Fig. 6.9 View from about the same location as Fig. 6.8, looking south, 1950s.

their understandings of a community that many at first glance were "scared" to enter. Yet, some distrust still remains. Members of the community are often suspicious of LSU. There was a time, not so long age, where blacks could not attend LSU. In fact there was a fence that divided the OSBR neighborhood from LSU's property. CUP has sought to repair some of these tensions and painful memories by working together to revitalize the neighborhood. As large new apartment buildings are going up along Nicholson Drive and Highland Road, the two main corridors through OSBR, there is a fear that LSU is extending its presence into the neighborhood (**Figs. 6.8-6.9**). This could potentially raise rents, increase housing costs and displace community residents. At a recent community meeting a resident voiced his concern that "OSBR is not LSU's parking lot on football Saturdays." There is also the perception that LSU's interest in the neighborhood is merely a superficial one—it is good "PR" to do good works in the local community. Questions remain, will LSU continue to support CUP projects; will they maintain an ongoing committed relationship with OSBR?

The Baton Rouge Area Foundation

While CUP, LSU and grassroots initiatives have worked over the past fifteen years in numerous ways to bring about components of urban renewal, in the spring of 2005, Plan Baton Rouge (an initiative of the non-profit BRAF) announced that it was launching a year-long strategic planning process that would coordinate the many efforts that were currently underway and provide an overall vision for OSBR. Gwen Hamilton, Plan Baton Rouge's senior director and a long-time resident of OSBR, is the liaison between the strategic plan consultant team and the many community partners. Along with the executive director of Plan Baton Rouge, a consultant team led by RKG Associates was hired to create a plan for community revitalization and an implementation strategy (**Fig. 6.10**). Hamilton recalled:

> In 2001, LSU received a Community Outreach Partnership Center Grant from the U.S. Department of Housing and Urban Development, enabling the University to focus on community organization, economic development, and neighborhood revitalization in the urban area adjacent to LSU. Meanwhile, an effort to revitalize downtown Baton Rouge—an adjacent area—was seeing its first series of successes. A collaboration between

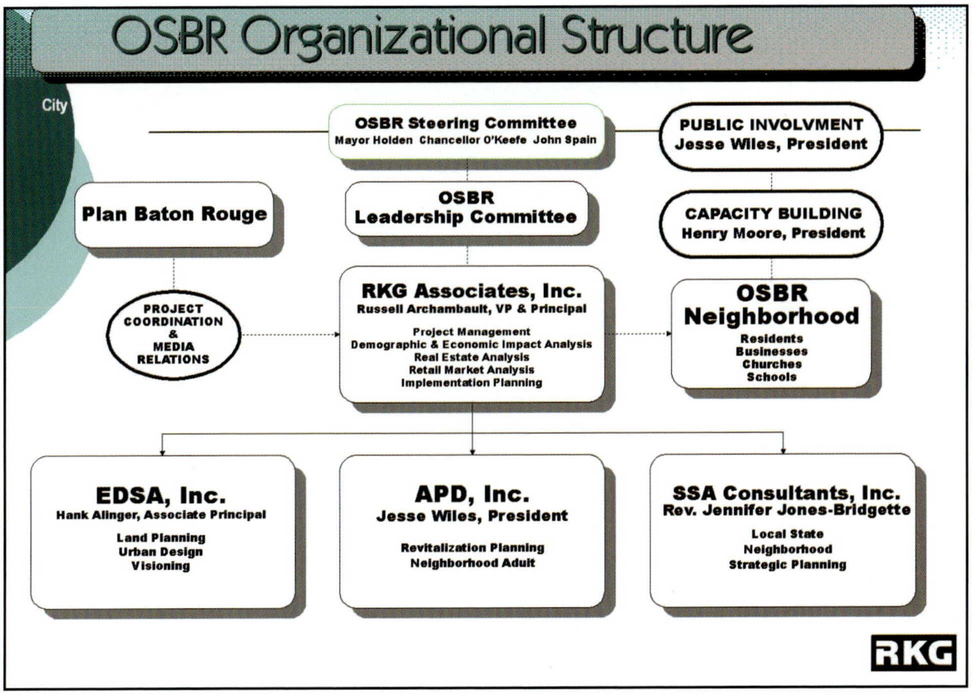

Fig. 6.10. OSBR planning process organizational structure for redevelopment planning.

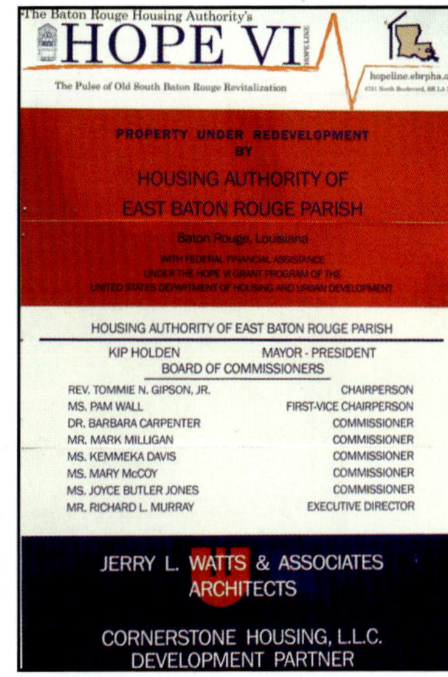

Fig. 6.11. Hope VI sign, Terrace Boulevard.

local and state government, the Baton Rouge Area Foundation, Plan Baton Rouge, and many others, resulted in the recognition of the importance of Old South Baton Rouge to the overall health and growth of the city, and began turning their attention to cultivating that neighborhood. Both groups—LSU and the downtown interest, have since worked to leverage their resources and experience into real benefits for the people of Old South Baton Rouge.

In addition to these initiatives, with the help of Cong. Richard Baker and the BRAF in 2003, the East Baton Rouge Parish Housing Authority secured a $18.6 million federal HOPE VI grant, which is being used to demolish the housing projects of the 1960s and improve the quality and availability of affordable housing (**Fig. 6.11**). In 2006, the old Maison Coteau apartments, the federal housing project built on Thomas Delpit in the 1960s, were torn down and are currently being replaced by twenty-five single, detached, and duplex homes (**Fig. 6.12**). Some of the single-family units being built here bear strong generalized resemblances to the vernacular forms of OSBR. Can this be considered part of the on-going process of cultural creolization (**Fig. 6.13**)?

According to Richard Murray, executive director of the East Baton Rouge housing authority "This represents the beginning of Phase I for Hope VI in Baton Rouge which will total forty-eight houses changing the landscape in this area and the lifestyle of the residents in a positive way" (http// hopeline.ebrpha.org). The Hope VI project goes beyond tearing down "projects." They will hire twenty young people to train them in construction development along with GED preparation and leadership development as well as assist residents with child care, home-buying, home maintenance and other outreach efforts. The major goal is to lessen the concentration of poverty by promoting mixed-income housing.

Within a relatively short period of time numerous groups converged on OSBR, houses began to be torn down, and outsiders appeared on a frequent basis with their notepads, cameras and questions. For community residents, especially the elderly, this flurry of activity was unsettling. While urban planners saw this as an "ideal" site for redevelopment due to its location between

Fig. 6.12. Hope VI project under construction, 2006.

Fig. 6.13. Hope VI Single Family residence.

downtown and LSU, many community members saw the potential for their neighborhood becoming "gentrified" (Preliminary Community Revitalization Plan, 2003 Master Plan Charrette). Renewal, instead of being seen as something positive was perceived as a threat. In addition to the distrust of outsiders and their real motives, residents worried that new commercial developments would chase out the last of the remaining local stores, and that LSU students would push residents out of the neighborhood. Fears of being displaced, especially among the elderly, and losing the traditional historical and social fabric of the neighborhood were foremost in the minds of community residents

Voices of Old South Baton Rouge:

Community Concerns about Development: Gwen Hamilton

With Plan Baton Rouge, CUP, and local officials working together, gaining direct input and support from residents and other stakeholders became the priority. RKG began to design a process that would rely on the direct input of the community, allowing stakeholders to voice their opinions or frustrations, and see their ideas contributing to a new vision for the area. They realized, from their past experiences in urban design, the importance of a process of community engagement and open communication—and, how that process would impact the long-term shape and success of their plan.

First, the consultants fashioned a comprehensive communications plan that would reach as many people as possible and rely on direct community input. An Old South Baton Rouge website (http://osbr.planbr.org) was created to provide updates, meeting notifications and minutes, a history of Old South Baton Rouge, and details on how to get involved in the planning process. Through a central mailing list, municipal officers, ministers, nonprofit and community organizations, broadcast and print media, residents, business owners, and other stakeholders were connected to current information. Lawn signs, community banners, newspaper advertisements, and other methods helped generate "word of mouth" buzz around the effort. These strategies, in an ongoing effort, continue to raise awareness of and build confidence in this process.

Primarily, consultants and planners have used interviews and community meetings to rally support behind the effort and get a clear vision of stakeholders concerns and needs. Prior to any planning activity, consultants conducted interviews with over one-hundred community stakeholders to get a better understanding of the area. They found that the planning process needed to increase the involvement of stakeholders beyond traditional community leadership (i.e. politicians, local officials, etc.), incorporate the strong history of Old South Baton Rouge, overcome feelings of distrust and skepticism, and promote better opportunities for young people.

Based on those pre-interview results, consultants began searching for avenues to reach out to the ministerial community, education community, and political leadership, and reconnect the community with its history. Four public involvement tracts were initiated: 1) meetings with leadership and steering committees; 2) grassroots capacity building workshops; 3) ministerial community breakfast meetings; and 4) general public community forums. Through these activities—hundreds of meetings spanning over a year's time, stakeholders helped create a plan that can work for everyone, one that is representative of their visions for the community.

as they prepared to gather for the first of a number of community meetings that were to be held by Plan Baton Rouge.

Fig. 6.14. Community Meeting Poster, 2006.

In May 2005, the first of three community meetings took place at Polk Elementary School with the goal of including community residents in the planning process (**Fig. 6.14, 6.15**). On May 3, over 300 residents gathered to tell the planners what kinds of changes they'd like to see. Residents focused on the positive aspects of the neighborhood like the many trees and green spaces and the rich history of McKinley; yet they had many suggestions for improvement, including-beautification, sidewalks, the need for grocery stores, more community policing, more recreational facilities, job training and placement, decent safe housing, social services, and input into decision-making. Many agreed that crime and a negative perception of OSBR have contributed to a lack of interest in the revitalization of the neighborhood. Two more community meetings were held in the summer and fall of 2005 (http://www.planbr.org).

Fig. 6.15. A Community Meeting.

On March 23, 2006 at the Baranco Clark YMCA in the heart of Old South Baton Rouge, Plan Baton Rouge (now the Center for Planning Excellence) unveiled the final Old South Baton Rouge Strategic Plan (**Fig. 6.16**). The Strategic Plan Steering Committee co-chairs were Mayor Melvin "Kip" Holden of the City of Baton Rouge, LSU Chancellor Sean O'Keefe, and Executive VP John Spain of BRAF. Both LSU Provost Risa Palm and President William Jenkins committed to stand behind the Strategic Plan and to advance its implementation. Community residents mingled with RKG consultants in the YMCA's gym where a sneak preview of the final plan was displayed

Fig. 6.16. Plan Baton Rouge Strategic Plan map.

on numerous poster boards. Residents looked at graphically enhanced colorful aerial maps that showed a vision of OSBR with a baseball park in the northeast corner, a pedestrian walkway along a renovated canal (**Map 6.1, Fig. 6.17**), parks, new shopping centers, a revitalized Lincoln Community Theatre Centre, and a "Brickyard Landing Discovery Center" at the Old City Dock. When the attention was turned to the speakers the message was overwhelmingly clear: "This is just the beginning!" As John Spain, Executive VP of BRAF, pointed out, it is not uncommon for redevelopment plans to stall out and to "sit on a shelf and collect dust" (*Advocate* 2006a). All agreed that this was not going to happen.

While a plan was now in place the question remained "who" was going to implement it, "where" would the money come from, and how, and what would the first steps be? Gwen Hamilton reflected:

> I mean, there are lots of competing priorities. Where do you start? When the plan was finished, there was no organized group of individuals who could take the plan and say, "We're going to take responsibility from a grass roots perspective to move this forward." So we chose, as a first step, to go forth and try to organize that group.

Between March and October 2006, a group of community members who had volunteered at the last community meeting to serve as a transition team interviewed twenty-six people for fifteen positions on the "Old South Baton Rouge Partnership Board." This board is now responsible for the implementation of the plan.

Already, there are changes in the neighborhood including the newly renovated McKinley High School Alumni Center, the new Carver Branch Library, and the Headstart Center. There is also a levee-top bike-trail that connects Old South Baton Rouge to both LSU and downtown, and the newly opened McKinley Middle Magnet. City Park is being renovated with four million dollars for the construction of new ball fields, basketball courts, and walking trails. In addition, developers are building new housing and retail spaces just north of LSU, and "property along Nicholson Drive is quickly being snapped up for redevelopment" (Baton Rouge Area Foundation 2006).

CUP recently focused its initiatives on businesses in OSBR. An all-day conference was held (on a Monday to make sure the barbers could come) with forty-four small businesses attending. Another focus of CUP has been organizing youth activities. The churches and ministers have taken on some of the crime strategy portion and the farmers' market portion. The focus is on grassroots organization and the neighborhood taking responsibility for revitalization. How will this occur among a group who has been marginalized in poverty and in many respects lacks the very resources to support themselves, let alone bring about economic revitalization? There are those in the neighborhood who feel the result of this plan will be gentrification. And if revitalization

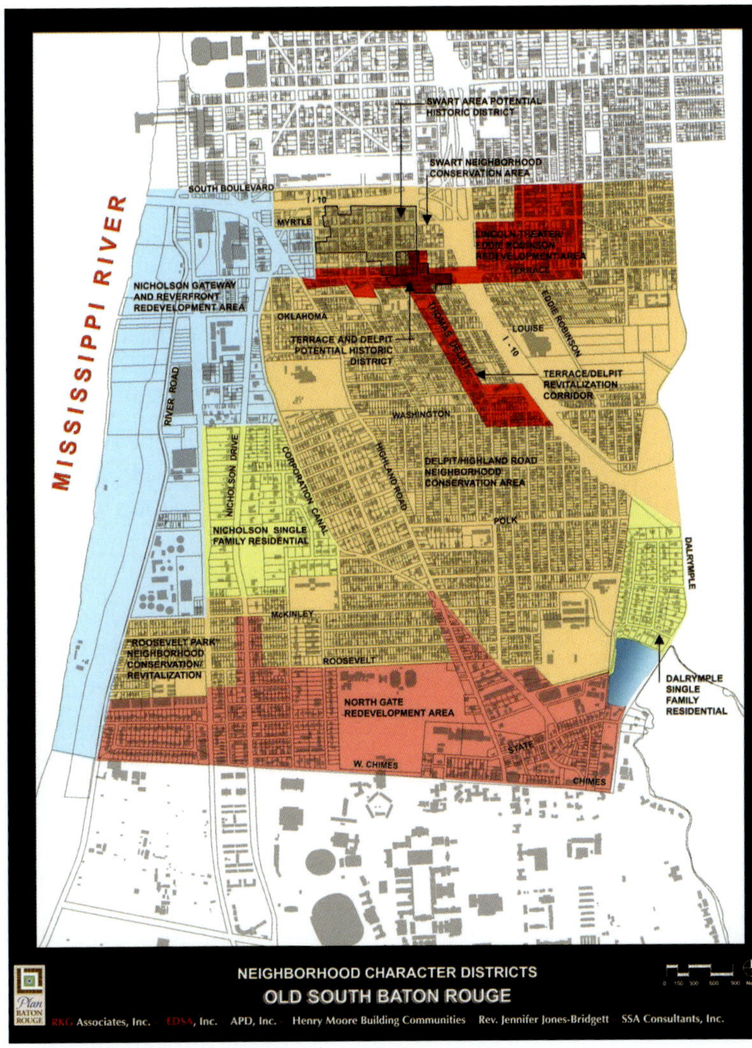

Map 6.1. OSBR subdistricts.

Fig. 6.17. The Corporation Canal.

was the goal, why wasn't the money for the strategic plan spent on rehabilitating houses? There are concerns that although there is a plan, money for implementation will not be forthcoming. When 40 percent of the residents are below poverty line, how can they leverage investors? Who will invest in a neighborhood that is seen as ridden with crime and blight? Who will benefit from investments that are made?

As the plan moves forward, stakeholders are implementing strategies to:

- Increase the rate of home ownership in Old South Baton Rouge and improve housing options for elderly residents;
- Improve housing and neighborhood conditions by supporting the initiatives of local businesses and residents, including reducing panhandling in the area;
- Minimize the impact of gentrification due to redevelopment;
- Train local people in the building trades and employ them to renovate homes in the neighborhood;
- Utilize available land resources as a catalyst for redevelopment, including the use of vacant, blighted, and adjudicated properties;
- Identify and preserve the best historic elements of Old South;
- Record and celebrate the rich local history;
- Establish a regulatory and administrative framework to preserve the area's historic properties;
- Stimulate public and private reinvestment, and increase job development;
- Provide assistance and incentives to new and existing business owners in the area;
- Improve the education, skills, and employment options available to residents;
- Correct deteriorating drainage systems and enhance the flow of traffic through the area;
- Provide continuing opportunities for the private sector and residents to engage in redevelopment activities; and
- Create more productive outlets for local youth that will help prepare them for future success.

According to Gwen Hamilton: "This process is truly unique. It has centered on combining the efforts of residents and neighboring stakeholders to generate a lasting, positive change in this historic, often neglected community. Over the next few years, we look forward to seeing the area emerge as a cutting-edge redevelopment model and leader in our city, state, and region."

How are these redevelopment efforts impacting the residents? Will there be a trickle-down effect stimulating new economic growth for the residents? Will home ownership increase? Will the city address issues of crime? And, will the enforcement of loitering ordinances discourage the street life of a community in which so much of it occurs in public spaces? Will the neighborhood remain primarily black, and if not, what would be the consequences of a majority non-black district? In the end, how will a "new" neighborhood emerge without erasing places that are central to the identities and memories of this community?

Conclusion: Rethinking Place and Preservation

In ten years, Old South Baton Rouge will reflect the New South.

Baton Rouge Area Foundation, 2006

In the end, communities do not stay the same, they are fluid, changing landscapes. Old South Baton Rouge will never be what it was! While there is a great deal of nostalgia, the past is the past. However, there is much that can be preserved, and the process has begun. Perhaps we might ask what will the community become? "What is the new OSBR?" Could it be the site of multi-ethnic diverse populations? Will it become a neighborhood of mixed income housing? Could it be the site of historic walking tours that honor the heritage of African American life under Jim Crow? Could historic markers mark sites of significance in the neighborhood? Might concentrations of vernacular architecture and public spaces comprise a basis for historic districts? Will businesses return to service the increasing needs of downtown and LSU? These efforts will have to be city wide. Until the larger community recognizes the importance of OSBR to its own identity, and that of the state and the nation, these efforts will be unrealized. Preservation is central to keeping alive the history that has shaped us all.

To embrace Jim Crow and segregation as part of our past is to engage in the memory work that must be done. The challenge is to represent this unique experience in American history as a way to understand ourselves and others as well as the larger landscape of American history. Is it possible to quantify such subjective life experiences and to communicate their joined meanings to a new generation, or to outsiders? This has been one of the difficulties facing the vernacular community. Historians have always favored the notion of great (white) men and great (European) artists approach to the establishment of significance of place. The National Register of Historic Places was essentially built out of such a perspective—an academically trained (dare we say, biased) specialists' perspective. When it comes to writing up a formal proposal about why a relatively disadvantaged cultural landscape, filled with small deteriorating wooden houses, should be preserved and supported with public funds, the case has always been, at the very least, hard to make in the competitive world of government decision-making. African Americans for the most part, do not experience value of place in the same way as wealthy and highly educated academics and bureaucrats do. Rather than focusing on the magnificent artistry of the individual structure, or the Cartesian order of the landscape, they speak in terms of the value of their shared community heritage. The geography of their community is reflected more in the personal experience of memory. Arguments about how the lives of so many people were shaped in a place, and the shared experiences of living in small houses, often do not carry much gravitas in the halls of government. The voices of the community may be less articulate and more subjective, they may depend more on oral histories and less on national pattern books, but they are no less important. They represent an undeniably significant component of our shared American history. They cannot be ignored.

in Old South Baton Rouge

PHOTOS BY JAMES W. TERRY, III

Gary Alley

SCHOOL BUS

9 THOMAS DELPIT

HILL TOP
BARBER SHOP

McKINLEY
PHYSICAL EDUCATION

2009 Martin Luther King, Jr. Day Activities

2009
Martin Luther King, Jr.
Day Activities

Appendix I

A Tour of Old South Baton Rouge with Joe Delpit

I can remember some businesses in and around the Chicken Shack, and some of them were quite popular for people in the community at that time. I remember that East Boulevard was basically a gravel street rather than a paved street. While I was quite young I was very observant of what was going on around me and I remember the Paramount X-Ray Cleaners was over on Harrison Street and they eventually moved over on East Boulevard. Mrs. Leslie Banks and Mr. Banks were the owner/operators of that laundry and they did an excellent job. Our neighbors also had a laundry; it was called Capitol Cleaners and it was operated by Mr. Shelby Rotolo and his family. Mr. Rotolo also had an amusement business with juke boxes that he would put out in different places and go by and collect rent. There was one of his juke boxes in our business.

Going further north up East Boulevard there was a medical center up there and a restaurant. Dr. George Butler who was a pharmacist and his brother Dr. Leo S. Butler owned that building. Dr. George Butler was a pharmacist, like I said, and he had Ideal Drug Store and he also had a restaurant in there. I don't remember the name of it but it was very beautiful in there, I remember that as a kid. It had a Caribbean atmosphere where they had like palm trees. I think they may have even called it the Palm Room or something like that, but as a kid I used to see it and it was beautiful. Then Dr. Butler had his doctor's office in there.

Inzenga's was where Scott's Tailor's was. Tony Inzenga. They had a grocery store there and were an Italian family. At this time there was a lot of Italian people that lived down here in the South Baton Rouge with black people. We lived together and worked together and played together and grew up together.

And then there was a clothing store that was on the corner of Louise and East Boulevard. I don't remember the name of that store. They later converted it to a pharmacy. Dr. James Bernard and his brother had a pharmacy there and Mr. Darensbourg was a pharmacist and they also had a medical office in it. And next to that later came to be Dr. Valarian Smith's dental office. That was much later after that time.

Going on up East Boulevard heading north there were a bunch of little businesses. There was the Spot Pool Hall and there was McKinley Bar where a lot of adults would go into. And further up there was Dimattia, another Italian family, who had a shoe store on the corner of Terrace and East Boulevard. And in between there, there was Sam's Grocery, owned and operated by another Italian fellow, Sam Gemreis (sp?). There was a club and restaurant that was operated right next to Sam's Grocery store on the right hand side of East Boulevard, I don't remember the name of it unfortunately. Mr. Charley Nash was the owner of it. I think they called it Wagon Wheel. In fact, they did call it Wagon Wheel.

On the opposite side of the street there was a little restaurant that was operated, I don't remember the name of that one now, it's a service station there now, Fina Service Station, but there was a restaurant right on that corner and they had pretty good food. And moving on up next to that Fina Station, Mr. Theodis White had a paint shop there. He had a very big business. He also was a paint contractor where he would do commercial work and residential work. He created lots of jobs for people. And he built a building next to that to build some more doctor's offices.

Going a little bit further down where the East Boulevard Housing Development is was the McKinley Theater. I used to go see cowboy pictures there, Hopalong Cassidy and Roy Rogers and all that stuff, years ago. And on the side there was a little alley, and behind McKinley Theater was Bar-row's Funeral Home and Luther's Motel. I don't know how that worked out, but they had a little motel and kind of like a little hotel/motel combination back there that would have been facing, I guess, Maximilian Street, but you would go to it through the alley by the old McKinley Theater.

Later, McKinley Theater was changed to what was called the Rhythm Club. The Rhythm Club was. the largest club probably at that time in Baton Rouge for sure, and possibly in the state, that black people went to. I don't know that for a fact, but the Rhythm Club was a club that held well over a thousand people and all sorts of nationally known artists came to the Rhythm Club—Sam Cooke, James Brown, B. B. King. I mean any and every body who was on the charts or who was hot at that time performed at the Rhythm Club.

Going a little bit further from the Rhythm Club there was a place that opened much later, it was a little small place called Nat's Lounge, and they opened that little place up and it turned out to be a pretty good little neighborhood lounge. Not many problems in the early years, but later on it became one that there were many problems [with], I guess like a lot of other things in our community.

Going on up to the corner of Terrace and East Boulevard, there was a service station owned and operated by Mr. Allen. Mr. Allen was an elderly white gentleman. We wasn't old when he first started, but he also had one of the few service stations in this area and he did an excellent job with it and the people in the community liked him quite a bit.

Going on across Terrace Street there was Bonfanti's Grocery on the corner of Terrace and East Boulevard. Louis Bonfanti and his family operated that. And going on down there was a shoe shop that Mr. Bonfanti owned, Tony Bonfanti, T.J. Bonfanti, and he operated for years. And I'm not sure if he sold it to a black man by the name of Herbert Williams, or if Mr. Williams just managed it, I don't remember how the relationship was, but Mr. Williams did take over that operation. Dimattia eventually closed out which was a shoe shop on the other side of the street. And over on Maximilian Street and Myrtle Street there was a drug store, I think it was called Capitol Drug Store and that drug store stayed there for years and years. Right in front of that drug store on Myrtle and Maximilian was a dentist office, Dr. B. V. Baranco, a local person who had a wonderful family and they all worked very hard in the community to make the community better, Dr. Baranco.

I guess going on up to Government Street I don't remember any other businesses. There were a few cafes on Government Street. One I remember was the Spot Cafe. And there was Dr. Israel who had a pharmacy. I don't remember the name of his pharmacy, but I think, it's Leonard Israel, had a pharmacy on Government and 13th. And between 13th and 12th there was about two restaurants, one was the Spot Cafe, and the other one was Ever Ready. I might be wrong about the Spot, that may have been somewhere else, but I think the Spot was operated by Mr. Byrd. Ever Ready Cafe, I don't remember the gentleman's name, but they were very popular, lots of people would go there to eat.

There was a bakery shop on Myrtle and East Boulevard, it was called Pan Dandy Bakery. And at later years, the Matrain's (sp?), who were Italians also, they opened up a grocery store on the corner of Myrtle and East Boulevard.

I'm gonna just go on from East Boulevard over as far as I can recall because I'd like to say something about the Lincoln Hotel and the Lincoln Restaurant The Lincoln Hotel was one of the finest places in Baton Rouge, of any hotel, that you could go to, white or black. The restaurant was immaculate, the rooms were just beautiful, and it was very well constructed. Dr. A. L. Chapman, who was a local physician, and his family operated that. After he died it seemed to have gone down and just went to zero. He also opened up the Lincoln Theater which was on Myrtle Street during that same time period. And the Lincoln Theatre was a really wonderful place. I mean it made us all so proud to have buildings like that in our community.

Coming down south there was a club called Apex Club, that's on the corner of Louise and McCalop. Mr. Macy Lamotte (sp?) had the Apex Club. The Apex Club was a very popular place were people would go and sit down, no problem whatsoever. [People would] enjoy themselves, a little cocktail after work, they just had a wonderful thing going on there. Mr. Lamotte also owned an amusement business like Mr. Rotolo did. Mr. Lamotte was an African American and he would go to different places and put in his juke boxes and they would split the take. In other words if my dad wanted to put in Mr. Lamotte's or Mr. Rotolo's machines in the Chicken Shack, then they would split whatever it was. If two hundred dollars came out of it then my father would keep a hundred and Mr. Rotolo would get a hundred and that's the way they operated in those times.

Coming down 13th street on the north side of Terrace there was a club called the Five Crown, the old Five Crown social club. It was a two story building and there too was a lot of live entertainment, some national, and a lot of local entertainers would perform there. It was a wonderful place at one time and like other things it got bad with shootings and drugs.

We also had another theater that was quite popular on North Boulevard, the Temple Theater and the Temple Roof Garden. This was not a what you would call a business per se, it was operated mostly by the Masons. The Masons would rent this facility to people in the community for dances and balls and that's where black folks went to have all of their formal balls and dances. There was a beautiful place up there plus they had all kind of entertainers that would come there. They even had athletic events up there. There was basketball on top of the Temple roof and some of the best players that ever came through Baton Rouge played there. And entertainers like B.B. King, Bobby Bland, Louis Armstrong, Duke Ellington, Cab Calloway, you name it, even Diana Washington and Etta James. These people would come there. When I was about sixteen I used to slip up on the Temple roof, I had no business being there, but I enjoyed it so very much. I mean just to be around those people—not to get no alcohol or nothing just to hear these people perform. There was no air conditioner at that time up there and they had the fire escape up on the building fire steps. They would come down and some of us would climb up those fire escapes and you would actually go through a window and slip in. And they wouldn't know that we were going up four stories, they wouldn't know that we were even in there but we would listen to that music, it was really wonderful.

Coming down 13th street, which is now Eddie Robinson Drive, there were some smaller little mom and pop type grocery stores. One of them I remember, when I was going to school we used to stop by their little neighborhood grocery store, was Davidson's grocery store on the corner of Julia and South Twelfth Street. Mr. Davidson would sell snacks and things like that, candy, and he had little sandwiches and things.

I understand over by Reddy Street school was Mr. Fleet's, now that's what most of the older people used to talk about now, I don't remember. I remember going to Mr. Fleet's store but I don't remember this—he used to make these big old sandwiches they tell me. He'd put peanut butter and jelly on french bread. And then he would have oil sausage. They tell me they used to take that oil sausage that come out of big jars and take that sausage and slap it on that bread and put that juice on it and say that's some of the best eating you ever had in your life.

Liberty Shoe Shop, which was right at Thirteenth and South Boulevard and was owned by Mr. Sam Williams. That shoe shop was there for the longest. Also another shoe shop on the corner of Government and Thirteenth Street was Darensbourg Shoe Store. Darensbourg's still operating, but they moved it from that location closer to Acadian Thruway. And one of the most successful businesses, and you're talking about good bread and donuts and those cinnamon rolls and things like that, was Lincoln Bakery shop. Mr. Allen Dalcourt, that man had some of the best bread, and all of the local restaurants used Mr. Dalcourt's bread.

One very significant restaurant, probably if they were still operating it would be the oldest business owned by a blacks in Baton Rouge, is on North Boulevard called Bernard's Chicken Loaf House. That business was very successful.

At that time things was segregated, your white and black restaurants, except at three restaurants I know that were owned by blacks—Chicken Shack, Bernard's Chicken Loaf House, and Percy's

Barbecue. Percy's Barbecue was down on Texas Street and that man had some of the best barbecue there was. But at those three restaurants you had a large number of whites, even though segregation was still in place. They would be coming to those restaurants and want to eat and sit down because the food was just that good. I can tell you those were some pretty good days now. Those three black men—Tommy Delpit, Joe Bernard, and Mr. Percy Franklin, all those guys stared delivery service years ago well before Domino Pizza and any of the other ones ever dreamed about it. And they did a great job at it.

Joe Delpit outside of his business headquarters on Lettsworth Street.

Appendix II

Percent of Negro Residences in Depressed Areas Lacking Basic Facilities in Baton Rouge in 1940

(Sociology 204 1940:58-60)

	Negro owner lacking:	Negro renters lacking:
1. Indoor toilet	76.1	68.8
2. Tub/shower	71.8	91.4
3. Running water	7.0	9.7
4. Hot water	91.5	95.6
5. Electricity	38.0	67.0
6. Refrigeration	49.3	43.0

Appendix III

Percent of All Negro Residences in Baton Rouge Lacking Basic Facilities in 1940

(Sociology 204 1940:73-75)

	Families of 5th graders lacking:	Families of high school student lacking:
1. Home ownership	53.3	32.0
2. Electricity in home	46.0	32.0
3. Glass in windows	30.7	13.3
4. Screens on windows	13.3	22.7
5. Child has own bedroom	95.4	94.7
6. Telephone in house	84.0	82.7
7. Daily newspaper	38.7	34.7
8. An automobile	67.8	60.0

Appendix IV
Churches of Old South Baton Rouge as of 1940

Mt. Zion First Baptist Church, 356 E. Blvd., Founded **1858**,
(was originally at 311 St. Maximilan)

Wesley United Methodist Church, 544 Government St., Founded **1866**

Bethel African Methodist Episcopal Church 1358 South Blvd., Founded **1867**

Shiloh Baptist Church, 185 Eddie Robinson, Founded **1872**
(first location: 317 Old Spanish Town Road and St. Mary, 1894 map)

Mt. Gillion Baptist Church, 346 E. Buchanan St., Founded **1876**

New Jerusalem Baptist Church, 1627 Thomas Delpit Ave., Founded **1898**

Calvary III Baptist Church, 1911 Georgia St., Founded **1904**

New Ark Baptist Church, 1344 Terrace St., Founded **1905**

St. Francis Xavier Catholic Church, Founded **1906**

Greater Mt. Gideon Baptist Church, 205 Alice St., Founded **1911**

Little Rising Sun Baptist Church, 12755 16th St., Founded **1912**

New Bethel Baptist Church, 1540 Matilda St., Founded **1913**

Neely United Methodist Church, 1755 Fig St. Founded **1914**

Greater Israelite Baptist Church, 1841 Thomas Delpit Ave., Founded **1915**

Progressive Baptist Church, 998 Julia St., Founded **1916**

Greater St. John Baptist Church, 2019 Colorado St., Founded **1919**

New St. John Missionary Baptist Church, 1455 South Blvd., Founded **1920**

Sweet Home Baptist Church, 343 W. Buchanan St., Founded **1923**

St. Joseph Baptist Church, 2424 Tennessee St., Founded **1927**

New Prospect Missionary Baptist Church, 1174 Terrace, Founded **1929**

Greater Beulah Baptist Church, 955 E. Polk St., Founded **1930**

Greater St. James Baptist Church, 1919 Arizona St., Founded **1932**

Fairview Baptist Church, 1636 Braddock St., Founded **1934**

Rose Hill Missionary Baptist Church, 1384 W. Grant St., Founded **1940**

Appendix V

One Square Mile

Submitted by: Carl E. Stewart, 1995

This is a list of notable people who came out of OSBR. Coach Carl E. Stewart—himself a native of the community—composed this list, in 1995, probably for the McKinley Alumni Association. We recognize that the list may omit many important contributors to the culture of the community, the state, and the nation. Coach Stewart concentrated his attention on professional figures, politicians, and educators. We include it as an example of a commemorative act which signifies the importance of the community through the legacy of its important sons and daughters.

Boundaries: At the time Dr. Gardner C. Taylor lived in this particular area of Baton Rouge and during subsequent years, the "ONE SQUARE MILE" was bounded on the WEST by East Boulevard and on the SOUTH by Washington Street; on the NORTH by North Boulevard and on the SOUTH by Washington Street. In some cases, our people will reside slightly outside of these boundaries to compensate for the fact that at least fifteen percent (15%) of this landscape was occupied by white people.

Louisiana, National and International Figures

1. Dr. Gardner C. Taylor
Europe St.—Leland College
Internationally acclimed Theologian

2. Eddie Robinson
Smith St.—Leland College
winningest football coach in America

1. Dr. Delores Spikes
S. 14th St.—Southern University
President of the Southern University System

4. Rep. Cleo Fields
Mary St.—Southern University
United States Congressman

5. Jude Patin
Julia St.—Southern University
General of the U.S. Army

6. Joe Brown
Louisa St.—McKinley High School
Lightweight Champion of the World, 1956

Joe Brown.

7. Dr. Emmitt Bashful
Rail Road Ave.—Southern University
Chancellor of Southern University, N.O., LA

8. Lenora Lafayette
Georgia St.—McKinley High School and Fisk University
Opera singer in Europe and the United States

9. Huel Perkins
Europe St..
Educational Administrator at Southern University and LSU

10. Don Chaney
Garfield St.—McKinley High School and the University of Houston
All-pro guard with the Boston Celtics and Coach of the Houston Rockets and the Detroit Pistons

11. Joseph A. Delpit
East Blvd.—McKinley High School
Baton Rouge City Councilman and Speaker Pro Tem of the Louisiana Legislature

12. Charles Honore
E. Washington St.—McKinley High School and Southern University
General U.S. Army

13. Lynn (Butler Smith) Whitfield
963 Terrece Anvene
Southern University / Howard University School of Drama
Emmy-winning Actress

14. Tyrus Thomas
McKinley High School, Louisiana State University
Professional basketball player with the Chicago Bulls.

Physicians

1. Dr. Louis James
S. 11th St.— McKinley High School and Southern University

2. Dr. Ceasar Piper
S. 12th St.—McKinley High School and Leland College

3. Dr. W.B. Bernard
Peach St.—McKinley High School, U.S. Army, Medical School

4. Dr. Jimmy Bernard
Peach St.—McKinley High School, U.S. Army, Medical School

5. Dr. Audry Fleet
13th St.—McKinley High School, Southern University, McHarry Medical School

6. Dr. Hastings Huggins—South 13th St.

7. Dr. Alvin Williams
McKinley High School, Southern University.

9. Dr. Donald Harris
East Blvd.—McKinley High School, Southern University, U.S. Army, Meharry Medical School

10. Dr. Henry Paul
McKinley High School, Southern University

11. Dr. Raymond Baranco
Southern University

12. Dr. Charles Pickett
McKinley High School, Southern University, Meharry Medical School

13. Dr. Clarence Avery
S. 15th St.—McKinley High School, Southern University, University of Southern Califronia

14. Dr. E.J. Mencer
S. 12th St.—McKinley High School, Meharry Medical School

15. Dr. Patrick Patin
Julia St.—McKinley High School, St. Francis Xavier, Meharry Medical School

16. Dr. Leo Butler ("Dean of Black Physicians")
Terrance St.—McKinley High School, Howard University Medical School

16. Dr. D'Orsay Devenport Bryant, Jr.
Bulter Building, East Blvd., Howard University School of Medicine

Dentists

1. Dr. David Hall
McKinley High School, Southern University and Meharry Medical School

2. Dr. Harry Lamotte
S. 15th St.

3. Dr. B.V. Baranco
St. Maximillian St.

4. Dr. Valarian Edward Smith
1469 East Blvd.—Howard University School of Dentistry
also a founder of the Baton Rouge Community Playhouse and Chorus

Pharmacists

1. George Butler, The Butler Drug Store
East Blvd.

2. Mr. Christy, Christy's Drug Store

3. Mr. Israel, Israel's Drug Store
Government St.

4. Mr. Conrad, Conrad's Drug Store

5. Mr. Lange, Lange's Drug Store
S. 13th St. and South Boulevard

Contractors

1. Louis Darensbourg
Julia St.—McKinley High School

2. Harvey Honore
Julia St.—McKinley High School

3. Alvin Guidry
S. 11th St.—St. Francis Xavier High School

4. Mr. Patin
Julia St.

Athletes

1. Eddie Robinson
McKinley High School, Leland College
Coaching: Smith School and Grambling College

Tyrus Thomas.

2. Carl Stewart
Grambling High School, Grambling State University, Livingston Alley
Coaching: McKinley High School and Southern University

3. George E. Mencer
McKinley High School and Leland
Coaching: McKinley High School

4. Don Chaney
McKinley High School and University of Houston
Coaching: Houston Rockets and Detroit Piston, NBA

5. Tommy Green
McKinley High School and Southern University
Coaching: Southern University

6. Willie Titus
McKinley High School, Southern University
Coaching: Woodlawn High School and McKinley High School

7. Tyrus Thomas
McKinley High School, Louisiana State University
Professional basketball player with the Chicago Bulls.

Lynn Whitfield.

Preforming Arts

1. Lenora Lafayette
Georgia St.—McKinley High School and Fisk University
Opera Star in Europe and the United States

2. Porter Kilbert
St. Maximillian St.—Southern University
Member of Duke Ellington Orchestra

3. Faye Burns
Southern University
Pianist and director of music for the Baton Rouge Community Chorus

4. Lynn (Butler Smith) Whitfield
963 Terrace Anvene
Southern University, Howard University School of Drama
Emmy-winning Actress

Special Recognition

1. Alzaga Vincent recieved her R.N. (nursing credentials) in the late 30's

2. Valeria Jean Butler
963 Terrace Ave., Southern University Laboratory, Howard University
First African American President of Louisiana Housing Finance Agancy and founder of the original Baton Rouge chapters of both *The Links* and *Jack & Jill*, the nation's premiere civic and social organizations for outstanding African-American women and children, respectively.

3. Sylvia Weatherspoon
Mckinley High School, Louisiana State University
Co-anchor of WBRZ News (Baton Rouge)

Sylvia Weatherspoon.

Figures and Maps

Chapter I

Chapter II

Chapter III

Chapter IV

Chapter V

Chapter VI

Cover Images

Front Cover: upper image, East Boulavard (Thomas Delpit), looking north from McKinley High School, 1950 by Chester Beaty, courtesy of the LSU Special Collections; lower image, McKinley High School Alumni Center.

Rear Cover: upper image, painted shotguns on upper 17th Street; lower image, Wayne Jones's mural of the Bus Boycott on Thomas Delpit Boulevard.

Bibliography

Advocate, the (daily). (1997). Baton Rouge.

---- (2005a). May 1.

---- (2005b). June 13.

---- (2006a). April 2.

---- (2006b). August 20.

Alomar, R. (1994). *Front yards in an African American neighborhood: An analysis of characteristics, use and patterns.* M.A. Thesis, Louisiana State University, Baton Rouge.

Anderson, J. (1988). *The education of blacks in the South, 1860-1935.* Chapel Hill: University of North Carolina Press.

Arp, W., III., & Boeckelman, K. (1997). Religiosity a source of black environmentalism and empowerment. *Journal of Black Studies, 28*(2), 255-267.

Bankston, C. L., & Caldas, Stephen. (2002). *A troubled dream: The promise and failure of school desegregation in Louisiana.* Nashville: Vanderbilt University Press.

Baton Rouge. (1899). *City directory.* Baton Rouge: City of Baton Rouge.

Baumbach, R. (1981). *The second battle of New Orleans: A history of the Vieux Carré riverfront expressway controversy.* University, AL: University of Alabama Press.

Bergeron, M. O., & Jackson, J. (1989). East Baton Rouge and Livingston Parishes. In *Folklife in the Florida Parishes.* Baton Rouge: Center for Regional Studies, Southeastern Louisiana University and the Louisiana Folklife Program, Division of the Arts. Pp. 39-43.

Blassingame, J. W. (1973). *Black New Orleans, 1860-1880.* Chicago: University of Chicago Press.

Brooks, E. (1984). *The women's movement in the black baptist church, 1880-1920.* Unpublished Ph.D. Dissertation, University of Rochester, Rochester.

Brown, H. R. (1969). *Die nigger die.* New York: Dial Press, Inc.

Butler, A. S. (2005). Fraternal and Benevolent Societies in Nineteenth-Century America. In T. L. Brown, G. S. Parks, & C. M. Phillips (Eds.), *African American fraternities and sororities: The legacy and the vision* (pp. 67-94). Lexington: The University of Kentucky Press.

Capital Region Planning Commission. (1968-1974). *A comprehensive plan for the capital region of Louisiana.* (numerous parts). Baton Rouge.

Carleton, M. T. (1981). *River capital: An illustrated history of Baton Rouge.* Woodland Hills, California: Windsor Publications, Inc.

Carney, J. (2001). *Black rice.* Cambridge, MA: Harvard University Press.

Chase, J. W. (1978). American heritage from Ante-Bellum black craftsmen. *Southern Folklore Quarterly, 42*(2), 135-36.

Chronicle. (1915). Baton Rouge: The future manufacturing metropolis of the awakened South. September.

City-Parish Planning Commisson. (1997). *Horizon five-year update final plan report, city of Baton Rouge, Parish of East Baton Rouge.* Baton Rouge.

---- (1971). *A community blight index.* Baton Rouge: Community Renewal Program.

---- (1945). *The city-parish plan, Baton Rouge, Louisiana.* St. Louis: Harland Bartholomew and Associates, City Planners.

Davis, A., & Dollard, J. (1940). *Children of bondage.* New York: Harper Torchbooks.

Davis, D. (1999). *Crossing over: An oral history of the desegregation experience of public school personnel in East Baton Rouge Louisiana.* Ph.D. Dissertation, Louisiana State University, Baton Rouge.

Deggs, Sister M. B. (2001). *No cross, no crown.* Bloomington: Indiana University Press.

Donlon, J. H. (2001). *Swinging in place: Porch life in Southern culture.* Chapel Hill: University of North Carolina Press.

Draughon, R., Jr., (1998). *Down by the river: A history of the Baton Rouge riverfront.* No. 1 of the series, "Preserving Louisiana's Heritage." New Orleans: R. Christopher Goodwin & Associates, Inc., for the US Army Corps of Engineers, New Orleans District.

Dormon, J. (Ed.). (1996). *Creoles of color of the Gulf South.* Knoxville: University of Tennessee Press.

Du Bois, W. E. B. (1969 [1903]). *The souls of black folk.* New York: Signet.

Edwards, J. (2001) Architectural Creolization: The meaning of Colonial Architecture. In M.-J. Amerlinck de Bontempo (Ed.), *Architectural anthropology* (pp. 86-120). Westport, CN: Greenwood Publishing.

---- (2002). In praise of the gallery and other African-American contributions to America's vernacular architecture. In J. Hankins and S. Maklansky (Eds.), *Raised to the trade, Creole building arts of New Orleans* (pp. 61-95). New Orleans: New Orleans Museum of Art.

---- (2006). Creole architecture: A comparative analysis of upper and lower Louisiana and Saint Domingue. *International Journal of Historical Archaeology, 10*(3), 1-31.

---- (2009). The most contested house in America. *Buildings and Landscapes, 16.*

Edwards, J., Kariouk, N . (2004). *A Creole lexicon: Architecture, landscape, people.* Baton Rouge: Louisiana State University Press.

Falk, W. W. (2004). *Rooted in place: Family and belonging in a southern black community.* New Brunswick, NJ: Rutgers University Press.

Elliot, C. (2006). Remembering Emerson Bell (1932-2006): Baton Rouge should have done better by him. *Baton Rouge Journal*, June.

Fairclough, A. (1999). *Race & democracy: The civil rights struggle in Louisiana 1915-1972.* Athens: University of Georgia Press.

Franz, D. E. (1993). *Beauregard Town: Linking residents to precedents.* Baton Rouge: Louisiana State University, School of Landscape Architecture. Final Project.

Frazier, J. M. (1937). *The history of negro education in the Parish of East Baton Rouge, Louisiana.* M.A. Thesis, State University of Iowa.

Free Dictionary, the. <http://encyclopedia.thefreedictionary.com/Quonset+hut> accessed 6/2/05.

Gaines, E. J. (1992 (1978)). *In my father's house.* New York: Vintage Books.

Gaston, R. W. (1971). *Dr. William Bass Hatcher, Louisiana educator.* Ph.D. Dissertation, Louisiana State University: Baton Rouge.

Gardner, J. (Ed.). (1983). *A better life: Italian-Americans in South Louisiana.* New Orleans: American-Italian Federation of the Southeast.

Gill, J. (1997). *Lords of misrule: Mardi Gras and the politics of race in New Orleans.* Jackson, MS: University Press of Mississippi.

Glassie, H. (2000). *Vernacular architecture.* Philadelphia and Bloomington: Indiana University Press.

Glissant, E. (1989). *Caribbean discourse: Selected essays.* Charlottesville, VA: University of Virginia Press.

Goodwin, R. C., & Hinks, S. (1993). *Cultural resources investigations for the Baton Rouge front levee enlargement and concrete slope pavement, item M-230 to 227-L, East Baton Rouge, Parish, Louisiana.* Archaeological Report to the U.S. Army Corps of Engineers. New Orleans: R. Christopher Goodwin and Associates.

Grandison, K. I. (1999). Beyond buildings: Landscape as cultural history in constructing the historical significance of place. In M. A. Tomlan (Ed.), *Preservation of what, for whom?* (pp. 159-68). Ithaca, NY: National Council for Preservation Education.

Haag, W. G. (1975). *The archaeology of the Baton Rouge civic center area.* Baton Rouge: A Report submitted to Capital Improvements Division, City of Baton Rouge.

Hall, G. M. (1992). *Africans in colonial Louisiana: The development of Afro-Creole culture in the eighteenth century.* Baton Rouge, Louisiana State University Press.

Harland Bartholomew and Associates, City Planners. (1945). *The 25 year city-parish plan for metropolitan Baton Rouge, Louisiana.* Saint Louis: for the City-Parish Planning Committee.

Harper Dickinson, G. (2005). Pledged to remember. In T. L. Brown, G. S. Parks, & C. M. Phillips (Eds.), *African American fraternities and sororities: The legacy and the vision* (pp. 11-36). Lexington: Univ. of Kentucky Press.

Harris, F. C. (1994). Something within: Religion as a mobilizer of African-American political activism. *Journal of Politics, 56*(1), 42.

Hayden, D. (1995). *Power of place: Urban landscapes and public history.* Cambridge, MA: MIT Press.

Hebert, M. J. (1999). *Beyond black and white: The civil rights movement in Baton Rouge, Louisiana, 1945-1972.* Ph.D. Dissertation, Louisiana State University, Baton Rouge.

Heck, R. (1966). *A guide to the development and historical architecture of Baton Rouge.* Baton Rouge: American Institute of Architects, Baton Rouge Chapter.

---- (1970). *Historic Baton Rouge: An urban planning perspective for the preservation of its heritage.* Baton Rouge: Community Renewal Program City-Parish Planning Commission.

Hendry, P. M., Edwards, J. D., et. al. (2005). *Assessing sites of historic significance in Old South Baton Rouge.* Baton Rouge: A report prepared for Plan Baton Rouge and RKG Consultants.

Hirsch, A. R., & Logsdon, J. (Eds.). *Creole New Orleans.* Baton Rouge: Louisiana State University Press.

Holloway, J. E. (Ed.). (1990). *Africanisms in American culture.* Bloomington, Indiana University Press.

Housing Authority of East Baton Rouge Parish. (2002). *Preliminary community revitalization plan: The Old South Baton Rouge community.* Baton Rouge: City and Parish of Baton Rouge.

Hurlbert, J., et. al. (1996). *The structure of social and economic isolation in underclass populations.* Baton Rouge: Louisiana State University Press.

Hutchinson, J. (1986). The cure for domestic neglect: Better homes in America, 1922-1935. In C. Wells (Ed.), *Perspectives in vernacular architecture II* (pp. 168-78). Columbia: University of Missouri Press.

Jackson, J. M. (1997). Like a river flowing with living water: Worshipping in the Mississippi Delta. In *Louisiana folklife festival program book.* Monroe: Louisiana Folklife Festival.

Jensen, W. L. (1972). *The impact of substantial land use changes.* Baton Rouge: Community Renewal Program of the City of Baton Rouge and the Parish of East Baton Rouge, Louisiana.

Johns, M., & Moore, R. (1962). *It happened in Baton Rouge, U.S.A.: A real life drama of our deep South today.* New York: Congress of Racial Equality.

Joyner, C. (1984). *Down by the riverside: A South Carolina slave community.* Urbana: University of Illinois Press.

Kebede, A. (2002). *Movement along the Baton Rouge fault.* M.S. Thesis, Louisiana State University, Baton Rouge: <http://etd.Louisiana State University.edu/docs/available/etd-1115102-090126/>.

Kein, S. (Ed.). (2000). *Creole: The history and legacy of Louisiana's free people of color.* Baton Rouge: Louisiana State University Press.

Kellogg, J. (1977). Negro urban clusters in the Postbellum South. *Geographical Review, 67*(3), 310-21.

King, A. (1995). *The bungalow: The production of a global culture* (2nd ed.). New York: Oxford University Press.

Kniffen, F. (1936). Louisiana house types. *Annals of the Association of American Geographers, 26*(1), 179-93.

Lancaster, C. (1986). The American bungalow. In D. Upton and J. Vlach (Eds.), *Common places: readings in American vernacular architecture* (pp. 79-106). Athens: University of Georgia Press.

Layton, R. (1997). *An introduction to theory in anthropology.* Cambridge: University of Cambridge Press.

LeBeuf, J.-P. (1961). *L'habitation des Fali, montagnards du Cameroun septentrional.* Paris: Librarie Hachette.

Lemmon, A. E., et. al. (Eds.). (2003). *Charting Louisiana: Five hundred yeas of maps.* New Orleans: The Historic New Orleans Collection.

Lewis, P. F. (1976). *New Orleans: The making of an urban landscape.* Cambridge, MA: Ballinger Publishing Co.

Lincoln, C. E., & Mamiya, L. H. (1990). *The black church in the African American experience.* Durham, NC: Duke University Press.

Litwack, L. (1998). *Trouble in mind: Black Southerners in the age of Jim Crow.* New York: Alfred A. Knopf.

Livermore, M., & Midgley, J. (1998). The contribution of universities to building sustainable communities: The community university partnership. In M. D. Hoff (Ed.), *Sustainable community development: Studies in economic, environmental, and cultural revitalization* (pp. 123-138). Boca Raton: Lewis Publishers.

Lofgren, C. A. (1987). *The Plessy case: A legal-historical interpretation.* Oxford: Oxford University Press.

Louisiana State University. Sociology 204 (Leo M. Favrot, Instructor; 7 graduate students) 1940. The negro in Baton Rouge: A study by the class in race and race relations (Unpublished Typescript).

Louisiana State University Libraries, Special Collections. (2001). A recaptured past: The Baton Rouge 1953 bus boycott. Electronic Resource: <http://www.lib.Louisiana State University.edu/special/exhibits/boycott/index.html>.

Lovell, O. E. (1961). *Crucial issues in Louisiana public education as reflected in selected Louisiana newspapers, 1898-1956.* Ph.D. Dissertation, Louisiana State University, Baton Rouge.

Lyons, E. and Cloues, Richard C. (1999). The cultural and historical mosaic and the concept of significance. In M. Tomlan (Ed.). *Preservation of what, for whom?* (pp. 37-48). Ithaca, NY: The National Council for Preservation Education.

McAlester, V. & L. (1984). *A field guide to American houses.* New York: Alfred A. Knopf.

MacDonald, R. R., Kemp, J., & Haas, E. (Eds.). (1979). *Louisiana's black heritage.* New Orleans: Louisiana State Museum.

McKinley High School Oral History Project. (1997). *Visions: The soul & spirit of South Baton Rouge.* Baton Rouge: McKinley High School Oral History Project.

McKinley High School Class of 1928. (1928). *The panther* (yearbook). Baton Rouge: McKinley High School.

McMillen, N. R. (1989). *Dark journey: Black Mississippians in the age of Jim Crow.* Urbana: University of Illinois Press.

McNeil, N. B. (1961). *A geographic study of the Baton Rouge fault, Baton Rouge, Louisiana.* M.S. Thesis, Louisiana State University, Baton Rouge.

Matthews, D. R., & Prothro, J. W. (1966). *Negroes and the new Southern politics.* New York: Race and World.

Meyers, R. (1976). *History of Baton Rouge, 1699-1812.* Baton Rouge: Louisiana State University Press.

Mills, G. B. (1977). *The Forgotten people: Cane River's Creoles of color.* Baton Rouge: Louisiana State University Press.

Morning advocate (daily). (1963). Baton Rouge. August 7.

Muller, R. A., & Rohli, R. (2002). Synoptic associations of regional flooding: Rainstorms in Louisiana, 1911-2000. *Southwestern Geographer,* 6(1), 1-31.

Murphy, L. G., Melton, J. G., & Ward, G. L. (1993). *Encyclopedia of African American religions.* New York: Garland Publishing, Inc.

Neyland, L. W. (1958). The negro in Louisiana since 1900: An economic and social study. Unpublished Ph.D. Dissertation, New York University.

Newton, M. (1985). Louisiana folk houses. In N. R. Spitzer (Ed.). *Louisiana folklife: A guide to the state* (pp. 179-90). Baton Rouge: Louisiana Folklife Program, Office of Cultural Development, Department of Culture, Recreation, and Tourism.

Palmié, S. (2006). Creolization and its discontents. *The Annual Review of Anthropology, 35*, 443-56.

Parent, W. (2004). *Inside the carnival: Unmasking Louisiana politics.* Baton Rouge: Louisiana State University Press.

Peek, P. (1978). Afro-American material culture and the Afro-American craftsman. *Southern Folklore Quarterly, 42*(2), 112-13.

Perkins, B. K. (2003). *Armand Duplantier en Amérique: A biographical time line.* Baton Rouge: Vintage Research.

---- (2004). *The early families of Magnolia Mound Plantation, 1786-1841, Baton Rouge, Louisiana.* Baton Rouge: Vintage Research.

Peterson, S.A. (1992). Church participation and political participation. *American Politics Quarterly, 20.*

Porche-Frilot, D. M. (2006). *Propelled by faith.* Ph.D. Dissertation, Louisiana State University, Baton Rouge.

Queen, E. L., Prothero, S. R., & Shattuck, G. H. (1996). *Encyclopedia of American religious history.* Boston: Proseworks.

Rabalais, P. P. with K. Watts. (N.D.). Joyful improvisations: The quilts of Anna Williams exhibit text. Textile and Costume Gallery. Baton Rouge: Louisiana State University.

Raboteau, A. (2004). *Slave religion: The "invisible institution" in the Antebellum South.* New York: Oxford University Press.

Rathburn, R. R. (1979). Italian immigrants in southeastern Louisiana. In N. R. Spitzer (Ed.). *Mississippi Delta ethnographic overview* (pp. 310-15). Baton Rouge: National Park Service.

Richter, W. L. (1999). Slavery in Baton Rouge, 1820-1860. In C. Vincent (Ed.), The African American experience in Louisiana, Part A. (pp. 505-520). *The Louisiana purchase bicentennial series in Louisiana history,* Vol. XI. Lafayette, LA: Center for Louisiana Studies.

Roach-Lankford, S. (1985). The regional folklife of north Louisiana. In N. R. Spitzer, (Ed.), *Louisiana folklife: A guide to the state* (pp. 87-102). Baton Rouge: Louisiana Folklife Program, Office of Cultural Development, Department of Culture, Recreation, and Tourism.

Rodrigue, S. F., & Phillips, F. (2006). *Historic Baton Rouge: An illustrated history.* San Antonio, TX: Historical Publishing Network.

Rohrer, J., & Edmonson, M. (1960). *The eighth generation: Cultures and personalities of New Orleans negroes.* New York: Harper.

Rose, J. (2006). *Rethinking representations of slave life in historical plantation museums: Towards a commemorative museum pedagogy.* Ph.D. Dissertation, Louisiana State University, Baton Rouge.

Sepia Socialite (newspaper). (1942). New Orleans.

Shuman, M. (P.I.). (1993). *A cultural resources survey of Arlington revetment and LSU berm levee improvement item, East Baton Rouge Parish, Louisiana.* New Orleans: U.S. Army Corps of Engineers Report No. COELMN/PD-91/01.

Simpson, P. (1997). Linoleum and lincrusta: The democratic coverings for floors and walls. In A. Adams and S. McMurry (Eds.), *Exploring everyday landscapes: Perspectives in vernacular architecture VII* (pp. 281-292). Knoxville: University of Tennessee Press.

Social Work, School of. (1942). *Social welfare resource book of Baton Rouge, Louisiana.* Baton Rouge: Louisiana State University.

Spitzer, N. (Ed.). (1979). *Mississippi Delta ethnographic overview.* New Orleans: National Park Service.

Staten, A., & Roach, Susan. (1997). "Take me to the water:" African American river baptism. In *Louisiana folklife festival program.* Monroe: Louisiana Folklife Festival.

Sternberg, M. A. (1996). *Along the river road: Past and present on Louisiana's historic byway.* Baton Rouge: Louisiana State University Press.

Sykes, J. *New Orleans free persons of color in Baton Rouge, 1850-1860.* Baton Rouge: Catholic Life Center Archives.

Taylor, E. L. (2000). *The words of Gardner Taylor.* Vol. 3. Valley Forge, PA: Judson Press.

Townes, E. (1993). *Womanist justice, womanist hope.* Atlanta: Scholars.

Trillin, C. (1978). An attempt to compile the definitive history of Dideés Restaurant. Excerpted in F. De Caro (Ed.), *Louisiana sojourns: Travelers' tales and literary journeys* (pp. 509-17). Baton Rouge: Louisiana State University Press.

Turner, S. (2000). *South Baton Rouge: A community at a crossroads.* Baton Rouge: Louisiana State University.

Uter, F. M. (1992). *A history of the Catholic church in Baton Rouge, 1792-1992.* Baton Rouge: Saint Joseph Cathedral.

Vincent, C. (1981). *A centennial history of Southern University and A & M College, 1880-1980.* Baton Rouge: Southern University.

Vlach, J. . (1975). *Sources of the shotgun house: African and Caribbean antecedents.* 2 vol. Ph.D. Dissertation, Indiana University, Bloomington.

---- (1981). Afro-American folk crafts in nineteenth century Texas. *Western Folklore, 40*(2), 149-161.

---- (1986). Afro-Americans. In Dell Upton (Ed.), *America's architectural roots: Ethnic groups that built America* (pp. 42-47). Washington D.C.: Preservation Press, National Trust for Historic Preservation.

---- (1990). Architecture. *The Afro-American tradition in decorative arts.* Athens: University of Georgia Press.

---- (1991). *By the work of their hands: Studies in Afro-American folklife.* Charlottesville: University Press of Virginia.

Wahlman, M. S. (1987). Africanisms in Afro-American visionary arts. In *Baking in the sun: Visionary images from the South* (pp. 28-43). Lafayette, LA: University Art Museum, University of Southwestern Louisiana.

Walkes, J. A. (1986). *Jno G. Lewis, Jr.—End of an era: The history of the Prince Hall Grand Lodge of Louisiana, 1842-1979.* Leavenworth: J. A. Walkes, Jr.

Washington, M. H., & Nunez, C. L. (2005). Education, racial uplift, and the rise of the Greek-letter tradition. In T. L. Brown, G. S. Parks, & C. M. Phillips (Eds.), *African American fraternities and sororities: The legacy and the vision* (pp. 137-180). Lexington: The University of Kentucky Press.

Watts, K. with E. Walker. (1995). *Anna Williams: Her quilts and their influence.* Paducah: American Quilter's Society.

Westmacott, R. (1991). Pattern and practice in traditional African American gardens in rural Georgia. *Landscape Journal, 10*, 2.

----(1992). *African-American gardens and yards in the rural South.* Nashville: University of Tennessee Press.

White, D. R. M. (1998). *Cultural gumbo: An ethnographic overview of Louisiana's Mississippi River Delta and selected adjacent areas.* New Orleans: The Jean Lafitte National Historical Park and Preserve.

Wiggins, W. (1983). The black folk church. In Richard M. Dorson (Ed.), *Handbook of American folklore* (pp. 145-154). Bloomington: Indiana University Press.

Wingfield, H. (1988). The historical and changing role of the black church: The social and political implications. *The Western Journal of Black Studies, 12*(3).

Woodward, C. V. (1951). *Origins of the New South, 1877-1913.* Baton Rouge: Louisiana State University Press.

Works Projects Administration in the State of Louisiana. Federal Writers' Project. (1940). *Louisiana, A guide to the state.* New York: Hastings House.

Oral History Interviews

Pat Baranco (2005).

Emerson Bell (2002).

Josephine (Cascio) Bonfanti (2005).

Bridget Jackson Brister (1997).

Edmae Delpit Butler (2002).

Dr. Barbara Carpenter (2002).

Inez Christentery (2005).

Joe Delpit (1996).

Keith Douglas (2002).

Hazel Freeman (1997).

Nona (Dumoille) Gray (2005).

Gwen Hamilton (2006).

Eula Mae Hatter (1997).

Louise Augustine Payne Haynes (2005).

Isabelle Herson (1995, 2002).

Eddie Johnson (1997).

Charles A. Jones, Sr. (2002).

Harriet Jones (2002).

Jennifer Jones (1997).

Mother Sarah Jones (1997).

Wayne Jones (2005, 2006).

Sadie Keel (1997).

Annie Kimble (1997).

Rev. Lionel Lee (1997).

Fred Matthews (1996).

Beryl McGhee (1997).

Claryce Minor (1997).

Jean Myles (2002).

Betty Parker (1996).

Brenda Patterson (1997).

Isaac Patterson (1997).

Huel Perkins (2006).

Virginia (Caruso) Pinocci (2005).

Charles Ricard (2005).

Ray Roy (2005).

Rev. Charles T. Smith (1997).

Donald R. Sterling (1997).

Isadore E. Tansil, Sr. (2002).

Welhelmenia G. Thompson (1997).

J. W. Vaughn (2002).

Ida Mae Whiten (1997).

Almenia Williams (1997).

Anna Williams (2002).

Kathy (Cascio) Wink (2005).

Acknowledgements

This book has been a community effort from the beginning. Our first thanks goes out to the many residents of Old South Baton Rouge who have so graciously shared their stories with us and tolerated our questions, our probing, our tape recorders, and our cameras. They opened their old photo albums to us, and invited us into their homes to talk about their experiences, the accomplishments of their families, and the history of the community. In no small measure, this is their book.

The McKinley High School Oral History Project (1995-2005) was responsible for 230 oral history interviews that provide the basis of this book. The project was co-sponsored by the LSU Department of Curriculum and Instruction, the Community University Partnership (CUP), and the LSU Libraries T. Harry Williams Center for Oral History. Grants from the Baton Rouge Job Training Partnership Office (JTPA) and the U.S. Department of Housing and Urban Development funded the various summer youth oral history projects which resulted in the oral histories that provide the foundation for this book. Special thanks to Cecile Guin, LCSW director, LSU School of Social Work Office of Social Service Research and Development for her support in obtaining funding. The collection was transferred to the Carver Branch of the East Baton Rouge Parish Public Library in the fall of 2005 so as to be more readily available in Old South Baton Rouge. This transfer was made possible by the work of graduate students enrolled in LSU's Social Work 7506-Community and Agency Contexts for Direct Practice taught by Dr. Pricilla Allen. The collection is also housed with LSU Libraries Special Collections, where they are made available to researchers for access and duplication.

We are grateful to the many McKinley High School students, principals, and community liaisons, who worked on this project over the course of ten years. The students were" Shawnda Hollins, Roderick Jones, Caremn Posey, Khary Carrell, Nedra Carter, Michael Goods, Rudolph Henry, Veonetta Jewell, Chasity Lovely, Heidi McGee, Shawnte Green, Shanta Jenkins, Rahshada Jenkins, Melvin Heard, Katina Welsh, Beau Bogart, Jamahl Fields, Erin Pourche, Courtney Zachary, Natalie Clark, Nita Clark, Cindi Edwards, Teona Edwards, Courtney Grimes, Jessica Mosby, Chrystal Perkins and Brandy C. Snowden. Of particular note were the special efforts our community liaisons Isadore Tansil and Fred Matthews. The T. Harry Williams Center at LSU supported this project from the beginning and particular thanks goes to Pamela Dean, Mary Hebert and the current director Jennifer Abraham. Faye Phillips, Germain Bienvenu, and other staff of the LSU Special Collections division of the library graciously tracked down obscure maps and illustrations from their collection and provided permission for them to be included in this volume. The Leo S. Butler Community Center provided permission for the use of their illustrations. Wayne Jones, a local artist, painted the frontispiece specifically for this volume. The Alumni Museum in the Old McKinley High School permitted us to reproduce several of their historic illustrations.

The College of Education at LSU worked in partnership with the Oral History Project and has given its unfailing support. Thanks to Dean Jayne Fleener as well as the many graduate students over the years who participated in the service learning projects associated with the Oral History Project, in particular: Molly Quinn, Toby Daspit, Julia Rose, Lavada Taylor, Tayari Kwa Salam, Elecia Lathon, Dorian McCoy, Nicholas Ng-A-Fook, Hillary Proknow and Rodrick Jones. Jan Shoemaker supported the service learning component of the Oral History Project from the beginning. Grant money received through the Women's and Gender Studies at LSU enhanced the interdisciplinary nature of this study by enlarging the number of faculty involved including Carolyn Ware, Tiwana Simpson, and Nghana Lewis. In the Department of Geography and Anthropology, thanks are due to the hard work of artist Mary Lee Eggart, and to anthropology students

Guiyuan Wang, Sylvia Mintz and geographer Charles Flannigan. The Community University Project under the leadership of Pat Smith has been unconditional in its support, together with the staff at the Leo Butler Center. Kristin Sanders of the Baton-Rouge City-Parish Planning Commission wrote two grant applications in support of this volume.

Several readers enhanced this work and took time to read all or parts of the manuscript including: Gaines Foster, Michelle Livermore, John Hendry, Hillary Procknow, Eddie Robinson, Lisa Delpit, Joe Delpit, Huel Perkins, Nathan Self and Jeff Bennett. Carolyn Bennett of the Foundation for Historic Louisiana also provided invaluable support and assistance. Funding was graciously supplied by Boo Thomas and Gwen Hamilton of the Baton Rouge Area Foundation, and by Russell Archambault of RKG Associates. We trust that our combined efforts have been able to portray the surprising strengths and value of this historic community, and that these efforts find acceptance in the Old South Baton Rouge community and beyond.

This book is based upon the McKinley High School Oral History Project (1995-2004), directed by Dr. Petra Munro Hendry. The results of this project are now archived in the Carver Branch of the East Baton Rouge Parish Library, and at the T. Harry Williams Center for Oral History, a division of the LSU Library Special Collections. It is also based upon a report prepared by Dr. Petra Munro Hendry, Dr. Jay D. Edwards, Dr. Charles Flannigan, Sylvia Mince and Dr. Julia Rose, 2005. The report was commissioned by the Baton Rouge Area Foundation and RKG Consultants as part of the Old South Baton Rouge Revitalization Plan. Funding from the College of Education in 2006 supported an expansion of the report into a full book manuscript, with the assistance of Carolyn Ware, Pat Smith, Gwen Hamilton, Elecia Lathon, Dorian McCoy, and Guiyuan Wang.

The authors of the chapters in this book are as follows: Chapter I, Community Culture and Social Change, Jay Edwards and Petra Hendry; Chapter II, Shaping the Cultural Landscape, Jay Edwards and Petra Hendry; Chapter III, Chapter IV, Remembering the History of Place, 1885- 1965, Petra Hendry; Chapter IV, The Architectural Character, Jay Edwards; Chapter V, Creating Culture and Community Petra Henry with Carolyn Ware, Elecia Lathon, and Dorian McCoy; Chapter VI, The Power of Place: Community Revitalization, Petra Hendry and Jay Edwards with Gwen Hamilton and Patricia Smith. Photography was supplied by Jay Edwards with Petra Hendry. Maps and artwork were supplied by Mary Lee Eggart of the Department of Geography and Anthropology, with Charles Flannigan. Historic Maps and aerial photographs were supplied by LSU Special Collections, the Cartographic Information Center of the LSU Library, and by Magnolia Mound Plantation. Additional images were supplied by the Louisiana State Library, the Fred B. Kniffen Lab of the Department of Geography and Anthropology of LSU, and from private collections of families of OSBR. The frontispiece is original artwork supplied by Wayne Jones.

About the Editors

Jay D. Edwards is Professor of Anthropology and director of the Fred B. Kniffen Cultural Resources Laboratory in the department of Geography & Anthropology, at LSU. He has taught courses there since 1967. He specializes is studies of the material culture and vernacular architecture of the Louisiana, the Gulf South, and the Atlantic World. His most recent previous book, co-authored with Nicolas Kariouk, is *A Creole Lexicon: Architecture, Landscape, People*, published by LSU Press in 2004. A recent article is "Shotgun: the most contested house in America," published in *Buildings and Landscapes* (2009), Vol. 16.

Petra Munro Hendry is the St. Bernard Chapter of the LSU Alumni Association Endowed Professor in the College of Education at Louisiana State University. Since 1991, she has been at LSU, where she teaches courses in Curriculum Theory, Curriculum History, Oral History Methodology and Gender Studies. She is the co-director of the Curriculum Theory Project, an interdisciplinary research initiative which endeavors to understand educational practice and reform within a broad social and cultural framework. Her scholarship examines the role of narrative in the construction of curriculum history, educational research and teachers' life histories. She is the author of *Subject to Fiction: Women Teachers' Life History Narratives and the Cultural Politics of Resistance* (Open University Press) and *Pedagogies of Resistance: Women Educator Activists 1880-1960* (Teachers College Press).

Index